SENTENCING MATTERS

Michael Tonry

OXFORD UNIVERSITY PRESS

New York   Oxford

Oxford University Press

Oxford   New York
Athens   Auckland   Bangkok   Bogotá   Bombay
Buenos Aires   Calcutta   Cape Town   Dar es Salaam
Delhi   Florence   Hong Kong   Istanbul   Karachi
Kuala Lumpur   Madras   Madrid   Melbourne
Mexico City   Nairobi   Paris   Singapore
Taipei   Tokyo   Toronto   Warsaw

and associated companies in
Berlin   Ibadan

Copyright © 1996 by Michael Tonry

First published in 1996 by Oxford University Press, Inc.
198 Madison Avenue, New York, New York 10016

First issued as an Oxford University Press paperback, 1997

Oxford is a registered trademark of Oxford University Press

Library of Congress Cataloging-in-Publication Data
Tonry, Michael H.
Sentencing matters / Michael Tonry.
p.   cm.—(Studies in crime and public policy)
Includes bibliographical references and index.
ISBN 0-19-509498-0
ISBN 0-19-512293-3 (pbk.)
1. Sentences (Criminal procedure)—United States.
2. Sentences (Criminal Procedure) I. Title. II. Series.
KF9685.T66 1996
345.73'0772—dc20   [347.305772]   95-5925

1 3 5 7 9 8 6 4 2

Printed in the United States of America
on acid-free paper

Preface

Sentencing has been in a process of "reform" for a quarter century, but there is no more agreement now than in 1975 about what is wrong or how it can be made right. Then as now liberals were concerned about disparities, racial and class bias, unfair processes, and excessively harsh punishments. Then as now conservatives believed that many punishments were too lenient, that procedures were too complicated and time-consuming, and that crime rates would fall if only more people were locked up and for longer times.

Traditional processes in which judges try, case by case, to fashion sentences that vindicate victims' interests, acknowledge offenders' circumstances, and take account of public safety concerns have lost favor. Both liberals and conservatives distrust those processes but for different reasons; liberals worry that judges will be arbitrary or prejudiced, conservatives that judges will be softhearted and lenient.

Reformers' passions and persistence continue unabated. In every state and the federal system, calls are made for sentencing guidelines, mandatory penalties, and "three-strikes" laws; for more use of community penalties; for crime reduction through deterrence and incapacitation; and for crime reduction through treatment and prevention.

The political debates have changed remarkably little in a quarter century. Many people have strong commonsense beliefs about sentencing and punishment, but it is often common sense uninformed by knowledge.

That is a pity, because we have learned a great deal in the past twenty-five years about sentencing processes, the crime-reductive effects of punishments, and what happens when sentencing laws are changed. From research and systematic observation in the United States and other Western countries, we have learned how to craft sentencing laws and punishment policies that are fair, respectful of human rights, and protective of public safety. We have also learned that the effort to replace fallible human judgments with rigid sentencing rules was a mistake and has caused as much injustice as the systems they replaced.

This book attempts to pull together that knowledge. Chapter 1, for readers in a hurry, summarizes the whole and develops major themes. Chapter 2 discusses research and experience concerning changes in state sentencing laws and practices, including creation of sentencing guidelines. Chapter 3 does the same for the federal justice system. Chapters 4 and 5 discuss intermediate sanctions, penalties that are more burdensome and intrusive than probation but less so than prison, and mandatory penalties, including "three-strikes" laws. Chapter 6 discusses judges'—often difficult and conflicted—roles in sentencing reform, and chapter 7 widens the focus to look at sentencing reform experience and research in a number of Western countries including Australia, Canada, England and Wales, Germany, the Netherlands, Scotland, Sweden, and the United States. Chapter 8 immodestly sketches the contours of a just and effective sentencing system for U. S. jurisdictions that would treat like cases alike and different cases differently.

Nonfiction books are written by individuals only in the most mundane senses. Most of what we know, certainly most of what I know and here try to relate, was learned from others. Even the bits we think we have gleaned by ourselves more often result from lapse of memory than from discovery. I have been fortunate in my tutors. Countless judges, corrections officials, prosecutors, and scholars have provided instruction over a quarter century and I am grateful to all of them. Roxanne Lieb and Dale Parent, founding directors of the Washington and Minnesota sentencing commissions, have patiently corrected my mistakes and clarified my confusions for fifteen years, and tried once more when I sent them this manuscript. Norval Morris, Lloyd Ohlin, David Boerner, Todd Clear, Richard Frase, Daniel J. Freed, Doris MacKenzie, Joan Petersilia, Andrew von Hirsch, and Ronald F. Wright read drafts of parts or all of this book and showed me how to make it better. I owe special thanks to Kate Hamilton, without whose organizational skills, graphics talents, and eye for detail this would be a poorer and later book.

It is customary at this point for humble writers to insist that colleagues bear no responsibility for a book's failings, though they may take credit for its strengths. It is less customary, but happens, for writers to suggest that any glory is entirely their own, any opprobrium the due of others. Neither posture entirely fits here, for many of those whose aid I gratefully acknowledge disagree fundamentally with various of my arguments, and as to those with equal vigor would disclaim credit and deny responsibility.

Earlier versions of parts of several chapters were published elsewhere: parts of chapters 2, 4, and 5 appeared in *Crime and Justice: A*

Review of Research, published by the University of Chicago Press; parts of chapter 3 appeared in *Crime and Delinquency*, published by Sage Publications, and in *The Federal Sentencing Reporter*, published by the University of California Press; and part of chapter 7 appeared in *The Politics of Sentencing Reform*, edited by Chris Clarkson and Rod Morgan and published in 1995 by Oxford University Press. Such sections as are reprinted are reprinted by permission. In all cases they have been updated, in most they have been substantially revised, and in some they have changed almost beyond recognition.

Castine, Maine　　　　　　　　　　　　　　　　　　　　　M. T.
June 1995

Contents

SENTENCING MATTERS

1

Sentencing Matters

Sentencing matters in the 1990s more than ever before. This is not because the values and interests at stake have changed. The state's interest in enforcing its laws, the defendant's interest in preserving his liberty, and the judge's responsibility justly to reconcile them are as they have always been. So is the mix of considerations that judges think important—the importance of the behavioral norms that were violated, the effects of the crime on the victim, and the amalgam of aggravating and mitigating circumstances that make a defendant more or less culpable and make one sentence more appropriate than another.

What has changed is the political salience of sentencing. Until twenty-five years ago, the word "sentencing" generally signified a slightly mysterious process which, it was all but universally agreed, involved individualized decisions that judges were uniquely competent to make. Sentencing laws were crafted to allow judges latitude to fashion penalties tailored to the circumstances of individual cases. In our time, both the need for individualized consideration and the special competence of judges have been contested.

Sentencing, as a result, has been radically refashioned in two ways. First, sentencing has become a recurrent subject of ideological conflict, partisan politics, and legislative action. Many elected officials are no longer willing to enact general laws on sentencing and defer to judges to apply them wisely. Modern laws often tell judges what sentence to impose rather than set boundaries within which sentencing choices are to be made. Election campaigns regularly feature candidates' promises to be "tough on crime" and to support harsher punishments. Every state since 1980 has enacted laws mandating minimum prison sentences based on the premises that harsher penalties will reduce crime rates and that judges cannot otherwise be trusted to impose them. Following Washington State voters' adoption in 1993 of a "three strikes and you're out" referendum that mandates life sentences for third-time felons, many other states considered such laws and some adopted them. The federal Violent Crime Control and Law Enforcement Act of 1994 contained a three-strikes provision, extended the death penalty to sixty additional crimes, and authorized $8 billion for construction of state prisons in a country in which the prison population had tripled between 1980 and 1995. And still many members of Congress returned to Washington after the 1994 elections promising to pass tougher laws.

Second, there has been a fundamental and ongoing shift in the past quarter century in sentencing processes and institutions. In 1970, every state and the federal system had an "indeterminate sentencing system" in which judges had wide discretion to decide who went to prison and to set maximum and sometimes minimum prison terms. Parole boards decided when prisoners were released. Beginning with Maine's abolition of parole in 1975, nearly every state has in some ways repudiated indeterminate sentencing and recast sentencing policies to set standards for judges' and parole boards' decisions and thereby to narrow or eliminate their discretion.

Although ideological and partisan politics have played some part in fostering the shift from indeterminate to (what is now, primarily for semantic contrast, called) determinate sentencing, the impetus for change has been broad-based. Proposals for sentencing change have come from many quarters. Penal abolitionists, humanitarians, and political liberals typically want reduced severity. Law enforcement officials, victims groups, and political conservatives want tougher penalties. Academics, civil rights advocates, and civil libertarians want them made fairer and want racial, sexual, and other unwarranted disparities reduced. Utilitarians and crime-control spokesmen want them made more effective. Nearly all want sentencing made more consistent, whether in the name of justice, efficiency, effectiveness, or economy.

More is known about the operation of determinate sentencing systems and about the effects of sentencing policy changes after twenty-five years of ferment than was known about indeterminate sentencing after seventy-five years. Partly this is because evaluation tools are available in our time that were not available to earlier generations, and partly it is because people want to know whether changes have achieved what they were designed to accomplish. Sizable literatures exist on the effects of various changes in sentencing institutions and practices, on the crime-preventive effects of changes in penalties, and on the operation and effects of noncustodial penalties. From them, we know how to create sentencing systems that are just and efficient and protective of public safety. Policy makers in many states are trying to use that knowledge to design better systems. Whether they succeed will depend on which of the pressures for sentencing change—partisan political calls for ever-increasing severity or nonpartisan calls for more just, efficient, and effective systems—proves more powerful and lasting.

A just sentencing system would be simultaneously respectful of the public interests in safety, crime prevention, and economy, and of the needs to assure that convicted offenders are treated fairly and consistently. Accumulated research and experience concerning the past twenty years of sentencing policy changes shows what such a system would look like.

First, legislatures would repeal all mandatory minimum penalties, including "three-strikes" laws.

Second, legislatures would invest the funds needed to establish credible, well-managed noncustodial penalties that can serve as sanctions intermediate between prison and probation.

Third, authority for creation of rules for sentencing would be delegated to an administrative agency, often but not necessarily called a sentencing commission.

Fourth, the sentencing commission would be directed to develop, promulgate, and monitor systems of sentencing rules, usually but not necessarily called sentencing guidelines.

Fifth, the sentencing commission would be directed to take account of existing and planned corrections resources, both community based and institutional, and to devise guidelines that are compatible in their projected implementation with the facilities and resources that are or will be available.

Sixth, the sentencing commission would be directed to devise guidelines for custodial penalties that set maximum presumptive terms of confinement for all cases and minimum presumptive terms only for the most serious crimes.

Seventh, the sentencing commission would be directed to devise guidelines for noncustodial penalties that permit judges to choose among noncustodial penalties for minor crimes and between them and periods of full or partial confinement for more serious crimes.

Eighth, enabling legislation and sentencing commission policy would establish a presumption that, within the range of sanctions set out in applicable guidelines, judges should impose the least punitive and intrusive appropriate sentence.

The proposals are more fully explained and justified in chapter 8. The intervening chapters contain the evidence on which these proposals are based. Here they are presented in brief on the rationale that fairness to readers requires that they know where a writer hopes to take them.

The rest of this chapter discusses the developments that underlay the proposals. Section I provides a backdrop by sketching the precipitants, forms, and effects of the past quarter century's sentencing policy changes. Section II discusses a wrong turn taken from the mid-1970s onward when support for "just deserts" theories and partisan calls for law and order combined to make many policy makers forget that offenders are three-dimensional human beings and not two-dimensional crime-and-criminal-history constructs.

I. Twenty-Five Years of Sentencing Ferment

Were a time machine available to bring a group of state and federal judges from the year 1971 to a national conference on sentencing in 1996, most of those judges would be astonished at a quarter century's changes and many, perhaps all, would be disapproving.

Their astonishment would result from the number and enormity of the changes they would learn about. Every American state and the federal system in 1970 had an indeterminate sentencing system in which a legislature enacted and amended the criminal code and set maximum penalties. Minimum penalties existed in a few jurisdictions, but they were widely disapproved; they generally required one- or two-year minimums except for mandatory life sentences in some jurisdictions for murder. Subject only to statutory maximums and occasional minimums, judges had authority to decide whether a convicted defendant was sentenced to probation (and with what conditions) or to jail or prison (and for what maximum term). A parole board would decide when prisoners were released; usually prisoners became eligible for release after serving a third of the maximum sentence, but they could be held until their maximum terms expired. Prison managers typically had authority to reduce maximum sentences by a third by awarding time off for good behavior ("good time"). For all practical purposes, appellate review of sentences and parole release decisions was nonexistent. Judges' and corrections officials' decisions were supposed to be governed by the unique circumstances of particular cases. Without rules governing decisions whose correct application could be examined, there was little that appellate courts could review except gross abuses of discretion or allegations of corruption; no bodies of case law on sentencing or parole appeals could or did accumulate.

In 1996, the time-traveling judges would learn that Congress in 1994 enacted legislation authorizing billions of federal dollars to those states that would abolish parole release, establish guidelines to constrain judicial sentencing discretion, and either abolish or narrow good time so that prisoners would serve at least 85 percent of their announced sentences. They would also learn that the federal system and many states had rejected indeterminate sentencing in principle and repealed much of its apparatus. Fifteen jurisdictions had adopted sentencing guidelines to limit judicial discretion; more than ten had eliminated parole release; another twenty-five had adopted parole guidelines; many had narrowed the ambit of good time; and all had enacted mandatory minimum sentence legislation (often requiring minimum ten-, twenty- or thirty-year terms and sometimes mandatory sentences of life-without-possibility-of-parole).

There can be little doubt that the time-traveling judges would disapprove of much of what they found in 1996. Partly this can be attributed to parochialism. Human beings tend to prefer the familiar over the new and what we know over what we don't. Because the broad outlines of indeterminate sentencing had been the same everywhere since 1930 (Rothman 1980), few judges at work in 1971 would have had experience with any other system.

Some of their objections would, however, concern matters of principle and conceptions of justice that transcend parochialism. Rigid sentencing laws, including mandatory penalties, they would argue, create unacceptable risks of injustice because they make it impossible to take account of important differences between defendants. For that reason, the U.S. Congress in 1970 repealed most mandatory minimum provisions in federal law.

Legislative passage of laws that specify penalties for particular cases is unwise, they would urge, because legislators are far likelier than judges to be influenced by short-term emotions and concern for political advantage. Chase Riveland, Washington State's longtime commissioner of corrections, encapsulates those concerns when he describes many modern tough-on-crime laws as "drive-by legislation." And, they would insist, narrow limits on judicial discretion are unsound because they shift more power into the already powerful hands of prosecutors who will exercise it less judiciously than judges would.

We can predict that these arguments would be made because many judges have opposed sentencing reforms from the early 1970s to today in these terms, and many judges (and nonjudges) still do. But there is one 1970s argument that is seldom heard—that there is no need for substantial changes to sentencing law and practice because there is no convincing evidence that indeterminate sentencing was afflicted by unwarranted sentencing disparities or racial and gender bias. This argument is seldom heard because it is no longer tenable.

Unwarranted disparities, explicable more in terms of the judge's personality, beliefs, and background than the offender's crime or criminal history, have repeatedly been demonstrated (Blumstein et al. 1983, chap. 2). There was substantial gender disparity in indeterminate sentencing—in favor of women (Nagel and Hagan 1983; Knapp 1984). The evidence is unclear on the causes of racial disparities, but their existence is well documented (Mann 1993; Tonry 1995a).

Finally, there is one 1970s argument—that tougher penalties will reduce crime rates—that is still heard, but mostly from campaigning conservative politicians and virtually never from crime-control researchers or from authoritative nonpartisan bodies. Political scientist James Q. Wilson, for example, for two decades America's leading conservative scholar of crime and punishment, in 1994 acknowledged, "Many (probably most) criminologists think we use prison too much and at too great cost and that this excessive use has had little beneficial effect on the crime rate" (Wilson 1994, p. 499).

No one doubts that having some penalties is better than having none. What is widely doubted is the proposition that changes in penalties have any significant effects on behavior. Most crime-control scholars are doubtful because that proposition is refuted by the clear weight of the research evidence and because every nonpartisan expert body in the United States, Canada, and England that has examined the evidence has reached that same conclusion. In 1993, the National Academy of Sciences Panel on Understanding and Control of Violent Behavior (Reiss and Roth 1993), paid for by the Bush administration's Department of Justice, noted that the average prison time per violent crime had *tripled* between 1975 and 1989 and asked, "What effect has increasing the prison population had on levels of violent crime?" The answer, "Apparently, very little." In 1978, the National Academy of Sciences Panel on Research on Deterrent and Incapacitative Effects (Blumstein, Cohen, and Nagin 1978), funded by the Ford administration's Department of Justice, concluded, "we cannot assert that the evidence warrants an affirmative conclusion regarding deterrence." Daniel Nagin (1978), that panel's principal consultant, was more explicit, "Policymakers in the criminal justice system are done a disservice if they are left with the impression that the empirical evidence . . . strongly supports the deterrence hypothesis."

Similar bodies in other English-speaking countries have reached the same conclusions. The English Home Office (1990), during Margaret Thatcher's time as prime minister, conducted a three-year review of evidence on the crime-control effects of penalties and concluded that the penalties' effects were so uncertain that they should have only minor influence on sentencing policy. As a result, Parliament enacted the Criminal Justice Act 1991, which replaced crime-control premises in English sentencing policy with a "just deserts" approach (Ashworth 1992*a*). A key passage in the Home Office report explained why: "Deterrence is a principle with much immediate appeal. . . . But much crime is committed on impulse . . . by offenders who live from moment to moment; their crimes are as impulsive as the rest of their feckless, sad, or pathetic lives. It is unrealistic to construct sentencing arrangements on the assumption that most offenders will weigh up the possibilities in advance and base their conduct on rational calculation."

Canada is the other English-speaking country that has recently had a conservative national government, led by Tory party prime minister Brian Mulroney. In 1993, the judiciary committee of Canada's parliament (Committee on Justice and the Solicitor General 1993), led by a member of Mulroney's party, recommended that Canada shift from an American-style law enforcement approach to crime to a European-style preventive approach. The report observed, "The United States affords a glaring example of the limited impact that criminal justice responses may have on crime. . . . If locking up those who violate the law contributed to safer societies then the United States should be the safest country in the world." There is overwhelming additional evidence to support the conclusions of the government-sponsored panels in Canada, England, and the United States; it is discussed at length in chapter 5.

The overall impression the time-traveling judges would take back with them would be shaped by whether they learned first about the federal or the state sentencing reforms. If they studied the changes wrought by the federal Sentencing Reform Act of 1984, and the U.S. Sentencing Commission it created, they would go back determined to fight the first signs of the sentencing reform movement. If they studied the experiences of states like Delaware, Minnesota, Pennsylvania, Oregon, and Washington, they would return apprehensive but with an understanding that meliorable injustices existed under indeterminate sentencing that could be mitigated without creating larger injustices in their place.

Before I describe what the travelers would learn, I should summarize the briefing book they would receive that would provide background to the ongoing debates they would encounter. Sentencing became a focus of criminal justice reform efforts in the mid-1970s, influenced by several contemporaneous developments. First, civil rights activists, concerned by what appeared to them to be racial and class bias and unwarranted disparities in sentencing and correctional administration, called for controls on the discretion of judges and other officials (e.g., American Friends Service Committee 1971). Second, social scientists reported that there was little systematic empirical evidence that corrections programs successfully reduced recidivism, which undermined the rehabilitative foundation on which indeterminate sentencing stood (e.g., Lipton, Martinson, and Wilks 1975). Third, proceduralists throughout the legal system were working to make legal processes fairer and decision makers more accountable, and argued that sentencing too should be subject to rules and review procedures (e.g., Davis 1969; O'Donnell, Churgin, and Curtis 1977). Fourth, political conservatives, concerned about a specter of "lenient judges," supported sentencing reforms as a way to set and enforce harsher sentencing standards (e.g., Wilson 1975, 1983).

Most of these developments shaped an influential book, *Criminal Sentences: Law without Order* (1972), by Judge Marvin Frankel, at that time a federal district court judge. On fairness grounds, he decried the absence of standards for the sentences that federal judges set and the related absence of meaningful opportunities for sentence appeals. He proposed creation of a specialized administrative agency called a sentencing commission that would develop rules for sentencing. The rules would be presumptively applicable and questions about their correct application would be subject to review by higher courts.

Judge Frankel's proposals were shaped by appreciation of the institutional properties of legislatures and administrative agencies. Administrative agencies over time develop specialized expertise that legislatures can not match and develop cadres of subject-matter specialists. Moreover, because commissioners are typically appointed for fixed terms and are ordinarily outside day-to-day political battles, administrative agencies can be somewhat insulated from emotionalism and short-term political pressures.

Judge Frankel's sentencing commission proposal has become the most widely adopted vehicle for sentencing reform. In the 1970s, several states—most notably Minnesota and Pennsylvania—created sentencing commissions. Several others—for example, Arizona, California, Illinois, and Indiana—replaced indeterminate sentencing with "statutory determinate sentencing" schemes in which criminal codes prescribed specific prison terms for particular crimes.

The comparative merits of the sentencing commission soon became clear. Evaluations in Minnesota and Pennsylvania (and later in Oregon and Washington) showed that use of sentencing guidelines reduced disparities generally and in particular reduced racial and gender disparities (this last might be seen by some as a mixed blessing since the effect was to increase sentences for women). In addition, many judges in those states came to favor guidelines because they provided a starting point for considering what sentences to impose and were seen to reduce disparities. By contrast, the statutory determinate sentencing systems were not shown to have had significant lasting effects.

More importantly, experience confirmed Judge Frankel's ideas about administrative sentencing agencies. Minnesota's commission adopted policies tying sentencing policy to available prison resources and managed to hold the prison population within capacity throughout the 1980s, when most states experienced record increases. The Washington (for a time), Oregon, and most recently Kansas commissions had similar success at partly insulating sentencing policy from political pressure and keeping prison populations and prison resources in balance. By contrast, in states like California where fine-grained sentencing policies were left in legislative hands, statutory sentencing provisions were made harsher nearly every year and the prison population climbed by 400 percent between 1980 and 1995 (Zimring and Hawkins 1995).

By 1996, the success of Judge Frankel's innovation was clear. Twenty-five states at one time or another had created commissions, guidelines were in effect or under development in nearly twenty states, and new commissions had begun work in 1994 in Oklahoma, Missouri, and Massachusetts (Frase 1995; Greene 1995a). No state adopted a statutory determinate sentencing scheme after 1980 and some that had done so, like Colorado, diluted its effects by reintroducing parole release (Wesson 1993).

Because the federal commission had the prior experiences of the states to draw on, ample resources, and the capacity to recruit staff from throughout the country, all of the auguries would have predicted that the U.S. Sentencing Commission would build on the state experiences and produce the most successful guidelines system to date. The commission managed to defy that prediction.

Few outside the federal commission would disagree that the federal guidelines have been a disaster. In a statement similar to many made by other judges, Second Circuit Court of Appeals judge José Cabranes (1992) wrote, "The sentencing guidelines system is a failure—a dismal failure, a fact well known and fully understood by virtually everyone who is associated with the federal judicial system." A Federal Judicial Center survey of federal judges released in 1994 showed that 58.9 percent of appellate judges and 68.5 percent of trial judges were "strongly" or "moderately" opposed to retention of "the current system of mandatory guidelines." Forty percent of appellate judges and 50 percent of trial judges wanted the guidelines eliminated entirely.

The Sentencing Reform Act of 1984 abolished parole release prospectively and directed the newly created sentencing commission to develop guidelines for federal sentencing. The highly detailed guidelines divide crimes into forty-three different categories and are both rigid and mechanical. The commission has forbidden judges to take account in sentencing of many considerations—such as the effect of the sentence on the defendant or the defendant's family; or the defendant's mental health or drug or alcohol dependence; or a severely deprived background or victimization by sexual abuse—that many judges (and most people) believe to be ethically relevant in a just system of sentencing. The guidelines are based not on the offense of which the defendant was convicted, but on his "actual offense behavior," including alleged crimes of which he was acquitted or never charged. The guidelines allow virtually no role for nonimprisonment sentences.

For all these reasons, the federal guidelines are deeply disliked by most federal judges and lawyers who practice in federal courts, and they are widely circumvented. Even commission-sponsored research demonstrates that prosecutors and judges disingenuously circumvent the guidelines in a third of cases (Nagel and Schulhofer 1992). The true rate is probably higher.

Staff of newly created state commissions report that negative stereotypes created by the federal guidelines have been a major obstacle to their work. Recent commissions in Arkansas, Texas, Ohio, and North Carolina adopted resolutions repudiating the federal guidelines as a model for any policies they might later develop (Orland and Reitz 1993). Both the North Carolina commission and the American Bar Association's Sentencing Standards Project (which proposed that states create sentencing commissions) avoided use of the word "guidelines" because of the negative connotations associated with the federal guidelines (Reitz and Reitz 1995; Tonry 1995*b*).

No one factor can explain why the federal guidelines have been so much less successful and accepted than state guidelines. Some judges use words like arrogant and hostile to describe the commission's attitude to the federal judiciary. Some observers argue that the failure was in management. With its ample resources, a better-managed commission that consulted more widely and made efforts to learn from the state experiences could have done better. Others suggest that inexperience may have been part of the problem. Only three of the seven commissioners had ever been a judge, only two had been a trial judge, and only one had imposed a sentence within the preceding twenty years. Still others, more conspiracy-minded, note that a number of the initial commissioners were long known to be aspirants for higher judicial office (two achieved their aspirations) and suggest that the guidelines were an effort to show that the commission's policies were consonant with the views of influential congressional conservatives (von Hirsch 1988; Freed and Miller 1989; U.S. General Accounting Office 1990*a*; Stith and Koh 1993; Tonry 1991, 1993*a*).

There is truth in all those explanations, but the most important explanation is contextual: the federal sentencing commission legislation was formulated and agreed on in one political era, in which Judge Frankel's ideals were widely shared, but implemented in a different political era in which they had little influence. The initial proposed federal commission legislation introduced in the Congress in 1974, Senate Bill 181, was a direct outgrowth of a Yale Law School seminar that attempted to convert Judge Frankel's ideas into proposed legislation (O'Donnell, Churgin, and Curtis 1977). After reintroduction in successive congresses as a stand-alone bill, the proposal was folded into the then-pending proposed federal criminal code. By 1979, Senators Edward Kennedy and Strom Thurmond, the ranking Democratic and Republican members of the Senate Judiciary Committee (who succeeded one another as chairs), agreed on compromises and the Senate passed the proposed federal code, including the sentencing commission provisions, by a large majority. Although the House of Representatives did not act, the Senate agreement held, and the code bill including the sentencing commission parts repeatedly thereafter passed both the Senate Judiciary Committee and the Senate by wide margins. Eventually the code bill was abandoned as unpassable but the more technocratic and less controversial commission parts were included in an omnibus crime bill that was enacted in 1984 (Stith and Koh 1993).

Unfortunately, when this bipartisan, good-government, rationalistic proposal, formulated in the mid-1970s and intended to make sentencing fairer and to distance sentencing policy from politics, took effect, the government in power did not hold those goals. The crime-control policies of the Reagan administration in 1985 when the commissioners were appointed were oriented more toward toughness than toward fairness. As the English playwright John Mortimer has put it, the champions of "law and order" apparently valued those goals in reverse order. It should not therefore be a surprise that the commissioners who were appointed chose not to try to insulate their policy-making process from congressional politics but instead to show that they, too, were tough on crime and had little sympathy for the views of "lenient" judges (an odd stereotype since a large percentage of federal district judges by 1987 when the guidelines took effect were Reagan appointees—as today a large percentage of the guidelines' fiercest critics are Reagan and Bush appointees).

So the picture the traveling judges would see is mixed: federal guidelines that at least match their worst preconceptions of what would happen if indeterminate sentencing were abandoned, and state guidelines that turned out—I believe they would conclude—surprisingly well.

Modern sentencing reform efforts might have been more successful but for two developments—one principled, one political—that Judge Frankel probably did not foresee. First, some other governing rationale for sentencing policy was bound to take the place left empty when rehabilitation lost favor. In both academic and policy circles, that place was taken (sometimes implicitly) by retribution or "just deserts," with unintended consequences that made sentencing in many jurisdictions harsher and more mechanical than is necessary or just. Second, to an extent not known since the 1930s, crime control became a central issue in American politics in the 1970s and remains a central issue to this day. Because law-abiding citizens understandably fear crime and resent criminals, "toughness" and "law and order" are popular slogans to run on and "leniency" and "soft on crime" are labels few candidates willingly accept. Because, however, increased toughness seldom has any perceptible effects on crime rates, unremitting concern for toughness has resulted in pressures only, and continually, to increase penalties. The interaction between these two developments has produced the rigidity and harshness that are the two features of modern sentencing that judges and other practitioners most dislike.

II. The Injustice of Just Deserts

The irony of "just deserts" is that it backfired. The overriding aim was to make sentencing principled and fair, and the logic was consistent with Judge Frankel's call for rules to govern sentencing. If indeterminate sentencing sometimes produced racial and class disparities, other unwarranted disparities, and sentences grossly out of proportion to the crimes of which offenders were convicted, there was much to be said for proposals to scale the severity of punishments to the seriousness of crimes and thereby to satisfy the first tenet of equal treatment: to "treat like cases alike." In practice the effect was to focus attention solely on offenders' crimes and criminal records, to the exclusion of ethically important differences in their circumstances, and thereby to fail the second tenet of equal treatment: to "treat different cases differently."

Reduced to their core elements, just deserts theories are based on the intuitively powerful idea that punishment should be *deserved*, the empirical premise that most people agree about the comparative seriousness of crimes, and the proposal that crimes be ranked in order of their seriousness and punishments proportioned to those rankings (von Hirsch 1976, 1985, 1993). In such a scheme, people convicted of comparable offenses would receive similar punishments, and people convicted of more serious offenses would receive harsher penalties than those convicted of less serious offenses. In practice, however, while most academic proponents of desert theories favor overall *reduction* in the severity of punishments (e.g., von Hirsch 1993), the result has been both to make punishment more severe and to create disparities as extreme as any that existed under indeterminate sentencing.

It would be unfair to assign all blame for overemphasis on the equality principle and underemphasis on the difference principle to just deserts theories. Those emphases are in part a by-product of the format in which new sentencing standards were expressed. Sentencing guidelines are typically set out in a two-dimensional grid. Because crimes and criminal records can be scaled for seriousness, and few other ethically relevant considerations can, the two axes of the grids are invariably measures of the seriousness of crimes and the extensiveness of criminal records. This is true of the federal sentencing guidelines, for example, even though the U.S. Sentencing Commission expressly rejected just deserts as the rationale for its guidelines. Thus, with or without express just deserts rationales, modern sentencing policies concentrate almost exclusively on crimes.

This strikes many judges, prosecutors, and defense lawyers—who typically believe that many characteristics of offenders besides their crimes are pertinent to just sentencing—as wrong and unjust. Forced to choose between their oaths to enforce the law, by imposing sentences they believe unjust, and to do justice, by willfully evading the law's commands, they often do the latter. As a result, many sentencing reforms premised in part on "truth in sentencing" produce deceptive sentencing.

All guidelines systems are not premised on just deserts rationales, but many of those that promulgate their guidelines in grids suffer from the same problems. The Kansas and Minnesota sentencing commissions, among others, expressly adopted just deserts rationales for their guidelines (Parent 1988; Kansas Sentencing Commission 1990, p. 4). The U.S. Sentencing Commission refused to adopt any rationale for its guidelines, explaining that it decided not to choose between just deserts and "crime-control" (deterrence and incapacitation) rationales because, "this choice was unnecessary because in most sentencing decisions the application of either philosophy will produce the same or similar results" (U.S. Sentencing Commission 1992*a*, p. 3). Yet all three commissions promulgated architecturally similar grids that prescribe standards for sentencing.

Reduced to their core elements, all sentencing guidelines grids are fundamentally the same: two-dimensional tables that classify crimes by their severity along one axis and criminal records by their extent along the other. Applicable sentences for any case are calculated by finding the cell where the applicable criminal record column intersects with the applicable offense severity row (for example, see table 1.1, the Washington State grid in effect in 1994). Guidelines grids vary in details. Although most divide crimes into ten or twelve categories, some use more; the federal guidelines—the extreme case—create forty-three levels of offense severity. They vary in ornateness. Although most, like Washington's, provide a range of presumptive sentences such as "twenty-one to twenty-seven months" for any offense severity/criminal record combination, those in North Carolina (1994) and Pennsylvania (1994) contain a range for "ordinary cases" and separate ranges for cases in which aggravating or mitigating considerations are present. Finally, they vary in severity. Offenders who in most state systems would be subject to presumptive prison sentences of a few months or years often face sentences of many years under the federal guidelines.

Whatever the detailed policies guidelines embody, however, the two-axis grid is a common feature and, in interaction with just-deserts rationales, produces unjust results and conduces to needlessly harsh sentences. Two things happen. First, because desert theories place primary emphasis on linking deserved punishments to the severity of crimes, in the interest of treating like cases alike, they lead to disregard of other ethically relevant differences between offenders—like their personal backgrounds and the effects of punishments on them and their families—and thereby often treat unlike cases alike. Second, the all-but-exclusive emphasis in guidelines grids on crimes and criminal records affects the psychology of sentencing and sentencers. Just as sunlight sometimes etiolates a leaf, leaving the veins distinct and bleaching out the surrounding tissue, desert theories and grids make crimes and criminal records distinct and the human characteristics of offenders invisible. Comparison of vein patterns may be useful, and enough, in classifying leaves, but in making crucial decisions about peoples' lives, comparison only of crimes and criminal records is not enough.

Ethical Differences Between Cases

Just deserts, sometimes characterized as expressing a "principle of proportionality" (von Hirsch 1992), is sound in theory but defective in practice. In an ideal world in which all citizens have equal opportunities for self-realization and material advancement, the idea that deserved punish-

Table 1.1. Washington State Sentencing Guidelines Grid, for Crimes Committed after June 30, 1990

Seriousness Level	Offender Score									
	0	1	2	3	4	5	6	7	8	9 or more
XV	Life Sentence without Parole/Death Penalty									
XIV	23y 4m 240–320	24y 4m 250–333	25y 4m 261–347	26y 4m 271–361	27y 4m 281–374	28y 4m 291–388	30y 4m 312–416	32y 10m 338–450	36y 370–493	40y 411–548
XIII	12y 123–164	13y 134–178	14y 144–192	15y 154–205	16y 165–219	17y 175–233	19y 195–260	21y 216–288	25y 257–342	29y 298–397
XII	9y 93–123	9y 11m 102–136	10y 9m 111–147	11y 8m 120–160	12y 6m 129–171	13y 5m 138–184	15y 9m 162–216	17y 3m 178–236	20y 3m 209–277	23y 3m 240–318
XI	7y 6m 78–102	8y 4m 86–114	9y 2m 95–125	9y 11m 102–136	10y 9m 111–147	11y 7m 120–158	14y 2m 146–194	15y 5m 159–211	17y 11m 185–245	20y 5m 210–280
X	5y 51–68	5y 6m 57–75	6y 62–82	6y 6m 67–89	7y 72–96	7y 6m 77–102	9y 6m 98–130	10y 6m 108–144	12y 6m 129–171	14y 6m 149–198
IX	3y 31–41	3y 6m 36–48	4y 41–54	4y 6m 46–61	5y 51–68	5y 6m 57–75	7y 6m 77–102	8y 6m 87–116	10y 6m 108–144	12y 6m 129–171
VIII	2y 21–27	2y 6m 26–34	3y 31–41	3y 6m 36–48	4y 41–54	4y 6m 46–61	6y 6m 67–89	7y 6m 77–102	8y 6m 87–116	10y 6m 108–144
VII	18m 15–20	2y 21–27	2y 6m 26–34	3y 31–41	3y 6m 36–48	4y 41–54	5y 6m 57–75	6y 6m 67–89	7y 6m 77–102	8y 6m 87–116
VI	13m 12+–14	18m 15–20	2y 21–27	2y 6m 26–34	3y 31–41	3y 6m 36–48	4y 6m 46–61	5y 6m 57–75	6y 6m 67–89	7y 6m 77–102
V	9m 6–12	13m 12+–14	15m 13–17	18m 15–20	2y 2m 22–29	3y 2m 33–43	4y 41–54	5y 51–68	6y 62–82	7y 72–96
IV	6m 3–9	9m 6–12	13m 12+–14	15m 13–17	18m 15–20	2y 2m 22–29	3y 2m 33–43	4y 2m 43–57	5y 2m 53–70	6y 2m 63–84
III	2m 1–3	5m 3–8	8m 4–12	11m 9–12	14m 12+–16	20m 17–22	2y 2m 22–29	3y 2m 33–43	4y 2m 43–57	5y 51–68
II	0–90 days	4m 2–6	6m 3–9	8m 4–12	13m 12+–14	16m 14–18	20m 17–22	2y 2m 22–29	3y 2m 33–43	4y 2m 43–57
I	0–60 days	0–90 days	3m 2–5	4m 2–6	5m 3–8	8m 4–12	13m 12+–14	16m 14–18	20m 17–22	2y 2m 22–29

Source: Washington State Sentencing Guidelines Commission (1991), table 1.

ments can be calibrated precisely to the offender's culpability, and that punishments should be apportioned accordingly, has much to commend it. Somewhat awkwardly for desert theories, however, ours is a world that in a number of respects falls short of the ideal.

For this reason, a number of leading philosophers who have written about punishment from a retributive perspective, though their views differ in important details, agree that retributive schemes cannot be justified in practice. British philosopher Antony Duff (1986, p. 294), for example, who then espoused a punishment philosophy that combined elements of retribution and moral education, rejected his own views in favor of a deterrence-based scheme: "Punishment is not justifiable within our present legal system; it will not be justifiable unless and until we have brought about deep and far-reaching social, political, legal, and moral changes in ourselves and our society."

American philosopher Jeffrey Murphy developed a retributive punishment theory based on the idea that offenders enjoy the benefits of organized society and other peoples' acceptance of the burdens of citizenship, and must be punished so that they do not gain an unfair advantage. If they enjoy the benefits of others' law-abiding behavior, they must accept the same burdens. Punishment is a process that appropriately attempts to put burdens and benefits back into balance. Nonetheless, in practice, Murphy (1973, p. 110) rejected the implications of his own theory because it could not deliver justice until "we have restructured society in such a way that criminals genuinely do correspond to the only model that will render punishment permissible—i.e., make sure that they are autonomous and that they do benefit in the requisite sense."

Philosophers writing from nonretributive premises often reach the same conclusion. English philosopher Ted Honderich (1989, pp. 238–39), for example, who in principle favors a punishment theory combining retributive and utilitarian elements, rejects it in practice: "There is nothing that can be called the question of [punishment's] moral justification which is left to be considered if one puts aside the great question of the distribution of goods in society." Oxford philosopher H. L. A. Hart (1968, p. 51), this century's most influential writer on punishment, after arguing that the criminal law did not and should not recognize a general defense of great economic temptation, nonetheless observed, for "those below a minimum level of economic prosperity . . . [perhaps] we should incorporate as a further excusing condition the pressure of gross forms of economic necessity."

That the problem of "just deserts in an unjust world," as it is sometimes called, is serious, is shown by its acknowledgment (though not acceptance) by Andrew von Hirsch (1986, p. 149), the most influential modern proponent of just deserts theories: "As long as a substantial segment of the population is denied adequate opportunities for a livelihood, any scheme for punishing must be morally flawed."

More generally, proponents of utilitarian punishment theories believe that no punishments should be imposed that are more harsh or intrusive than is necessary. This is sometimes called a "principle of parsimony," and is based on the belief that the infliction of suffering on anyone, including wrongdoers, is wrong and can be justified only when some greater good is thereby accomplished (Tonry 1994). Jeremy Bentham, the nineteenth-century philosopher to whom modern utilitarian theories can be traced, wrote, "Upon the principle of utility, if [punishment] ought at all to be admitted, it ought only to be admitted in as far as it promises to exclude some greater evil" (Bentham 1843).

Among modern writers, Norval Morris (1974) most fully takes account of parsimony in his theory of limiting retributivism. While just deserts considerations can often help us identify "undeserved punishments" (because manifestly too severe or too lenient), he argues, they offer little guidance on determination of "deserved punishments." Accordingly, just sentencing policies for all crimes should set upper limits, calibrated to prevent infliction of undeserved punishments, and for some serious crimes should set lower limits, but otherwise should allow judges to adjust sentences to take account of ethically relevant differences between offenders.

Most judges and practicing lawyers subscribe to views like Morris's. That is why they so often believe rigid sentencing guidelines and mandatory minimum penalties are unjust. And *that* is why, as the findings of numerous studies discussed in chapters 2, 3, and 5 attest, they are often prepared to manipulate and evade rigid sentencing guidelines and mandatory penalties to achieve what they consider just results in individual cases.

Even accepting for purposes of argument, however, that desert theories can be justified, in practice they suffer from important additional defects. The first arises from their sole reliance on current and (to a much lesser extent) past criminality for the calculation of deserved punishments. The problem, as English philosopher Nigel Walker (1991) has pointed out, is that "retributive reasoning would lead" not to standardized lists of crimes and punishments but "instead to 'a personal price list' which would take into account not only gradations of harm but offenders' culpability and sensibility." Walker sometimes writes of the Recording Angel who will determine our futures at life's end and suggests that a genuinely retributive assessment of an offender's culpability and deserved punishment would encompass all the things the Recording Angel would find relevant.

Like the Recording Angel's, most peoples' judgments of others' blameworthiness depend on knowledge of their circumstances. A suburban stockbroker who sells cocaine elicits different judgments of moral culpability than does a disadvantaged ghetto youth who sells the same amount. A mentally retarded, easily led boy who participates in a street mugging may elicit different culpability judgments than does the gang member who persuaded him to participate. A formerly abused wife who attacks her drunken husband with a knife elicits different culpability judgments than when the knife is in the husband's hand. And so on; circumstances matter in attributions of blameworthiness.

Likewise, the collateral effects of sentences on people other than the wrongdoer matter. In just deserts principle, two offenders who commit the same offense and have similar criminal records deserve the same penalty. If applicable guidelines specify a two-year prison sentence, both should receive it. If one, however, is unemployed and has no permanent residence, and the other works and supports a family, many people will want to treat them differently. Partly, this is because the second seems more stable, more integrated into society, and somehow more worthy. Partly also, and equally important, it is because the second offender's spouse and children—who have committed no crime—will also suffer. They will lose a partner and parent for so long as the offender is in prison and may possibly lose a home and a car and be forced onto welfare. The offender, besides losing his liberty while in prison, may find when he gets out that he has also lost his family.

Judges, prosecutors, and other officials make decisions about whole people, and not about generic offenders who have committed offense X and have criminal history Y. Not surprisingly, they often feel moved to take the individual offender's circumstances into account in deciding what to do.

Another defect with systems that mechanically scale crimes to punishments is that punishments are no more standardized than are offenders. In objective terms, punishments that technically are the same may be very different. A "generic" two-year prison sentence, for example, depending on a jurisdiction's resources and the amount of authority delegated to its corrections department, may range from time spent in a crowded, fear-ridden maximum security prison under lockup twenty-three hours per day to confinement under electronic monitoring in the offender's home, with medium and minimum security prisons, forestry camps, and halfway houses in between. All count as two years' deprivation of liberty, but all offenders and most observers see them as vastly different.

In subjective terms as well, two years' imprisonment in a single setting will have very different meanings to different offenders who have committed the same crime. Two years' imprisonment in a maximum security prison may be a rite of passage for a Los Angeles gang member. For an attractive, effeminate twenty-year-old, it may mean the terror of repeated sexual victimization. For a forty-year-old head of household, it may mean the loss of a job and a home and a family. For an unhealthy seventy-five-year-old, it may be a death sentence.

A critic might respond to these observations with accusations of perfectionism. No human institution will ever deliver perfect justice, even assuming there was wide agreement as to what that was, and just deserts theories are better than anything else that has been tried. The response is that there must be a conception of criminal justice that is better than one that fails to take account of ethically relevant differences between defendants and that fails to acknowledge qualitative differences in nominally identical penalties and in their effects on individuals.

The Psychology of Two-Dimensional Grids

Use of two-dimensional grids to express sentencing standards has impoverished sentencing, irrespective of the philosophical premise, because grids affect the way that people—policy makers, practitioners, and bystanders alike—think about sentencing. This does not mean that grids should be abandoned but only that their drawbacks and dangers should be recognized. They are efficient devices for condensing and communicating vast amounts of information. They are also, however, blunt instruments when applied to sentencing operations for which scalpels are often needed.

The two-axis grid reifies thinking about punishment into a calculus that takes account only of criminality. Under indeterminate sentencing, the goal of individualization of punishment to achieve rehabilitative ends, combined with an absence of sentencing rules, forced judges to adopt a holistic approach. That approach led to unwarranted disparities and unacceptable risks of invidious bias and capriciousness, but at its best it allowed judges to take account of the crime, all of the relevant circumstances, and the likely consequences of alternate possible sentences. In the nature of things, the two-axis grid focuses people's primary attention on the considerations represented by those two axes, to the exclusion of other considerations.

This focusing effect is inversely related to people's distance from individual sentencing decisions. Judges and lawyers are intimately involved in sentencing and, depending on their personalities and experience, to a greater or lesser extent resent and resist the reification of individuals into crime-and-criminal-history amalgams. Appellate courts are further removed and, seeing only lawyers and paper, are more comfortable than trial judges in treating people as stereotypes rather than as individuals. This may be one reason why federal trial judges have been much more vocal in their opposition to the mechanistic federal guidelines than federal appellate judges have been.

Academics and politicians are even further removed from sentencing and even more likely to forget that there are people behind crime-and-criminal-record categories. The work of Princeton University political scientist John DiIulio offers an example. He has many times written that "more than 95 percent of state prisoners are violent criminals, repeat criminals (with two or more felony convictions), or violent repeat criminals" (e.g., DiIulio 1994, a *Wall Street Journal* article entitled "Let 'Em Rot"). The statement is untrue; the 1991 survey of state prison inmates conducted by the Bureau of Justice Statistics, on which DiIulio claims his statement is based (Beck et al. 1993), to the contrary says, "About 38 percent of all inmates had not been incarcerated before: 19 percent were sentenced for the first time [i.e., this was a first conviction]; 19 percent had [previously been sentenced] to probation." DiIulio's numbers are facially inconsistent with the data source on which they are ostensibly based.

More interesting, however, is DiIulio's explanation for his claim. He points out that the Bureau of Justice Statistics report elsewhere indicates that 94 percent of prisoners had as an adult *or as a juvenile* been sentenced to incarceration or *to probation*. Thus presumably unconsciously he has included among "repeat criminals (with two or more felony convictions)" first-time prisoners whose only prior record consists of a juvenile court proceeding for a property offense that resulted in probation. By legal definition, a person whose record consists only of a prior juvenile court "adjudication" has no "prior felony convictions." DiIulio has also included first-time prisoners who are nuisance property offenders with prior misdemeanor convictions or who are minor offenders with prior felony convictions for such things as shoplifting or sale of marijuana in small amounts.

A cast of mind is revealed by the phrase "violent criminals, repeat criminals (with two or more felony convictions), or violent repeat criminals." A standard rule of interpretation of legal texts, *ejusdem generis*, presumes that items listed in a series are to be treated as of comparable weight or nature. DiIulio's point presumably ("Let 'Em Rot" may be evidence) is that most people in prisons are dangerous people who do not deserve sympathy. Two of his three categories, "violent criminals" and "repeat violent criminals," illustrate that point. Sandwiched between them, however, and implicitly a category of equivalent danger, are "repeat criminals" who as it turns out include both people with no prior adult convictions (only juvenile court adjudications, many for property crimes) and people whose only adult convictions involve trifling property crimes.

The reality is that all people in prison are not equally dangerous. In 1991, again drawing on the Bureau of Justice Statistics survey, 49 percent of prisoners had been convicted of violent crimes and another 13 percent were in prison for property or drug crimes but had previously been convicted (or in juvenile court, been adjudicated) of a violent crime. Thus 62 percent had at some time had a conviction or adjudication for a violent crime. This offers a starting point for calculating the percentage of genuinely dangerous prisoners, but most fair-minded adjustments would be downward. For many years, half or more of murders involved otherwise noncriminal people killing family members or friends in emotionally charged circumstances; these murderers tend to be docile prisoners and crime-free in their later lives. Many juvenile court adjudications for violence involve fights between young people who leave their inability to control their anger behind as they mature. And so on. Not all prisoners with violence in their records are the dangerous predators that DiIulio's rhetoric conjures up.

I discussed DiIulio's claim for several paragraphs not only to demonstrate its inaccuracy—only he knows whether the misstatements are willful or the product of overzealous argument—but also to illustrate the way that many conservative politicians and academics seem to have lost sight of the human dimensions and consequences of sentencing.

The recent tendency to formulate sentencing policy primarily in terms of current and past crimes bears part of the blame for overclaiming like DiIulio's. Thinking about sentencing abstractly in terms only of crimes and criminal records makes it easy to forget that the abstract category is only an analytical convenience and that the offenders facing sentencing are real people.

This may also be one reason the members of the federal sentencing commission were comfortable creating a system of sentencing in which, under sections 5H1.1–5H1.6 (U.S. Sentencing Commission 1992*a*), "education and vocational skills [and age, and mental and emotional conditions, and physical condition including drug dependence and alcohol abuse, and family ties and responsibilities, among others] are not ordinarily relevant in determining whether a sentence should be outside the applicable guideline range." The essence of the problem is captured in the title of a recent article on the federal guidelines by Professor Stephen Schulhofer (who is among a handful of academic observers who in general support the federal guidelines): "Assessing the Federal Sentencing Process: The Problem Is Uniformity, Not Disparity."

Another unfortunate effect of the two-dimensional grid is entirely mundane. In the nature of things an axis of a grid can express only qualities that are linear. Crimes and criminal records can be expressed on a linear scale that starts at zero and increases in intuitively plausible ways. Murder is worse than rape which is worse than robbery which is worse than burglary which is worse than grand theft which is worse than petty theft and so on. Likewise, having five prior convictions is worse than four which is worse than three. Reasonable people quickly reach agreement about the scaling of crimes and criminal records.

Conversely, a grid axis cannot handle factors that are not linear, and many ethically relevant considerations in sentencing cannot be expressed in a linear way. Their relevance at all, and whether they are aggravating or mitigating circumstances, varies depending on the case. Take employment. The relevance of employment to sentencing varies with circumstances. Most people believe it is irrelevant that a wealthy securities law violator will, if imprisoned, lose his or her job. If anything, that person's employment history and prospects are aggravating circumstances: such crimes involve a violation of trust, and the offender's economic well-being makes the crimes difficult to explain in terms other than greed.

People have widely divergent views on whether a lower-middle-class head of household's job loss, if imprisoned, is relevant. From the perspective of the effects of imprisonment on the defendant's spouse and children, and the increased likelihood that the family will break up and be made bankrupt and welfare dependent, job loss is a mitigating circumstance. From the perspectives that employed defendants are often middle-class, and more likely than unemployed defendants to be white, concern about racial and class disparities may make job loss appear irrelevant.

Finally, most people find impending job loss if imprisoned a mitigating consideration in the case of an employed minority defendant who has overcome an inadequate education, a deprived childhood, and adolescent drug dependence to work his way up a blue-collar ladder to become a service station mechanic, and who has over a period of years managed to support a partner and out-of-wedlock children.

Many other regularly recurring circumstances are situationally relevant to just sentencing but not universally relevant. Mental abnormality may be a mitigating circumstance when it makes the defendant susceptible to manipulation by others, but an aggravating circumstance when it reduces a defendant's ability to control aggressive impulses. Excess alcohol consumption may be a mitigating circumstance when a defendant convicted of manslaughter is an alcoholic, an aggravating circumstance when the defendant was a social drinker who refused friends' pleas to drive him home, and irrelevant when a chronically abusive man while drunk assaults his wife. Age may be a relevant circumstance when the defendant is seventeen and impressionable and when the defendant is seventy-five and infirm but irrelevant in distinguishing between twenty-five- and thirty-five-year-olds. Being an employed head of household may be irrelevant when the charge is stranger rape and relevant when the charge is embezzlement.

There is no reason why guidelines systems cannot allow judges to take account of meaningful differences between offenders and offenses. Many do, by allowing judges more latitude than the federal guidelines permit, by allowing more room for departures from guidelines for reasons stated, and by establishing policy statements that offer guidance on how various nonlinear considerations might be applicable to different kinds of cases.

Just deserts theories cannot be assigned all the blame for the rigidity and lack of subtlety of many guidelines systems, but they must accept some of the responsibility. By offering policy makers a rationale for sentencing that reduced relevant considerations to two that can be scaled on the axes of grids, they reified three-dimensional defendants into two-dimensional abstractions. When policy makers think of abstractions rather than people, it is easy to respond to an electoral opponent's possible "soft on crime" accusations by voting to increase sentences or to establish mandatory penalties. This danger may be greatest in times when public concern about crime is high, or when politicians are inclined to appeal more to people's fears than to their aspirations. If a two-dimensional grid is chalked onto a legislative committee room's blackboard, it takes little effort to erase numbers and replace them with higher ones (Zimring 1976).

The sentencing innovations of the past quarter century have achieved notable gains. Guidelines in some states have reduced racial, gender, and other disparities, have made judges more accountable for their decisions, and have facilitated development of systems of appellate review of sentencing. Commissions in some states, as Judge Frankel predicted, have developed specialized expertise and to some degree insulated policy from short-term political pressures. If the federal experience with a sentencing commission and guidelines has been disastrous, it is outweighed by the happier experiences in the states.

Unfortunately, the past quarter century's innovations have also diminished the quality of justice dispensed in criminal courts. Our predecessors knew that mandatory penalties are seldom effective deterrents, sometimes produce palpably unjust punishments, and often result in disingenuous actions by judges and lawyers to blunt their effect. Many policy makers forgot those lessons and are only now relearning them. Countless individual offenders and the integrity of sentencing have suffered as a result. Similarly, the mechanism of the two-axis grid and the law-and-order politics of the last two decades have too often converted offenders into abstractions and produced a penal system of a severity unmatched in the Western world.

2

Reforming Sentencing

The sentencing commission is alive and well. Proposed by Judge Marvin Frankel more than twenty years ago as a device for reducing sentencing disparities and judicial "lawlessness," sentencing commissions were to be specialized administrative agencies charged with setting standards for sentencing (Frankel 1972). Some commissions have operated much as Judge Frankel hoped they would; they have achieved and maintained specialized institutional competence, have to a degree insulated sentencing policy from short-term "crime of the week" political pressures, and have maintained a focus on comprehensive systemwide policy making. Guidelines promulgated by commissions have altered sentencing patterns and practices, have reduced sentencing disparities including those related to gender and race, and have shown that sentencing policies can be linked to correctional and other resources, thereby enhancing governmental accountability and protecting the public purse.

Many readers may be surprised by the preceding summary of experience with sentencing commissions and their guidelines. The controversial story of the best-known commission, the U.S. Sentencing Commission, is well known. The U.S. commission's guidelines are easily the most disliked sentencing reform initiative in the United States in this century. How, a reader might reasonably ask, can the commission idea be a success if its most prominent example is so controversial?

The answer is that the experience of the U.S. commission is misleading. First, the federal commission is but one of twenty-five that have been established and of a dozen or more now in existence. In some states, notably including Delaware, Minnesota, Oregon, Pennsylvania, and Washington, the experience has been much happier. Second, and as important for assessment of the viability of Judge Frankel's proposal, the evidence documenting the policy failures and unpopularity of the U.S. guidelines at the same time demonstrates the institutional capacities of sentencing commissions. However misguided the U.S. Sentencing Commission's policies, and however ineffective its efforts to elicit acceptance from practitioners, it has become a specialized agency of technical competence and has managed through its guidelines radically to alter sentencing practices in the federal courts.

The sentencing commission idea will survive the federal debacle. Policy makers can and do distinguish the merits and promise of Judge Frankel's proposal from the demerits and failures of the U.S. federal experience. When commissions in Texas and Arkansas began work, for example, "the inevitable initial resistance inspired by the unpopular federal effort was dealt with by rapid agreements within the commissions that the commissions would not develop standards that resembled the federal sentencing guidelines system" (Knapp 1993, p. 680). Ohio's commission early on "rejected the rigid sentencing grid favored by the federal system" (Orland and Reitz 1993, p. 838). Robin Lubitz, executive director of the North Carolina commission, has explained that its proposals "omitted the word 'guidelines' because of the unpopularity of the federal guidelines" (Orland and Reitz 1993, p. 838).

Sentencing commissions are not the only organizations that have felt a need to disavow the federal example. The recently approved American Bar Association Standards for Sentencing (3rd edition) propose that every state establish a sentencing commission charged "to develop a more specific set of provisions that guide sentencing courts to presumptive sentences" (American Bar Association 1994, Standard 18–4.1[a]). The Standards, however, carefully avoid use of the word "guidelines." The proposed commission would not "promulgate sentencing guidelines"; instead it would perform an "intermediate function" between the legislature and the courts (Standard 18–4.1). Early drafts had used the words "guideline function," but, "When the proposed Standards reached the ABA Criminal Justice Council [Kevin and Curtis Reitz, co-reporters for the Standards, explain], there was firm sentiment that the word 'guidelines' not be used. The Council feared that the use of the word would signal the ABA's endorsement of the *federal* sentencing guidelines, which are by far the best known and least popular sentencing system in the nation" (emphasis in original; Reitz and Reitz 1995, p. 129).

Despite the unhappy federal experience, sentencing reform remains on the policy agendas of many jurisdictions in the United States and elsewhere. The Criminal Justice Act 1991, which took effect in October 1992, was a major reconstitution of sentencing laws and practices in England and Wales (Wasik and Taylor 1991; Ashworth 1992*a;* Thomas 1995). In Australia, although the 1980 call of the Australian Law Reform Commission for abolition of parole fell on deaf ears, in 1989 New South Wales (Gorta 1992, 1993) enacted truth-in-sentencing laws not greatly different from those in some American states; in 1991 Victoria enacted the Sentencing Act of 1991, which made significant changes to that state's sentencing laws (Fox 1991; Freiberg 1993). Although the 1987 recommendation of a Canadian national commission that Canada establish a permanent sentencing commission was not adopted by the Canadian Parliament (Canadian Sentencing Commission 1987, chap. 14), major sentencing reform legislation has been repeatedly considered (see, e.g., Roberts and von Hirsch 1993; Doob 1994).

In American states, the sentencing commission is the only institutional survivor of two decades' experimentation with comprehensive approaches to sentencing reform. During the 1970s, four different reform approaches contended (Blumstein et al. 1983, chap. 3). Parole guidelines, the earliest, dating initially from the late 1960s, were an effort to reduce disparities in prison sentences by structuring the discretion of parole boards in setting release dates. A number of states, notably including Oregon, Washington, and Minnesota, and the federal system adopted parole guidelines (e.g., Gottfredson, Wilkins, and Hoffman 1978; Arthur D. Little, Inc. 1981; Bottomley 1990). Because parole boards, however, have no jurisdiction over jail sentences or nonincarcerative penalties, or over the decision whether to incarcerate in state prisons, parole guidelines were at best a partial solution to sentencing disparities and were repealed in the jurisdictions mentioned, to be replaced by sentencing guidelines. Some states continue to develop and to use parole guidelines, but they are promoted as relevant to parole administration and not as a stand-alone sentencing reform.

Next in order, expressly building on experience with parole guidelines and dating initially from pilot projects in Denver and Vermont in the mid-1970s, were sentencing guidelines that were "voluntary" in the two senses that they were developed by judges without a statutory mandate and that judicial compliance with them was entirely discretionary with the individual judge (Wilkins et al. 1978; Kress 1980). By the early 1980s, voluntary guidelines had been developed in most states (Blumstein et al. 1983, pp. 138–39), sometimes at the state level (e.g., Maryland, Florida, Massachusetts, Michigan, New Jersey, Utah, and Wisconsin) and more often at county or judicial district levels (Shane-DuBow, Brown, and Olsen 1985). The voluntary guidelines were often created by judges in hopes that by putting their own houses in order they would forestall passage of mandatory or determinate sentencing laws (e.g., Carrow et al. 1985, pp. 126–27). Evaluations showed that voluntary guidelines typically had little or no demonstrable effect on sentences imposed (Rich et al. 1982; Blumstein et al. 1983, chap. 4; Carrow 1984; Carrow et al. 1985), and in most places they were abandoned. They continue in effect in a number of states, including Michigan, Utah, Virginia, and Wisconsin, but no evaluations have been published. The notable exception to the generally pessimistic story of voluntary guidelines is in Delaware, where they took effect in the mid-1980s and appear to have normative and collegial, albeit not formal legal, authority (e.g., Quinn 1990, 1992; Gebelein 1991). In Delaware, also, no major independent or other evaluations have been published.

Third in sequence were statutory determinate sentencing schemes dating from the mid- to late 1970s like those in California, Illinois, Indiana, and North Carolina. They were diversely specific, ranging from California where initially, for example, robbery was specified to warrant a three-year prison term in the ordinary case, but two or four years if mitigating or aggravating circumstances were present, to Indiana where statutes prescribed ranges of ten to forty years for some offenses (Blumstein et al. 1983, chap. 3). Few of the statutory schemes were subjected to independent evaluations by outsiders. The exceptions are California, where many evaluations were conducted (for a complete list, see Cohen and Tonry 1983, table 7–15), and North Carolina, where Stevens Clarke and colleagues completed a number of evaluations (Clarke et al. 1983; Clarke 1984, 1987). In both states, statutory determinate sentencing laws reduced sentencing disparities and (remarkably, in retrospect) led to short-term reductions in average sentence lengths. Nonetheless, no state known to me (and I have said this often in places where, if I am wrong, I should have been corrected) has adopted a statutory determinate sentencing system for nearly fifteen years.

After nearly two decades of experimentation, the guideline-setting sentencing commission is the only reform strategy that commands widespread support and continues to be the subject of new legislation. Legislation to establish the first two commissions, in Minnesota and Pennsylvania, was enacted in 1978. In other places I have told the story of sentencing commissions through the mid-1980s (Tonry 1987, 1988). Suffice to say that by 1987, presumptive guidelines created by sentencing commissions were in place in Minnesota, Washington, and (after an initial legislative rejection) Pennsylvania. Voluntary guidelines in Maryland and Florida, which had been created with federal demonstration project money, were adopted statewide; Florida's were converted into (nominally) presumptive guidelines, and the judicial steering committee that oversaw the demonstration project evolved into a sentencing commission (Carrow et al. 1985). Entities called sentencing commissions had been created in South Carolina (von Hirsch, Knapp, and Tonry 1987, pp. 24–25, 117–24), New York (Griset 1991), Connecticut (Shane-DuBow, Brown, and Olsen 1985), and Maine (von Hirsch, Knapp, and Tonry 1987, pp. 20–21), but either decided not to develop guidelines (Maine and Connecticut) or tried to do so but were unable to persuade state legislatures to ratify the guidelines proposed (New York and South Carolina).

The pace of sentencing commission activity increased after the mid-

1980s. The federal legislation was passed in 1984, commissioners were appointed in 1985, and the guidelines took effect in 1987. Oregon's guidelines took effect in 1989. After 1990, guidelines created by sentencing commissions took effect in Arkansas, Louisiana, North Carolina, and, after legislative rejection of initial proposed guidelines, in Kansas in 1993 (Gottlieb 1991, 1993). At the time of writing, sentencing commissions are at work in Massachusetts, Missouri, Ohio, Oklahoma, and South Carolina (not to be confused with the earlier unsuccessful commission).

By 1995, counting those states where sentencing commissions failed (or did not try) to win legislative adoption of proposed guidelines, more than half the states have created sentencing commissions. Table 2.1, based on work by Richard Frase of the University of Minnesota Law School, summarizes sentencing guidelines developments in the states as matters stood in mid-1994. Twenty-two states had, or were at work on, voluntary or presumptive guidelines (Frase 1995).

Supreme Court Justice Louis Brandeis once observed that "it is one of the happy incidents of the federal system that a single, courageous state may, if its citizens choose, serve as a laboratory and try social and economic experiments without risk to the rest of the country" (*New State Ice Co. v. Liebmann*, 285 U.S. 262, 311 [1932]). Amid discussion, development, promulgation, enactment, rejection, celebration, and denunciation of America's experiments with sentencing commissions, it seems a good time to take stock of what has happened to Judge Frankel's suggestion that sentencing policy be made the subject of administrative rule making.

Numerous entities of different sorts have been called sentencing commissions, but my focus here is principally on those that fall within Judge Frankel's proposals. He called for statutory creation of an administrative body charged with developing rules for sentencing that would be presumptively applicable, subject to a judge's authority to impose some other sentence if reasons were given, with that judgment being subject to review on appeal by a higher court (von Hirsch, Knapp, and Tonry 1987, chap. 1). Nearly twenty commissions fit that definition (including those in Maine, South Carolina, and New Mexico, which did not result in adoption of guidelines). Excluded are commissions with more general charges to consider sentencing or corrections issues, or both, and formulate recommendations. The most celebrated commission of this type was the Canadian Sentencing Commission (1987); notable American instances occurred in New York (Griset 1991) and Texas (Reynolds 1993).

The rest of this chapter consists of three sections. The first examines experience with sentencing commissions in relation to the effects of their guidelines on sentencing patterns and correctional practices and in relation to their institutional properties (specialized competence, insulation

Table 2.1. Summary of State Sentencing Guidelines Systems

Jurisdiction	Effective Date	Scope and Distinctive Features
Utah	1979	voluntary; retains parole board; no permanent commission until 1983; linked to correctional resources since 1993
Alaska	1/1/80	no permanent sentencing commission; statutory guidelines' scope expanded by case law
Minnesota	5/1/80	designed not to exceed 95 percent of prison capacity; extensive database and research
Pennsylvania	7/22/82	also covers misdemeanors; broad ranges and departure standards; retains parole board, encourages nonprison sanctions since 1994
Florida	10/1/83	formerly voluntary; overhauled in 1994
Maryland	1983	voluntary; retains parole board
Michigan	1/17/84	voluntary; retains parole board
Washington	7/1/84	includes upper limits on nonprison sanctions, some defined exchange rates, and vague, voluntary charging standards; resource-impact assessment required
Wisconsin	11/1/85	voluntary; descriptive (modeled on existing practices); retains parole board (abandoned 1995)
Delaware	10/10/87	voluntary; narrative (not grid) format; also covers misdemeanors and some nonprison sanctions; linked to resources
Oregon	11/1/89	grid includes upper limits on custodial nonprison sanctions, with some defined exchange rates; linked to resources; many new mandatory minimums added in 1994
Tennessee	11/1/89	also covers misdemeanors; retains parole board; sentences linked to resources (abandoned 1995)
Virginia	1/1/91	voluntary; judicially controlled, and parole board retained, until 1995; resource-impact assessments required since 1995
Louisiana	1/1/92	includes intermediate sanction guidelines and exchange rates; linked to resources (abandoned 1995)
Kansas	7/1/93	sentences linked to resources
Arkansas	1/1/94	voluntary; detailed enabling statute; resource-impact assessments required
North Carolina	10/1/94	also covers most misdemeanors; sentences linked to resources
Massachusetts, Missouri, Ohio Oklahoma, and South Carolina	(in process)	all enabling statues encourage resource matching; Ohio commission rejected grid format; Massachusetts and Missouri statues retain parole board

Source: Adapted from Frase (1995).

from short-term emotionalism and political pressures, a systemic approach to policy making). The second section canvasses the major policy issues that current commissions have addressed and that future commissions must resolve. The third provides a diagnosis of the state of health of Judge Frankel's proposal and its long-term prospects.

Before continuing, a prefatory note concerning sources is necessary. The scholarly and evaluation literatures on sentencing commissions and their guidelines are slight. Besides Judge Frankel's book, only three others have discussed commissions (as opposed to their guidelines) in any detail (O'Donnell, Churgin, and Curtis 1977; von Hirsch, Knapp, and Tonry 1987; Parent 1988) and only a handful of articles have (Tonry 1979, 1991; Frankel and Orland 1984; Wright 1991, 1994). Private foundations and the federal research-sponsoring agencies have shown little interest in sentencing for many years and, as a result, little has been added to the literature since the 1980s. The only major exception concerns the U.S. Sentencing Commission, on which a modest evaluation literature (e.g., Schulhofer and Nagel 1989; Heaney 1991; Karle and Sager 1991; U.S. Sentencing Commission 1991*a*, 1991*b*; Dunworth and Weisselberg 1992; Meierhoefer 1992; Nagel and Schulhofer 1992; U.S. General Accounting Office 1992) and a sizeable policy literature (e.g., Alschuler 1991; Wright 1991; Freed 1992; Doob 1995; Tonry 1993*a*) have accumulated. The bimonthly *Federal Sentencing Reporter* published by the University of California Press for the Vera Institute of Justice is a treasure trove of otherwise fugitive reports and analyses of the federal sentencing commission and its guidelines; the December 1992 issue is devoted entirely to evaluation issues. In addition, most sentencing commissions collect monitoring data in greater or lesser detail and publish annual or more frequent statistical reports. There are a handful of recent empirical writings by others, using commission data, in Minnesota (e.g., Frase 1991*a*, 1993*a*, 1993*b*, 1994) and Washington (Boerner 1993), and a small number of articles have described the policies and processes of state sentencing commissions (Kramer and Scirica 1985; Parent 1988; Bogan 1990, 1991; Griset 1991; Lieb 1991, 1993; Dailey 1992; Kramer 1992; Gottlieb 1993; Wright and Ellis 1993; Wright 1995; Greene 1995*a*) and the federal sentencing commission (Breyer 1988, 1992; von Hirsch 1988; Freed and Miller 1989; Tonry 1991, 1993*a*). Finally, six scholarly journals have recently devoted symposium issues to sentencing: the *Yale Law Journal* (vol. 101, no. 8), the *University of Southern California Law Review* (vol. 66, no. 1), the *University of California Davis Law Review* (vol. 25, no. 3), the *Wake Forest Law Review* (1993, April), the *University of Colorado Law Review* (1993, April), and the *Journal of Criminal Justice Ethics* (Winter/Spring 1994). This chapter draws on these sources and also on personal contacts with state and federal policy makers and practitioners.

I. Experience with Commissions

The crux of Judge Frankel's proposal concerned the institutional capacities of administrative agencies. Rule-making authority has been delegated by legislatures in the United States to countless state and federal agencies on the basis that, better than any legislature, they can achieve and maintain specialized competence concerning complex subjects, they have some degree of insulation from short-term popular emotions and political pressures, and they can adopt comprehensive, long-term approaches to policy making. Because the sentencing commission was proposed as a tool for establishing standards for sentencing and reducing disparities, any stock-taking must consider two questions. First, have commissions successfully developed and implemented sentencing guidelines that have changed sentencing practices and reduced disparities? Second, as administrative agencies, have sentencing commissions developed specialized competence, achieved some insulation from knee-jerk politics, and adopted comprehensive, long-term approaches to policy making?

Effects on Sentencing Practices

Guidelines developed by commissions have changed sentencing practices and patterns, reduced disparities, ameliorated racial and gender differences, and helped states control their prison populations. That statement camouflages deep disagreements about the wisdom of decisions made by commissions. In the federal system, for example, numerous observers charge that the new sentencing patterns are too severe and that the new practices are undesirable because lawyers and judges commonly, and foreseeably, manipulate the guidelines to avoid imposing sentences that they believe are too harsh (Federal Courts Study Committee 1990; Freed 1992; Nagel and Schulhofer 1992; Tonry 1993*a*). In the federal, Minnesota, and Oregon systems, critics argue that disparities have been reduced by violating the second half of the equality injunction ("and treat different cases differently"). Racial and gender differences have been reduced but, controlling for current offenses and criminal histories, women and whites continue more often to receive mitigated sentences than do men and blacks and, conversely, men and blacks more often receive aggravated sentences. Gender differences have diminished but only by increasing the relative severity of women's punishments compared with preguidelines patterns in which women's sentences were typically less severe than men's (e.g., Knapp 1984, pp. 67–68). Racial differences have diminished in some jurisdictions, but only by limiting standard sentencing criteria to current offense and criminal history information (which in any case has a systematically unfavorable disparate impact on black defendants) and by forbidding judges to adjust sentences on the basis of biographical information such as education, employment, and family status. While the latter policy lessens chances of preferential treatment of nondisadvantaged defendants, in many individual cases it penalizes disadvantaged defendants who have to some degree overcome dismal life chances. Finally, although some jurisdictions have managed to regulate their prison populations, some never tried, and the U.S. commission, despite a statutory directive, failed to do so.

Nonetheless, while reasonable people can disagree about the wisdom of policies that commissions have adopted and regret that they have not been more successful at reducing unwarranted disparities and eliminating harsher treatment of minority defendants, no informed person can disagree that commissions and their guidelines have altered sentencing practices and patterns.

Conformity with Guidelines

Data are available from four states and the federal system on judges' compliance with guidelines. It is clear that judges in a large majority of cases will conform the sentences they announce to applicable authorized sentencing ranges. That assertion requires two important caveats. First, guideline developers have often insisted that guidelines should be disregarded when a case's special features warrant different treatment (Gottfredson, Wilkins, and Hoffman 1978); they are after all guidelines, not mandatory penalties, and judges' reasons for imposing some other sentence can be stated for the record and examined by higher courts. From this perspective, a guidelines system that elicited 100 percent compliance would be undesirable because judges would not be distinguishing among cases as they should.

Second, if judges are willing to give plea bargaining free rein, compliance may be more apparent than real. Guidelines make sentencing predictable. Picture a guidelines grid as a dartboard. As an example, figure 2.1 shows the initial 1989 Oregon grid. Each cell specifies a range of presumptively appropriate sentences; to fix the game counsel need only be sure that their dart hits the right cell. This they can do by means of charge dismissals. If counsel negotiate a fifteen-month prison sentence, and the applicable sentencing range for offense X is fourteen to sixteen months, the defendant need only plead guilty to X and the prosecutor to dismiss any other charges to assure the agreed sentence. Of course, different prosecutors may offer different deals to like-situated offenders, who may therefore plead guilty to offense Y or offense Z. So long as the judge imposes the agreed sentence from within the applicable guideline range in every case, nominal compliance will be absolute, however disparate the sentences like-situated offenders receive.

Crime Seriousness Scale			Criminal History Scale								
			Multiple (3+) Felony Person Offender	Repeat (2) Felony Person Offender	Single (1) Felony Person W/Felony Non-Person Offender	Single (1) Felony Person Offender	Multiple (4+) Felony Non-Person Offender	Repeat (2-3) Felony Non-Person Offender	Significant Minor Criminal Record	Minor Criminal Record	Minor Misdemeanor or No Criminal Record
			A	B	C	D	E	F	G	H	I
Murder	11		225-269	196-224	178-194	149-177	149-177	135-148	129-134	122-128	120-121
Manslaughter I, Assault I, Rape I, Arson I	10		121-130	116-120	111-115	91-110	81-90	71-80	66-70	61-65	58-60
Rape I, Assault I, Kidnapping I, Arson I, Burglary I, Robbery I	9		66-72	61-65	56-60	51-55	46-50	41-45	39-40	37-38	34-36
Manslaughter II, Sexual Abuse I, Assault II, Rape II, Using Child in Display of Sexual Conduct, Drugs—Minor, Cult./Manuf./Del., Comp., Prostitution, Neg. Homicide	8		41-45	35-40	29-34	27-28	25-26	23-24	21-22	19-20	16-18
Extortion, Coercion, Supplying Contraband, Escape I	7		31-36	25-30	21-24	19-20	16-18	180 90	180 90	180 90	180 90
Robbery II, Assault III, Rape III, Bribe Receiving, Intimidation, Property Crimes (more than $50,000), Drug Possession	6		25-30	19-24	15-18	13-14	10-12	180 90	180 90	180 90	180 90
Robbery III, Theft by Receiving, Trafficking Stolen Vehicles, Property Crimes ($10,000 - $49,999)	5		15-16	13-14	11-12	9-10	6-8	180 90	120 60	120 60	120 60
Failure to Appear I, Custodial Interference II, Property Crimes ($5,000 - $9,999), Drugs—Cult./Manuf./Del.	4		10 10	8-9	120 60	120 60	120 60	120 60	120 60	120 60	120 60
Abandon Child, Abuse of Corpse, Criminal Nonsupport, Property Crimes ($1,000 - $4,999)	3		120 60	120 60	120 60	120 60	120 60	120 60	90 30	90 30	90 30
Dealing Child Pornography, Violation of Wildlife Laws, Welfare Fraud, Property Crimes (less than $1,000)	2		90 30	90 30	90 30	90 30	90 30	90 30	90 30	90 30	90 30
Altering Firearm ID, Habitual Offender Violation, Bigamy, Paramilitary Activity, Drugs—Possession	1		90 30	90 30	90 30	90 30	90 30	90 30	90 30	90 30	90 30

Notes: In blocks above the solid black line, numbers are presumptive prison sentences expressed as a range of months. In blocks below the solid black line, upper numbers are the maximum number of custody units that may be imposed; lower numbers are the maximum number of jail days that may be imposed.

Figure 2.1. Oregon Sentencing Guidelines Grid, 1989. *Source:* Ashford and Mosbaek (1991).

There is considerable evidence that counsel do bargain around guidelines, which makes before-and-after-guidelines comparisons of sentencing difficult; the meaning of a plea to, say, second-degree aggravated assault may be different before and under guidelines. Comparisons of plea bargaining in Minnesota before and under guidelines showed a marked shift away from sentence bargaining and toward charge bargaining (Knapp

1984, chap. 6). Richard Frase, in a quantitative analysis of Minnesota sentencing patterns through 1989, concluded, "It appears likely that whatever plea-trial disparities there were before the guidelines went into effect continued to exist in the early post-guidelines years, and still exist today; plea bargaining, and its accompanying charge and sentence disparities, is 'alive and well' in Minnesota" (1993*a*, p. 34).

In Washington State, as table 2.2 shows, there was a marked shift in offense-of-conviction patterns after the guidelines took effect. In general, convictions of offenses subject to presumptive state-prison sentences declined, and convictions of other offenses increased. Before guidelines, 12.4 percent of cases fell within the eight highest severity levels. Afterwards only 7.4 percent—a 40 percent drop. Similarly, among the six lowest offense levels, in which the presumption generally is against state incarceration, there was a marked shift toward more convictions for the least serious crimes, for which the guidelines did not call for any incarceration.

In Pennsylvania, a more subtle pattern appeared, which shows how guidelines can accommodate different patterns of plea bargaining. Table

Table 2.2. Conviction Offenses by Seriousness Levels, 1982 and 1985 (%)

Level	FY 1982	January–June 1985	Difference
XIV	.2	.1	–.1
XIII	.5	.3	–.2
XII	.3	.2	–.1
XI	.1	.2	+.1
X	.9	.4	–.5
IX	5.6	3.6	–2.0
VIII	1.4	.6	–.8
VII	3.4	2.0	–1.4
VI	4.7	5.7	+1.0
V	.8	.7	–.1
IV	10.6	9.7	–.9
III	8.3	10.1	+1.8
II	34.5	33.3	–1.2
I	28.7	31.1	+2.4
Unranked	.0	1.9	+1.9
Total	100.0	99.9	

Source: Washington State Sentencing Guidelines Commission (1985), p. 3.

Note: Level XIV is the most serious category (aggravated murder). Percentages do not equal 100 due to rounding. FY = fiscal year.

Table 2.3. Statewide Conformity in Pennsylvania in 1983 and 1986, Selected Offenses (%)

Offense	Standard Range		Aggravated Range		Mitigated Range		Departure Up		Departure Down	
	1983	1986	1983	1986	1983	1986	1983	1986	1983	1986
Aggravated assault										
Felony 2	36	47	4	5	12	12	2	3	46	33
Felony 3	100	N.A.	0	N.A.	0	N.A.	0	N.A.	0	N.A.
Misdemeanor 1	70	71	1	2	10	8	0	1	19	18
Arson										
Felony 1	13	33	0	4	10	16	0	3	77	44
Felony 2	62	48	0	8	11	10	5	1	22	33
Burglary										
ogs 7	39	40	3	4	25	18	3	9	29	29
ogs 6	49	56	3	4	14	13	4	5	31	22
ogs 5	78	77	2	4	5	5	2	3	12	11
Retail theft										
Felony 3	62	65	2	2	9	12	1	0	25	20
Misdemeanor 1	91	96	0	0	4	1	0	0	5	2
Robbery										
Felony 1	48	59	6	7	10	10	15	11	25	12
Felony 2	67	73	4	4	6	7	6	4	20	12
Felony 3	85	87	1	3	4	3	2	2	17	5

Sources: Pennsylvania Commission on Sentencing (1984), table 1; Pennsylvania Commission on Sentencing (1987), table 4.

Note: ogs = offense gravity scale; N.A. - not available.

2.3 shows guideline compliance in Pennsylvania in 1983 and 1986. Pennsylvania guidelines established standard, aggravated, and mitigated ranges for every offense (North Carolina in 1994 implemented a similar system) and, like most jurisdictions, recognized various severity levels of some crimes (e.g., first-, second-, and third-degree robbery). Two patterns stand out from table 2.3. For most sets of offenses, fewer than half of those convicted of the most serious grade of the offense received sentences within the standard range; mitigated-range sentences were high, and downward departures were very high. Among those convicted of the lowest-grade offense in each set, from 62 to 96 percent received standard-range sentences; mitigated-range and downward-departure sentences were much less common. The most plausible explanation is that these patterns reveal the operation of diverse plea negotiation conventions within Pennsylvania. Where sentence bargaining is common, defendants plead guilty to the most serious offense charged with an understanding that the judge will impose a mitigated sentence or depart downward. Where charge bargaining is common, defendants plead to a charge that bears a presumptive penalty they will accept, and judges then impose a standard-range sentence.

In theory, plea bargains should not distort application of the federal guidelines because the guidelines are based on the defendant's "relevant conduct" as determined by a preponderance of the evidence at sentencing and not merely on the conviction offense. Nonetheless, there is substantial evidence from research sponsored by the U.S. commission (Schulhofer and Nagel 1989; U.S. Sentencing Commission 1991*a*, chap. 6; Nagel and Schulhofer 1992) and research by others (Heaney 1991) that counsel, often with tacit judicial approval, do bargain around the guidelines. Sometimes this is done by having the defendant plead guilty to an offense for which the maximum lawful sentence is less than the applicable guideline range. Sometimes it is done by counsel stipulating to facts that omit details that require a stiffer sentence, like weapon use or victim injury or a larger quantity of drugs. Sometimes it is done by understandings that the judge will ignore the guidelines and that neither party will appeal. Sometimes it is done in even more byzantine ways. Rule 5.k.1., for example, allows the judge to disregard the guidelines altogether if the prosecutor files a motion requesting a mitigated sentence because of the defendant's "substantial assistance to the government"; if the prosecutor's real motive is to avoid an unduly harsh sentence, observers can not know whether the claimed "substantial assistance" was provided or was useful. Although no one has devised a credible estimate of how often the guidelines are deceptively evaded, commission-sponsored research acknowledges that bargaining distorts guideline application in at least 25 to 35 percent of cases (Nagel and Schulhofer 1992).

Keeping in mind therefore that compliance rates may mean less than appears, table 2.4 shows compliance and departure rates for selected recent years for Minnesota, Oregon, Pennsylvania, Washington, and the

Table 2.4. Departure Rates, American Guidelines Systems, Recent Years (%)

Jurisdiction	Ad hoc Aggravated Departures	Approved Aggravated Sentences	Standard Sentences	Approved Mitigated Sentences	Ad hoc Mitigated Sentences
Federal (1994)	1.2	…	71.7	19.5	7.6
Minnesota (1992)*	2.7	…	88.8	…	8.4
Minnesota (1992)†	8.6	…	71.5	…	19.9
Oregon (1991)	3	…	94	…	3
Pennsylvania (1992)	2.3	5.8	70.9	9.2	11.9
Washington (1993)	1.6	…	90.2	(15.4)††	8.2

Sources: Ashford and Mosbaek (1991), pp. 31, 37; Minnesota Sentencing Guidelines Commission (1994), pp. 33, 40; Pennsylvania Commission on Sentencing (1993*b*), table 4; U. S. Sentencing Commission (1995), p. 78; Washington State Sentencing Guidelines Commission (1994*b*), table 10.

*Dispositional departures only (state incarceration or not).

†Durational departures (length of prison sentence).

††Many exceptional sentences involving no jail time are reported as "standard" sentences, and some as "mitigated" departures.

federal system. Departure rates are low in every jurisdiction, which shows that guidelines have moral force in each of them. Judges sworn to enforce the law are presumably more comfortable not "departing" from guidelines that the legislature has adopted or ratified. Not much else can be concluded from table 2.4. Because guideline ranges vary substantially from Minnesota's very narrow ones (e.g., for rape with no prior record: eighty-one to ninety-one months) to Pennsylvania's very broad combination of standard, aggravated, and mitigated ranges (e.g., for rape with no prior record: twenty-seven to seventy-five months), comparisons of departure rates across jurisdictions offer no comparative insights into sentencing consistency. Moreover, jurisdictions count departures in different ways. In the federal system, sentence reductions awarded defendants for "substantial assistance to the government" are not considered departures. Nor in Pennsylvania are sentences in the aggravated and mitigated ranges considered departures. Nor in Washington are sentence reductions under "First-Time Offender Waiver" and "Sex Offender Sentencing Option" provisions.

Once all the caveats are taken into account, and ignoring plea-bargaining complications, it would appear that the greatest levels of guidelines compliance occur in Oregon and Minnesota. Here too, unfortunately, things are not as simple as appears. As Frase has pointed out (1991a, 1993a, p. 17 and figs. 4–6), gross compliance rates are misleading; a better inquiry would focus on departures from what to what. He shows, for example, that in Minnesota rates of mitigated dispositional departures (that is, non-state-prison sentences when the guidelines specify state prison) annually represented 3 to 7 percent of all felony sentences between 1981 and 1989, but represented from 19 to 33 percent of all presumptive prison sentences. This is because guidelines presume imprisonment for only approximately 20 percent of convicted felons. If, therefore, 7 percent of all cases are mitigated dispositional departures, they represent a third of those presumed bound for prison.

One last permutation on compliance-and-departure calculations is to disaggregate for types of offense. Pennsylvania's guidelines, for example, cover felonies and misdemeanors. Although 87 percent of Pennsylvania sentences in 1983 fell within the applicable guideline ranges, when the data are broken down, 97 percent of misdemeanor sentences were compliant but only 79 percent of felony sentences (Tonry 1988, table 8). Significantly lower compliance rates characterized escape (40 percent), arson (64 percent), involuntary deviate sexual intercourse (68 percent), and aggravated assault (70 percent) (Tonry 1988, table 9). Data for 1991 show an 85 percent overall compliance rate, which breaks down much as the 1983 data did (Pennsylvania Commission on Sentencing 1993a, table 9).

For all the qualifications, however, judges much more often than not impose sentences that comply with applicable guidelines.

Disparity Reduction

Every sentencing commission claims that its guidelines have reduced sentencing disparities compared with sentencing patterns before guidelines took effect. Research on disparities, however, faces a number of formidable problems, some of which mirror the problems posed by data on compliance with guidelines. First, promulgation of guidelines may affect plea bargaining and before-and-after comparisons may be confounded if charging and bargaining practices change with the guidelines (Frase 1993a, p. 302). If second-degree aggravated assaults are systematically different before and under guidelines, analyses of disparities in sentencing for that offense may involve apples-and-oranges comparisons. If, for example, less serious second-degree assaults under guidelines more often result in pleas to less serious charges than before, cases resulting in convictions of second-degree assault may be more homogeneously serious and apparently reduced disparity may be a product of that greater homogeneity. Second, as was true during most of the last decade, if public and officials' attitudes toward offenders become more punitive over time, sentences are likely to become harsher with or without guidelines, and that rising tide complicates disparity analyses. Third, and most important, is a combined conceptual and methodological problem. Most disparity-reduction analyses use the offense severity and criminal history classifications that are expressed in the relevant guidelines as the basis of comparisons, rather than comprehensive statistical models of sentencing before and after guidelines, and this inevitably exaggerates the extent to which disparities have been reduced. This last problem has greatest relevance to the federal guidelines; evaluations of the federal sentencing guidelines by the U.S. Sentencing Commission (1991a) and the U.S. General Accounting Office (1992) illustrate the problem, and it is discussed in some detail below.

Because the evidence is clearer in the states and because the federal guidelines present special problems for disparity analyses, I discuss them in separate subsections. First, however, some prefatory remarks about disparity studies are in order. Most of the analyses discussed are efforts to compare sentencing disparities in the first year, or few years, under a guidelines system with sentencing in some period before guidelines took effect. As time goes by, it becomes increasingly difficult, and soon impossible, to reach conclusions about disparities. After a few years, hypothetical comparisons must be made with sentencing patterns as they would have been had guidelines not been adopted. This is impossible to do. The public and political attitudes and sensibilities that led to the creation of a sentencing commission would presumably have influenced sentencing patterns without guidelines. In addition, political and policy environments change over time, and these changes would also alter sentencing patterns with or without guidelines.

Disparity reduction in the states. There are plausible grounds for believing that the state guidelines in their early years reduced disparities. In Minnesota, where more evaluations have been conducted than in any other state, an evaluation of the first four years' experience concluded, "disparity in sentencing decreased under the sentencing guidelines. This reduction in disparity is indicated by increased sentence uniformity and proportionality" (Knapp 1984, pp. v–vi). Outside evaluators agreed: Minnesota "was largely successful in reducing preguideline disparities in those decisions that fall within the scope of the guidelines" (Miethe and Moore 1985, p. 360). Frase, drawing on data for 1981 to 1989, concluded that "the Minnesota guidelines have achieved, and continue to achieve" most of their goals, including disparity reduction, and "have been modestly successful in achieving greater honesty and uniformity in sentencing" (Frase 1993*a*, p. 3).

No independent evaluations have been published concerning the Oregon, Pennsylvania, Washington, and Delaware guidelines, but each commission, relying on its regularly collected monitoring data, has concluded that disparities declined. The Washington commission, relying on 1985 data, concluded, "the Sentencing Reform Act has clearly increased consistency in the imprisonment decision" (Washington State Sentencing Guidelines Commission 1986, p. 7). Looking back over the first six years' experience with guidelines, the Washington commission reported, "the high degree of compliance with sentencing guidelines has reduced variability in sentencing among counties and among judges" (Washington State Sentencing Guidelines Commission 1992*b*, p. 12). On the early years of the Pennsylvania guidelines, its commission concluded for 1983, "it appears that Pennsylvania's guidelines are accomplishing their intended goal of reducing unwarranted sentencing disparity" (Pennsylvania Commission on Sentencing 1984, p. i), and for 1984, "sentences became more uniform throughout the state" (Pennsylvania Commission on Sentencing 1985, p. i). John Kramer and Robin Lubitz (1985) agreed. Finally, reporting on the first fifteen months' guidelines experience in Oregon, its commission concluded, "the guidelines have increased uniformity in sentencing considerably. Dispositional variability for offenders with identical crime seriousness and criminal history scores has been reduced by 45 percent over the variability under the pre-guidelines system" (Ashford and Mosbaek 1991, p. viii). More recent data show that increased consistency has continued (Bogan and Factor 1995).

In Delaware, no evaluation has been published of the effects of its voluntary guidelines on disparities. However, a number of publications by the chairman (Gebelein 1991) and director (Quinn 1990, 1992) of Delaware's Sentencing Accountability Commission list "consistency and certainty" among the guidelines' goals and present data showing that the guidelines have succeeded in increasing use of incarceration for violent offenders and use of intermediate punishments for nonviolent offenders.

This at least arguably supports an inference of greater consistency in Delaware sentencing.

Most likely, sentencing guidelines reduced disparities in all these jurisdictions compared with what they would have been without guidelines. Judge Frankel's complaints about lawlessness in sentencing presumably strike a responsive chord in most judges and lawyers. Because guidelines set standards for sentences where none existed, it would be astonishing if they had no effect on sentencing decisions. Even when plea bargaining, which is nearly ubiquitous in American courts, is taken into account, it is likely that the bargaining takes place in the shadow of the guidelines and that the bargained sentences are more consistent than they otherwise would have been. Nonetheless, the evaluation research evidence on this question is less definitive than it appears or than its celebrants claim.

Disparity reduction in the federal system. The evidence on federal sentencing disparities is mixed, and the best conclusion at present is that we do not know whether disparities have increased or decreased (Rhodes 1992; Weisburd 1992; Tonry 1993*a*). Although the U.S. commission, on the basis of an evaluation of the first four years' experience with federal guidelines, claims "the data . . . show significant reductions in disparity" (U.S. Sentencing Commission 1991*a*, p. 419), there is reason to doubt that conclusion. Because both the U.S. commission and the U.S. General Accounting Office (GAO) devoted extensive efforts to measuring changes in sentencing disparities, I discuss the subject at some length.

For a discussion of the federal evaluation to be intelligible to readers not already familiar with the federal guidelines, some description of the system is necessary. In setting sentences, judges are first supposed to consult a schedule for the particular offense (table 2.5 shows the schedule for robbery) that specifies a "base offense level." Then, on the basis of various offense circumstances, such as whether the offender was armed and if so with what, whether the weapon was used and with what injurious result, and the value of any property taken, the offense level is adjusted upward or downward (almost always upward). Next the judge must determine the offender's criminal history score (mostly a measure of prior criminality). Finally the judge is to consult a two-dimensional grid (see table 2.6) to learn the presumptive sentence for the offender, given the offender's adjusted offense level and his or her criminal history. Thus, a hypothetical offender who was convicted of robbery (base offense level twenty in table 2.6) of $15,000 (increase by one level) of a bank (increase by two levels), in which he possessed and discharged a firearm (increase by seven levels), causing a minor injury (increase by two levels), would, with no prior record, fall within level thirty-two and be presumed to receive a prison sentence between 121 and 151 months.

The federal guidelines, uniquely among American guideline systems, are based not on the offense to which the defendant pled guilty or of

Table 2.5. Robbery, Extortion, and Blackmail

§ 2B3.1 Robbery

a) Base offense level: 20

b) Specific offense characteristics

1. If the property of a financial institution or post office was taken, or if the taking of such property was an object of the offense, increase by 2 levels.
2. (A) If a firearm was discharged, increase by 7 levels; (B) if a firearm was otherwise used, increase by 6 levels; (C) if a firearm was brandished, displayed, or possessed, increase by 5 levels; (D) if a dangerous weapon was otherwise used, increase by 4 levels; (E) if a dangerous weapon was brandished, displayed, or possessed, increase by 3 levels; or (F) if an expressed threat of death was made, increase by 2 levels.
3. If any victim sustained bodily injury, increase the offense level according to the seriousness of the injury:

Degree of bodily injury and increase in level

A) Bodily injury, add 2 levels
B) Serious bodily injury, add 4 levels
C) Permanent or life-threatening bodily injury, add 6 levels
D) If the degree of injury is between that specified in subdivisions A and B, add 3 levels; or
E) If the degree of injury is between that specified in subdivisions B and C, add 5 levels.

Provided, however, that the cumulative adjustments from (2) and (3) shall not exceed 11 levels.

4. (A) If any person was abducted to facilitate commission of the offense or to facilitate escape, increase by 4 levels; or (B) if any person was physically restrained to facilitate commission of the offense or to facilitate escape, increase by 2 levels.
5. If a firearm, destructive device, or controlled substance was taken, or if the taking of such item was an object of the offense, increase by 1 level.
6. If the loss exceeded $10,000, increase the offense level as follows:

	Loss (Apply the Greatest)	Increase in Level
A)	$10,000 or less	no increase
B)	More than $10,000	add 1
C)	More than $50,000	add 2
D)	More than $250,000	add 3
E)	More than $800,000	add 4
F)	More than $1,500,000	add 5
G)	More than $2,500,000	add 6
H)	More than $5,000,000	add 7

Source: U. S. Sentencing Commission (1992*a*).

which he was convicted at trial, but on "actual offense behavior," which the commission calls "relevant conduct." Judge William Wilkins, the commission's long-time chairman, and John Steer, for many years its general counsel, have explained that the relevant conduct approach was intended to offset efforts by prosecutors to manipulate the guidelines by

Table 2.6. U.S. Sentencing Commission Sentencing Table (in Months of Imprisonment)

Offense level	Criminal History Category (Criminal History Points)					
	I (0 or 1)	II (2 or 3)	III (4, 5, 6)	IV (7, 8, 9)	V (10, 11, 12)	VI (13 or more)
1	0–6	0–6	0–6	0–6	0–6	0–6
2	0–6	0–6	0–6	0–6	0–6	1–7
3	0–6	0–6	0–6	0–6	2–8	3–9
4	0–6	0–6	0–6	2–8	4–10	6–12
5	0–6	0–6	1–7	4–10	6–12	9–15
6	0–6	1–7	2–8	6–12	9–15	12–18
7	1–7	2–8	4–10	8–14	12–18	15–21
8	2–8	4–10	6–12	10–16	15–21	18–24
9	4–10	6–12	8–14	12–18	18–24	21–27
10	6–12	8–14	10–16	15–21	21–27	24–30
11	8–14	10–16	12–18	18–24	24–30	27–33
12	10–16	12–18	15–21	21–27	27–33	30–37
13	12–18	15–21	18–24	24–30	30–37	33–41
14	15–21	18–24	21–27	27–33	33–41	37–46
15	18–24	21–27	24–30	30–37	37–46	41–51
16	21–27	24–30	27–33	33–41	41–51	46–57
17	24–30	27–33	30–37	37–46	46–57	51–63
18	27–33	30–37	33–41	41–51	51–63	57–71
19	30–37	33–41	37–46	46–57	57–71	63–78
20	33–41	37–46	41–51	51–63	63–78	70–87

21	37–46	41–51	46–57	57–71	70–87	77–96
22	41–51	46–57	51–63	63–78	77–96	84–105
23	46–57	51–63	57–71	70–87	84–105	92–115
24	51–63	57–71	63–78	77–96	92–115	100–125
25	57–71	63–78	70–87	84–105	100–125	110–137
26	63–78	70–87	78–97	92–115	110–137	120–150
27	70–87	78–97	87–108	100–125	120–150	130–162
28	78–97	87–108	97–121	100–137	130–162	140–175
29	87–108	97–121	108–135	121–151	140–175	151–188
30	97–121	108–135	121–151	135–168	151–188	168–210
31	108–135	121–151	135–168	151–188	168–210	188–235
32	121–151	135–168	151–188	168–210	188–235	210–262
33	135–168	151–188	168–210	188–235	210–262	235–293
34	151–188	168–210	188–235	210–262	235–293	262–327
35	168–210	188–235	210–262	235–293	262–327	292–365
36	188–235	210–262	235–293	262–327	292–365	324–405
37	210–262	235–293	262–327	292–365	324–405	360–life
38	235–293	262–327	292–365	324–405	360–life	360–life
39	262–327	292–365	324–405	360–life	360–life	360–life
40	292–365	324–405	360–life	360–life	360–life	360–life
41	324–405	360–life	360–life	360–life	360–life	360–life
42	360–life	360–life	360–life	360–life	360–life	360–life
43	life	life	life	life	life	life

Source: U. S. Sentencing Commission (1992*a*).

dismissing charges to achieve a conviction offense that, under the guidelines, prescribed the preferred sentence (Wilkins and Steer 1990).

The complexity of the federal guidelines and their reliance on relevant conduct present nearly insuperable difficulties for a before-and-after disparity analysis. Information concerning drug quantity or purity or the presence of an unused firearm or the occurrence of uncharged crimes, all of which are "relevant conduct" and have incremental punitive significance, was often not material before the guidelines took effect. Consequently, there was no reason for probation officers to obtain or record such information, and for periods before November 1987 it is not systematically and reliably available. The GAO observed, "significant differences in much of the offender data available made it difficult to reliably match and compare groups of preguidelines and guidelines offenders. Preguideline offender data focused on personal information, such as socioeconomic status and family and community ties, that was supposed to be irrelevant under the guidelines in all or most cases. Conversely, most of the detailed data available on guidelines offenders, such as role in the offense, were not available for preguidelines cases" (1992, p. 10).

The commission and GAO approached disparities in two ways: by asking participants whether they believed disparities had been reduced and by conducting sophisticated quantitative analyses. All that can be learned from the interviews and surveys is that prosecutors and probation officers were likelier to believe that disparities had been reduced than were judges and defense lawyers. Table 2.7 shows answers to questions about reduced disparities from GAO interviews in four sites, commission interviews in twelve sites, and a commission mail survey.

Table 2.7 shows that most judges and defense counsel did not believe disparities to have been reduced (significant and slight majorities of prosecutors and probation officers disagreed). An earlier analysis of the guidelines by the Federal Courts Study Committee (1990) reported that many judges and the committee itself believed that disparities had increased.

Table 2.7. Percentage of Practitioners Who Believe Unwarranted Disparities Have Been Reduced

Data Source	Judges	Prosecutors	Federal Defenders	Private Attorneys	Probation Officers
USSC interviews	50	76	41	32	59
USSC mail survey	32	51	11	19	52
GAO interviews	20	83	(————37————)		50

Sources: For USSC interviews, U. S. Sentencing Commission (1991*b*), table 27; for USSC mail survey, U. S. Sentencing Commission (1991 *b*), table 28; for GAO interviews, U. S. General Accounting Office (1992), table 3.

Note: USSC = U. S. Sentencing Commission; GAO = U. S. General Accounting Office.

The quantitative analyses were also inconclusive. The GAO's conclusion, based both on examination of the U.S. commission's statistical analyses and reanalysis of the commission's data is that "limitations and inconsistencies in the data available for preguidelines and guideline offenders made it impossible to determine how effective the sentencing guidelines have been in reducing overall sentencing disparity" (1992, p. 10).

The commission would put a different gloss on its and the GAO's findings on disparity reduction. The GAO entitled its report *Sentencing Guidelines: Central Questions Remain Unanswered*. Commission Chairman Wilkins urged instead that the report be entitled, "Sentencing Guidelines: Disparity Reduced, but Some Questions Remain" (U.S. General Accounting Office 1992, p. 182).

The insurmountable problem that comparable pre- and postguidelines data are not available served as the basis for the GAO's agnosticism, though it noted that commission analyses showed reduction in disparities for some selected offenses. The GAO's own analysis showed that "unwarranted disparity continued" in relation to offenders' race, gender, employment status, age, and marital status (1992, p. 12).

Because of data limitations, the commission confined its empirical analyses of disparity reduction to four categories of robbery (with no or moderate criminal history, with and without a weapon), two categories of embezzlement ($10,000 to $20,000 loss, $20,000 to $40,000 loss), heroin trafficking (100 to 400 grams), and cocaine trafficking (500 to 2,000 grams). Sample sizes were tiny (preguidelines samples were 17, 13, 25, 18, 27, 36, 40, and 44 cases; postguidelines samples were 80, 38, 57, 24, 56, 71, 72, and 81 cases). Sentences from downward departures for "substantial assistance to the government" were excluded from the analysis. For each of the eight offenses examined, sentences "pre-" and "post-" guidelines (both sentences announced and sentences "expected to be served") were characterized in terms of means, medians, and the range in months within which the middle 80 percent of cases fell. The breadth of the ranges of the middle 80 percent of sentences declined for all eight offenses, though for five of those offenses the decline was not statistically significant. As commentators have stressed, the "not statistically significant" caveat means that the apparent reduction in disparity in five of the eight offenses studied may result from random chance and have nothing to do with the guidelines (Rhodes 1992; Weisburd 1992).

There are, unhappily, five reasons why even these modest findings are suspect. The first two are the inherent data limitations mentioned earlier and the tiny sample sizes. The third is that the commission's own process evaluation and several other studies (Schulhofer and Nagel 1989; Nagel and Schulhofer 1992) suggest that "substantial assistance" notions are commonly used to permit judges to impose sentences less severe than guideline sentences that the judge and the prosecutor consider too severe. In fiscal year 1993, of all disposed cases, 16.9 percent were downward departures for substantial assistance; 33.6 percent of drug trafficking dispositions were substantial assistance departures (U.S. Sentencing Commission 1994, tables 66, 67). Since judges are completely free of the guidelines once a substantial assistance motion is filed, opportunity for disparity is great. Excluding those departures from the disparity analysis inevitably understates the degree of variation in sentences, especially for drug cases.

The interaction between disparities and substantial assistance departures is complex. Low-level drug couriers and dealers seldom have useful assistance to provide and comparatively seldom benefit. People high in the distribution chain often can provide assistance and accordingly often receive sentences less severe than those received by their underlings.

The fourth problem is that two of the offenses examined, heroin and cocaine trafficking, became subject to mandatory minimum five-year sentences after the cases in the preguidelines sample were decided. Thus any apparent reduction in disparity for those offenses is likelier to result from passage of the mandatory minimum legislation than from implementation of the guidelines.

The fifth, and most important, problem is conceptual. "Unwarranted disparity" is not defined in the Sentencing Reform Act of 1984, and the commission selected a self-serving definition that inevitably exaggerated disparity reduction. Much research on sentencing disparities uses multivariate analyses and mathematical models to describe sentencing patterns before and after a policy or law change (e.g., Blumstein et al. 1983, chap. 2). Observed differences, assuming they are statistically significant and theoretically plausible, are then attributed to the change. The commission, instead, defined unwarranted disparities solely in terms of its own guidelines' offense and criminal history characteristics.

The commission's approach is misleading for two reasons. First, because federal law and guidelines now set very precise standards for sentences in relation to offenses and criminal history, and the previous law had only maximum authorized sanctions and a few mandatory minimums, it would be astonishing if the new guidelines had no effect on sentencing patterns. Previously there were no targets to shoot at, but under guidelines there are. Unless judges completely ignored the guidelines, sentences should on average have become closer to the targets. Second, however, the commission's approach might completely miss increases in disparity in relation to variables other than current offense and criminal history characteristics.

Anthony Doob (1995), for example, hypothesizes a situation in which preguideline sentencing decisions were premised solely on rehabilitative considerations and, in light of the relevant criteria, perfectly consistent. By using its culpability-based offense and criminal history categories to measure disparities, and superimposing them on the preguidelines data, the commission's methodology would miss the prior perfect consistency (by reference to different criteria) and most likely and unsurprisingly conclude that sentences were less disparate by its criteria after guidelines than before.

Suppose, for another example, that before the guidelines took effect, employed offenders with dependent children typically received lighter sentences because of judges' concern for the effects of a prison sentence on spouses, children, and household stability (as Wheeler, Mann, and Sarat [1991] suggest). The federal guidelines, which forbid judges to take account of employment prospects or family status, may have made the effects of employment plus dependents less consistent than before the guidelines; some judges foreseeably will circumvent the guidelines to achieve sentences that appear to them just and that follow the previous conventions, while others will adhere to the guidelines. Thus, in relation to employment and family status, sentencing under the guidelines will be more, not less, disparate than under the old system. By defining and looking for "unwarranted disparities" as it did, the commission undertook an impoverished look at disparity that was likely to produce a finding that disparities declined.

These methodological, measurement, and conceptual problems increased the odds that the commission would find that unwarranted disparities have declined. That statistically significant findings of reduced disparities were achieved for only three of eight selected crimes suggests that disparities have not declined very much or at all, or, as the GAO more cautiously concluded, that decline cannot be demonstrated.

Absence of evidence is not, of course, evidence of absence. My best guess is that the state commissions are right and that sentencing in their states became more consistent and that disparities declined. It is harder to be sure about the federal guidelines because their complexity, rigidity, and severity have fostered such wholesale circumvention that much case disposition has been forced below ground, and it is unclear how reliable federal data are on the characteristics of disposed cases.

Sentencing Patterns

Most commissions have adopted "prescriptive" guidelines that are intended to change existing sentencing patterns (rather than "descriptive" guidelines intended to reproduce, with greater consistency, past sentencing practices). Minnesota and Washington sought to increase use of imprisonment for violent offenses and to decrease it for property offenses. Both states assert that their monitoring data show that those objectives were achieved in the guidelines' early years (Knapp 1984, p. 31; Washington State Sentencing Guidelines Commission 1986, fig. 1; these analyses are discussed in some detail in Tonry [1988], pp. 306–9). Oregon had the same goals and found that the proportion of offenders convicted of felonies against persons who received state-prison sentences increased from 34 percent before guidelines, to 48 percent under guidelines while the proportion of property felons sentenced to state prisons declined from 19 to 9 percent; imprisonment for sex abuse felonies tripled from 13 to 42 percent (Ashford and Mosbaek 1991, pp. viii, 11). Data for 1993 show that these changed patterns continued (Bogan and Factor 1995, table 1). Pennsylvania sought to increase sentencing severity and appears to have succeeded; for most serious crimes, the proportion of convicted offenders incarcerated and their average minimum sentences before parole eligibility increased after the guidelines took effect (Pennsylvania Commission on Sentencing 1987, table 19). In Delaware, published monitoring data are less detailed than elsewhere but, as figure 2.2 shows, after the guidelines took effect the proportion of violent offenders among Delaware prisoners increased and the proportion of nonviolent offenders decreased (Gebelein 1991, p. 12). The U.S. Sentencing Commission also attempted to increase sentencing severity by decreasing use of probation, increasing the proportion of offenders incarcerated, and greatly increasing sentence lengths; it succeeded on all counts (U.S. Sentencing Commission 1991*a*; Tonry 1993*a*).

The effects of changes in sentencing patterns appear to vary with the abruptness of the new policies' departure from past practices. Where that change is modest, as in the initial guidelines in Pennsylvania, practices appear likely to revert to their prior patterns once the system has settled down. Where the change is sharp and the new sentencing policies are much more severe than past practice, there has been less evidence of reversion.

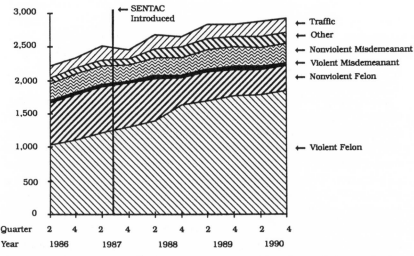

Figure 2.2. Composition of Delaware's Incarcerated Population before and after Effective Date of SENTAC Guidelines. *Source:* Gebelein (1991).

Published analyses are available from three jurisdictions—Minnesota, Washington, and the federal system—that describe system acceptance or rejection of substantial changes to sentencing policies. In Minnesota, amidst the commission's general policy of emphasizing prison use for violent offenses and deemphasizing its use for property offenses, major controversies included decisions to reduce the use of imprisonment for property offenders and to prescribe lengthy prison terms for sex offenders, especially for intrafamilial sex offenders. Richard Frase (1993*a*) tells both stories; in each, the commission's policy changes were resisted.

Prosecutors actively resisted the policy decision to preclude imprisonment for most property offenders. Under the initial guidelines, minor property offenders were prison bound only if they had accumulated many prior convictions. A common prosecutorial strategy, in response, was to build criminal histories. A shoplifter might, for example, contrary to an earlier practice of taking a plea to one offense with other charges being dismissed, be required to plead guilty to five offenses; the next time that offender was convicted of shoplifting, his five prior convictions would produce a presumptive prison sentence. The commission responded by changing the criminal history scoring rules so as to offset the bargaining pattern change (Parent 1988). This time prosecutors responded by insisting on guilty pleas to multiple charges and arguing that the sentence for the last contemporaneous plea must take account of the defendant's minutes-earlier prior convictions. In *State v. Hernandez*, 311 N.W. 2d 478 (1981), the Minnesota Supreme Court upheld that practice and the prosecutors won. By 1983, the proportion of property offenders imprisoned had risen to preguidelines levels and continued to rise through 1989 (Frase 1993*a*, p. 38).

The intrafamilial sex offense story is less tortured, but the moral is no less clear. Responding to heightened public concern, the commission prescribed prison sentences for most persons convicted of sexual offenses, regardless of the offender's prior record. Child sex abuse cases are especially complicated because of practitioners' recognition of many offenders' psychopathology, concern for maintaining households, and fear of making children feel guilty for having caused a parent's imprisonment and broken up the family. As a result, departure rates for child sex abuse cases have been high throughout the guidelines period and in 1987, despite the guidelines presumption of lengthy prison terms, the imprisonment rate for intrafamilial sex abuse cases was only 40 percent and the rate for nonfamilial statutory rape cases was only 58 percent (Frase 1993*a*). Frase's analysis does not demonstrate that sentences for sex offenders did not increase; they did, for those offenders for whom downward departures did not occur. Minnesota's sex-offender policies thus increased disparities among persons convicted of child sexual abuse offenses but, among those imprisoned, increased penalties.

David Boerner has shown how changes in guideline severity adopted in Washington were quickly followed by increases in average sentence severity. Because criminal code changes that increase penalties must be made prospectively, for constitutional reasons, during transition periods grandfathered cases must be sentenced under the earlier, less harsh, standards and new cases under the new standards, allowing for a quasi-experimental examination of the effects of the new standards. Figure 2.3 shows sentencing patterns from 1988 to 1992 for second-degree burglaries committed before and after the effective date of 1990 guideline amendments. Those amendments divided second-degree burglary into residential and nonresidential types and increased penalties for each. Average sentences for residential burglary increased substantially, while sentences for grandfathered cases (both nonresidential and residential) increased only slightly. Figure 2.4 shows comparable data for sentencing in first-degree statutory rape and first-degree "rape of child" cases from 1987 to 1992. Boerner writes that these offenses are comparable because code changes in 1988 that increased penalties also relabeled statutory rape as "rape of a child; the behavior covered by each of the degrees is essentially the same" (Boerner 1993, p. 25). Sentences for grandfathered cases under the original 1984 guidelines fluctuated but remained essentially the same through 1992, while cases sentenced under the 1988 guideline revision were substantially higher.

Boerner gives many such examples, all of which tend to demonstrate that changes in guidelines' sentence severity were quickly followed by increases in the severity of sentences for affected offenses. As always, the

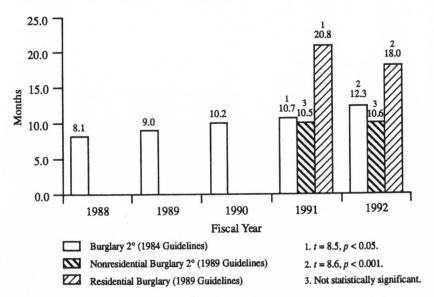

Figure 2.3. Average Sentence Length, Burglary. *Source:* Boerner (1993).

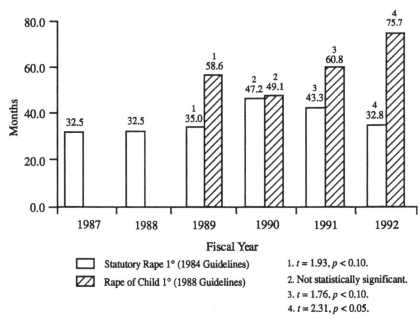

Figure 2.4. Average Sentence Length, Statutory Rape, and Rape of Child. *Source:* Boerner (1993).

data tell less than an omniscient observer would want to know. Because Boerner's data are average sentences received by incarcerated offenders sentenced for the designated offenses, it is impossible to know whether and how often the harsher sentences were avoided by plea bargains in which the defendant was allowed to plead guilty to a less serious offense than would have happened before the guideline revisions took effect. It would, however, require an unrealistically cynical hypothesis thereby to explain away all or most of the apparent increases in sentencing severity, leaving the conclusion that Washington's guideline changes did indeed significantly increase sentencing severity.

If the Washington data leave any doubt that sentencing policy changes through guidelines can alter sentencing practices, the U.S. Sentencing Commission experience should remove that doubt. The commission chose greatly to increase the proportion of offenders sentenced to imprisonment and greatly to increase the average lengths of prison sentences. It succeeded in both objectives.

The commission's evaluation showed that overall the percentage of convicted federal offenders sentenced to probation declined from 52 percent in late 1984 to 35 percent in June 1990. The commission in its four-year evaluation isolates only three offenses for separate study (drugs, robbery, and "economic offenses"); use of nonincarcerative sentences fell sharply for each.

Reduction in the use of probation as a sentence was even greater than the commission reports. The commission's evaluation overstates the use of probation, presumably by counting split sentences that include some period of incarceration as a condition as "probation." The commission's 1991 annual report (1992*b*, table 23) shows that only 14.5 percent of offenders in 1991 received "probation-only" sentences. According to the commission's 1993 annual report, 22.7 percent of cases resulted in "probation" sentences and 14.8 percent in "'straight' probation (i.e., no confinement condition)" (U.S. Sentencing Commission 1994, p. 67). Although the four-year evaluation does not report probation-only sentences before the guidelines took effect, some insight can be gained by comparing 1985 probation-only rates for selected offenses with 1991 rates. The 1985 data were reported by the commission in 1987. The first number in each of the following pairs is the 1985 probation-only rate; the second is the 1991 rate: robbery—18 percent, 0.3 percent; fraud—59 percent, 22 percent; immigration—41 percent, 16.8 percent (U.S. Sentencing Commission 1987*a*, p. 68; 1992*b*, table 3).

The severity of prison sentences likewise increased. The commission reports that the mean "expected to be served" sentence for all offenders increased from twenty-four months in July 1984 to forty-six months in June 1990 (1991*a*, p. 378). Prison sentences for drug offenses increased by 248 percent from 1984 to 1990 and from an average sixty months for robbery in 1984 to seventy-eight months in 1990. Although the commission's evaluation does not discuss other offenses, most offense categories would probably demonstrate stark increases.

The record, though not uncomplicated, shows that commissions through their policy choices can alter sentencing patterns substantially. That this can happen despite deep judicial dislike of the new policies is illustrated by the federal experience in which several judges have resigned rather than impose sentences they believe are unduly harsh. A California judge in tears imposed a lengthy sentence because the guidelines required it and then resigned; one not unrepresentative appellate judge voted to uphold an aggregate 140 years imprisonment for four defendants, only to observe, "these sentences defy reason, but as I have already noted—such is our system" (Bright 1993).

Racial and Gender Differences

Every sentencing commission has included reduction or elimination of racial and gender discrimination in sentencing among its goals (e.g., Minnesota Sentencing Guidelines Commission 1980), and most claim to a considerable extent to have succeeded. The Minnesota commission's three-year evaluation concluded that racial differences in sentencing declined under guidelines; nonetheless, minority defendants were likelier than whites to be imprisoned when the presumptive sentence prescribed non-state-imprisonment, minority defendants received longer sentences than similarly categorized whites, and men received longer prison sentences than similarly categorized women (Knapp 1984, p. 61). Terance Miethe and Charles Moore (1985, pp. 352–55), using the same data but more sophisticated statistical techniques, agreed that overall racial and gender differences declined under guidelines. Frase (1993*a*, p. 306), using the commission's monitoring data through 1989, also agreed that racial and gender differences diminished compared with preguidelines practices but painted a more complex picture. Women continued to receive gentler handling; they were less than half as likely to be subject to aggravated departures and more likely to benefit from mitigated departures. Black defendants had equal or higher aggravated departure rates compared with whites in each of five years studied and lower mitigated departure rates in all five years.

Washington's evaluation revealed similar patterns. The initial evaluation found an overall decline in racial differences in sentencing but that "substantial racial and gender disparity was found in the use of sentencing alternatives"; whites were almost twice as likely as blacks to benefit from special mitigating provisions for first-time and some sex offenders (Washington State Sentencing Guidelines Commission 1987, p. 59). In a ten-year review of Washington sentencing reforms, although concluding that racial and gender differences had diminished, the commission in 1992 acknowledged "significant gender and ethnic differences in the application of options" to incarceration (Washington State Sentencing Guidelines Commission 1992*b*, p. 12).

The Oregon racial data from the first fifteen months' guidelines experience are difficult to disentangle because most analyses compare whites and "minorities," a category that includes blacks, Hispanics, Asians, and Native Americans, groups whose patterns of criminality vary substantially. In addition, most of the data are presented in tabular form without controls or multivariate analyses to take account of systematic differences in the kinds of crimes and criminal histories that characterize various groups. Noting that the data are crude, the following can be observed. First, the overall probability of state incarceration for whites fell from 17 percent before guidelines to 12 percent under guidelines. For minorities, the rate fell slightly from 23.9 percent to 23 percent (with six-point decreases for blacks and Asians and three- and five-point increases for Native Americans and Hispanics) (Ashford and Mosbaek 1991, p. 47). Whites were slightly less likely than minority defendants to receive upward dispositional departures, slightly more likely to receive downward dispositional departures, and much more likely to benefit from an "optional probation" alternatives program (Ashford and Mosbaek 1991, pp. 49–52). As whites are to minority defendants in Oregon sentencing, so women are to men: women were less likely to receive upward departures, more likely to receive downward departures, and more likely to be sentenced to optional probation. Both leniency patterns—whites compared to nonwhites and women to men—have continued (Bogan and Factor 1995, p. 13).

Curiously, although the U.S. Sentencing Commission's self-evaluation and the GAO reanalyses of the commission's data involved much more sophisticated data-analytic methods than any of the state evaluations, the research design precluded any overall conclusions about racial and gender disparities. The commission's basic study, recall, was of disparity before and under guidelines using the commission's offense severity and criminal history schemes as the measure of consistency, but focusing on eight categories of cases involving small numbers in each category. As a result, the rote conclusion (1991*a*, pp. 302, 324) was that "cell sizes were inadequate to test or no significant relationships were found with respect to . . . race, gender, age." Exclusion from the analysis of departures for "substantial assistance to the government" leaves open the possibility that those mitigated sentences are skewed in terms of race or gender. In addition, as with the general disparity analysis, there is no basis for generalizing from the specific offenses the commission analyzed to federal offenders generally (U.S. General Accounting Office 1992, p. 64).

Because of the small sample sizes, the numbers of mitigated departures were insignificant, and no meaningful analyses of race and gender effects in departures could be made. In relation to disparities within the guidelines (i.e., whether some racial or gender groups are likelier to receive sentences at the top or bottom of the guideline ranges), the commission found that "race was found to be statistically significant across all offense categories [but] . . . only slight variations between sentencing of black and white offenders were found." However, "women were statistically more likely to receive sentences at the bottom of the range" (U.S. Sentencing Commission 1991*a*, p. 324).

The GAO, in a more sophisticated analysis, concluded that "blacks were more likely than whites to receive sentences at the bottom or top of the guidelines range rather than in the middle" and that "females were twice as likely (i.e., 1.91 times as likely, to be exact) as males to receive sentences at the bottom rather than in the middle of the range" (U.S. General Accounting Office 1992, p. 92).

The commission somewhat formalistically disagreed with the GAO's depiction of sentencing differences within guidelines as disparity, arguing that Congress authorized guideline ranges in which the maximum sentence was 25 percent longer than the minimum and accordingly by definition there could be no "unwarranted disparities," on racial or any other grounds, among sentences within applicable ranges (U.S. General Accounting Office 1992). Probably the fairest summary of the federal evaluations is that they are inconclusive on the effect of guidelines on racial disparities and consistent with state evaluations in finding gender disparities in favor of women.

The available evidence thus shows that guidelines have reduced but not eliminated racial and gender disparities in sentencing and that whites more often than nonwhites, and women than men, benefit from alternatives to incarceration and mitigated departures from guidelines. The difficulties in all this are that racial sentencing comparisons are confounded by systematic socioeconomic differences between races and that both racial and gender comparisons are confounded by group differences in criminality. Because blacks for reasons both of racial discrimination and social disadvantage tend to be likelier than whites to participate in common law crimes and to accumulate criminal records, guidelines based primarily on the current crime and the past criminal record in the nature of things treat blacks more severely than whites (and a parallel pattern distinguishes men from women). These differences are illustrated by tables 2.8 and 2.9 from Oregon's fifteen-month evaluation. The most extensive prior record category is "A." "I" is the least.

In order to combat racial disparities in sentencing, most sentencing commissions have forbidden judges to give weight in sentencing to socioeconomic factors such as education, employment, and family stability, which are known to be correlated with race, in order not systematically to disadvantage members of minority groups. Unfortunately, the "neutral" criteria of current offense and criminal history have the same effect. Since most guideline disparity analyses control for criminal history, they define

Table 2.8. Criminal History Classification by Race, Oregon (%)

Criminal History Category	Race					
	White	Hispanic	Black	Native American	Asian	Total
A	.5	.4	3.9	.8	.0	.7
B	1.8	1.3	4.9	1.7	.0	1.9
C	5.6	3.2	12.7	9.9	6.9	5.9
D	3.1	2.0	6.0	11.6	.0	3.3
E	8.7	3.6	8.3	7.4	.0	7.9
F	13.4	9.4	13.0	22.3	10.3	12.9
G	21.0	17.4	15.3	18.2	20.7	20.0
H	14.9	9.1	11.7	17.4	3.4	13.8
I	30.9	53.6	24.4	10.7	58.6	33.5
Total	100.0	100.0	100.0	100.0	100.0	100.0
Number	4,300	834	386	121	29	5,670

Source: Ashford and Mosbaek (1991), p. 49.

Note: Cases where criminal history is missing have been excluded; $p < .0001$.

Table 2.9. Criminal History Classification by Gender, Oregon (%)

Criminal History Category	Gender		Total
	Male	Female	
A	.9	.0	.7
B	2.1	.4	1.9
C	6.7	1.4	5.9
D	3.7	2.0	3.4
E	8.7	4.2	8.1
F	13.3	12.4	13.2
G	20.3	17.5	19.9
H	13.3	16.7	13.8
I	31.0	45.4	33.1
Total	100.0	100.0	100.0
Number	5,200	910	6,110

Source: Ashford and Mosbaek (1991), p. 56.

Note: Cases where criminal history is missing have been excluded; $p < .0001$.

away much of the differentially adverse sentencing experienced by members of minority groups as "not disparity."

Prison Populations

The Oregon, Washington, Minnesota, and federal commissions operated under enabling legislation that directed them to give substantial consideration to the impact of their guidelines on correctional resources, which was generally interpreted to refer to prison beds and capacity. The federal commission ignored that charge, despite unambiguous language in Section 994(g) of the Sentencing Reform Act of 1984: "The sentencing guidelines prescribed under this chapter shall be formulated to minimize the likelihood that the federal prison population will exceed the capacity of the federal prisons," and promulgated guidelines that were predicted to triple the federal prison population within a decade (U.S. Sentencing Commission 1987*a*, chap. 7). The states heeded their charges and, rarities among American states, as figure 2.5 shows, managed from the effective dates of their guidelines to hold prison populations within capacity for extended periods (and Oregon through 1994). In Minnesota and Washington, sensational crimes in each state in 1989 provoked anticrime hysteria, and the legislatures increased penalties for many crimes; both prison populations thereafter rose rapidly (Frase 1993*b*; Lieb 1993).

Nonetheless, the experience in Washington, Oregon, and Minnesota

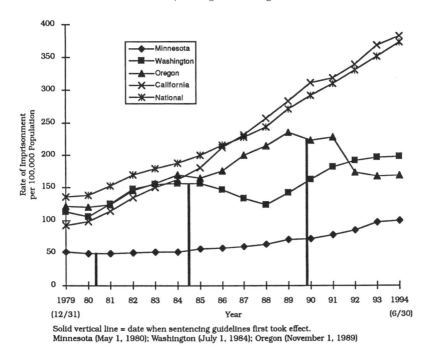

Figure 2.5. Rate of Prison Population Growth for Selected States and Nationally, 1979–94. *Sources:* Bureau of Justice Statistics (1994*a*, 1994*b*), Maguire and Pastore (1993).

shows that sentencing commissions and their guidelines can adopt policy approaches that treat prison beds as scarce and expensive resources and that those policies can succeed in constraining prison population growth and associated public spending.

Effectiveness as Administrative Agencies

Were there not a federal sentencing commission, no one would question that Judge Frankel's proposed new approach to formulation of sentencing policy has been markedly successful, both substantively and institutionally. In 1978, just a few years after the appearance of Judge Frankel's book, *Criminal Sentences: Law without Order,* and long before passage of the Federal Sentencing Reform Act of 1984, Minnesota and Pennsylvania enacted sentencing commission legislation and, in 1980 and 1982, respectively, guidelines took effect. As noted earlier in this chapter, many other states have established commissions, promulgated guidelines, or both.

Of guidelines now in effect, those in Minnesota, Pennsylvania, Washington, and Oregon have been in operation long enough that evidence concerning their operation is available. The preceding pages showed that commissions have in significant degree achieved many of their substantive policy goals. State commissions have also achieved Judge Frankel's institutional purposes. They have established and sustained specialized technical competence. In all four states, the commissions have survived to serve as their state's principal forum for sentencing policy proposals. Each has developed a monitoring system and has from time to time considered or implemented guidelines changes to respond to implementation problems revealed by monitoring programs. Each conducts regular training sessions. Each publishes annual statistical reports. Minnesota's commission in 1984 prepared the most sophisticated evaluation of a state sentencing initiative ever published (Knapp 1984). All four are wrestling with current policy issues. Pennsylvania in 1994 completed a major overhaul of its guidelines and some of their underlying policy premises (Pennsylvania Commission on Sentencing 1993*b*, pp. 3–7) and became the first state to incorporate intermediate sanctions into its guidelines (1994). Oregon and Washington have worked on guidelines for misdemeanants and for non-state-prison-bound felons (Bogan 1991; Washington State Sentencing Guidelines Commission 1992*b*). Minnesota has been working for years on nonincarceration guidelines, drug-offense policy, and day fines (e.g., Minnesota Sentencing Guidelines Commission 1991*b*, 1992).

The state commissions have served to some degree to insulate sentencing policy from short-term emotionalism and law-and-order sloganeering. Sentencing policies did eventually change in both Minnesota and Washington to reflect the law-and-order politics of the 1990s; perhaps it is no coincidence that penalties in both states increased substantially in 1989, only months after Willie Horton's voter-galvanizing appearance in the 1988 presidential campaign. In Minnesota, the anticrime reaction was so strong that the legislature amended the enabling legislation to make "public safety" the primary factor in setting sentencing standards and, while allowing some role for resource concerns, provided that resources should no longer warrant "substantial" consideration (Frase 1993*b*).

No legislative delegation of rule-making authority to administrative agencies can forever or completely insulate policy from partisan political influence, nor should it. Powerful and determined political forces can overrule an agency's policies directly through legislation or indirectly through informal political pressure or appointment of new commissioners committed to different policies. In the short term, however, especially in the face of less powerful or less determined opposition, administrative agencies can buffer policy from episodic emotions and sometimes can protect elected officials from constituent pressures. Especially in the past dozen years in the United States, criminal justice policies have been highly contentious. Political pressures and emotions tend to support increased penalties for currently topical crimes and to provide little support for comprehensive unemotional approaches to crime-control policies. Where the political will exists to try to buffer sentencing policies from short-term emotions, the experience in the states shows that commissions can provide that buffer—as long as the supportive political will survives.

The state sentencing commissions also adopted comprehensive systems approaches to sentencing policy. Minnesota, Washington, and Oregon all fitted their sentencing policies to available (or planned) prison resources, taking the theretofore unknown but unassailable position that responsible policy making requires that states face up to the programmatic and financial implications of the sentencing policies they adopt. Policy can be tailored to fit resources, or resources can be expanded to meet projected needs; one way or the other a "resource constraint" policy requires conscious and responsible decision making. This practice was conspicuously absent in the 1980s in most American states, where punishments were repeatedly raised without regard to resources and foreseeably resulted in unprecedented prison overcrowding and federal court intervention. As a result of the resource constraint policy, some of the commissions had consciously to reduce penalties for some crimes when pressures arose to increase penalties for others.

To this point, the experience of the federal and state commissions is institutionally similar. Where the experience differs is in the quality of the guidelines the state commissions produced, their successful efforts to win (at least) grudging support from judges and other practitioners, their success in achieving an institutional esprit among commission staff, and their abilities to insulate policy from politics at least for a time (e.g., Tonry 1991, 1993*b*). Three points of difference stand out.

First, unlike the federal guidelines, which remain deeply unpopular with judges and lawyers nine years after their effective date, the guidelines in Washington, Delaware, Pennsylvania, Minnesota, and Oregon are generally supported by criminal court practitioners. In no state is there heated debate about the guidelines' desirability and legitimacy and in no state is there significant organized opposition to them.

Second, as noted earlier, until legislative changes in Washington and Minnesota led to toughened guidelines, those states successfully maintained prison populations within available capacity and maintained lower than average incarceration rate increases, thereby avoiding out-of-control corrections spending and federal court intervention. In Oregon, population control continued through 1994. By contrast, the U.S. commission ignored its statutory directive to link policy to resources and, as a result, the federal prison population nearly doubled between 1987 and 1994, and the federal prisons in 1992 were operating at 158 percent of capacity (Bureau of Justice Statistics 1992*b*).

Third, unlike the state commissions, the U.S. Sentencing Commission suffered from internal dissension, high staff turnover, ineffective management, and political infighting (see chapter 3). The state commissions have been remarkably stable. The Pennsylvania commission's director, appointed in 1978, remained in place late in 1995, and several of the senior staff remained with the commission for ten years or longer. The current director of the Minnesota commission was promoted from within and has worked with the commission for more than a decade. The Washington commission's director in 1994 was its initial research director, and the initial director remains active in sentencing policy deliberations. The director of the Oregon Criminal Justice Council, under the auspices of which Oregon's guidelines were developed, held that position for many years after the state's guidelines were promulgated.

The U.S. Sentencing Commission experience has been less stable and less harmonious. The U.S. General Accounting Office (1990*a*), when asked by Congress to assess the commission's management and operations, found "organizational disarray." In four years the commission had four staff directors and one interim director and was without a research director for one and a half years. "According to former staff directors, it was difficult to manage in an environment where they could not maintain authority over staff because of commissioners' involvement," the GAO observed. Moreover, "part of the problem has been finding qualified candidates who would be willing to take the [research director's] position, given perceptions that the working environment is complicated by commissioner involvement and other matters" (p. 15). The May 1990 issue of the *Federal Sentencing Reporter* reprints critical statements about the commission's management from numerous agencies and spokesmen. Two members of the commission and one ex officio member have resigned on principle over the commission's failures (Robinson 1987; Block 1989).

To be sure, not all state sentencing commissions have succeeded. Some, like those in New York and South Carolina, developed guidelines but could not persuade legislatures to adopt them. In Pennsylvania and Kansas, legislatures rejected initial sets of proposed guidelines. In some states—for example, Florida—the guidelines are not well respected and are of little influence (Florida Legislature 1991). In 1994, commissions and guidelines were abolished in Tennessee and Wisconsin.

If the controversies associated with the U.S. Sentencing Commission and the wisdom of its policies are set aside, from a purely technical perspective even it can be seen as an institutional success. Successful administrative agencies achieve and maintain specialized competence concerning complex subjects (that is why they are created), they have some degree of insulation from short-term political emotions and pressures (that is why typically their members are appointed for fixed terms and can only be removed for cause), and they can adopt comprehensive and long-term approaches to policy making (this also is why they are created and why public funds are spent to develop cadres of policy experts).

From that perspective, even the U.S. commission has been at least a partial success. No one can doubt that it has achieved specialized competence. Through its rule-making processes, it has proposed and promulgated hundreds of changes to its guidelines, policy statements, and supporting commentary in efforts to rein in what it sees as willfully noncompliant judges and to fine-tune its policies. Through its monitoring and evaluation staffs, it has assembled mountains of data and published numerous annual and evaluation reports, at least some of which, notably its report on mandatory penalties (1991*b*), demonstrate high levels of technical competence and policy sophistication.

The commission has taken a comprehensive systems approach to policy making, as is evidenced by its efforts to devise guidelines for all federal offenses, to monitor the guidelines' implementation, to counterbalance the plea-bargaining strategies of prosecutors and defense counsel, and to train probation officers to serve as guardians of the guidelines.

The most powerful evidence that the U.S. commission has succeeded institutionally is that federal sentencing practices have been radically altered. No matter how misguided the guidelines and despite their inability to win support from the people who must implement them (which means they will fail in the long term), the guidelines have succeeded in recasting federal sentencing. Sentencing patterns changed as the commission intended: the proportion of cases sentenced to probation declined greatly, and average prison terms for many offenses became longer.

Where Judge Frankel's model failed in the federal system was in respect of political insulation. Most proponents of guidelines have seen its one-step-removed-from-politics character as a great strength (e.g., Frankel and Orland 1984). The U.S. commission, by contrast, made no effort to insulate its policies from law-and-order politics and short-term emotions. One sign of this is a repeated invocation by the commission of the "reduction of undue leniency" in sentencing as one of the guidelines' primary objectives. For example, in a typical statement, the U.S. commission indicated in 1991 that, "the goals of the Sentencing Reform Act of 1984 were to reduce unwarranted disparity, increase certainty and severity, and correct past patterns of undue leniency" (1991*c*, p. i), even though the Sentencing Reform Act of 1984 includes no language about "correcting undue leniency" among its enumerated statutory purposes (18 USCA 3553[a][2]; 28 USCA, chap. 58, 991[b]). The commission apparently decided that the U.S. Department of Justice and the most law-and-order members of the U.S. Congress were its primary constituency, and it established and attempted to enforce policies that pleased that constituency. This is presumably why the commission ignored a statutory directive that it should tie its policies to available correctional resources,[1]

1. #994(g): "The Commission in promulgating guidelines . . . shall take into account the nature and capacity of the penal, correctional, and other services and facilities available. . . . The sentencing guidelines prescribed under this chapter shall be formulated to minimize the likelihood that the federal prison population will exceed the capacity of the federal prisons."

why it chose to ignore a statutory presumption against incarceration of first offenders not convicted of violent or other serious crimes,[2] and why it reacted to harsh mandatory minimum penalty provisions for many drug offenses by making the guidelines even harsher (e.g., Tonry 1992*a*).

Thus the federal experience shows that, as an institution, a sentencing commission can operate much as do administrative agencies on other subjects. The state experience supports that conclusion but also shows that commissions can develop successful sentencing policies that win the support of practitioners, that tie policy to resource allocation, and that achieve substantively sound sentencing policies.

II. Issues Facing Commissions

For the foreseeable future, sentencing commissions are here to stay. Their guidelines have been completely successful nowhere, in part because there can be no consensus about the meaning of success. So long as people have discussed punishment there have been major differences in perspective between those who see the criminal law and sentencing primarily or exclusively as institutions concerned with alleged offenders' moral culpability and those who see the criminal law and sentencing primarily as institutions concerned with prevention of crime and maximization of public safety. Even without fundamental differences in punishment philosophy, differences in officials' perspectives breed disagreements. Legislators and sentencing commissioners are concerned with policy in the aggregate. If disparity reduction is the goal, clear, bright-line standards are the simplest to express and against which to measure progress. Judges, lawyers, and defendants are concerned with situationally just or appropriate penalties and often find clear and simple standards arbitrary and simplistic. Disagreements about punishment purposes and differences in perspective make it impossible to achieve perfect compliance with guidelines. Commissions have, however, managed to make sentencing more accountable, more consistent, and less disparate in its impact on minority group members, and those are not small achievements.

As the sentencing commission enters its third decade, two sets of policy issues must continue to be addressed. One set of issues poses fundamental policy-making challenges—plea bargaining, intermediate punishments, misdemeanor guidelines—that no commission has fully addressed. Another, however, involves issues on which there has been slow but steady progress, on which commissions have gradually refined their approaches,

2. #994(j): "The Commission shall insure that the guidelines reflect the general appropriateness of imposing a sentence other than imprisonment in cases in which a defendant is a first offender who has not been convicted of a crime of violence or an otherwise serious offense."

and on which commissions have learned from one another. This section sketches the contours of both these sets of issues. Discussing them in detail would require another chapter, and to my knowledge there is no published literature (except, perhaps, Parent [1988] and for some issues Morris and Tonry [1990]).

Major Systemic Issues

Four major systemic issues affecting sentencing guidelines have faced sentencing commissions from the outset. On one, the desirability of tying sentencing policy and its projected operations to correctional resources, there is slow but steady movement toward choosing to do so. As table 2.1 showed, most newly created commissions have been directed to take account of resource constraints in setting sentencing policies. Other major systemic issues—controlling prosecutorial discretion under guidelines and developing guidelines for misdemeanors and for nonincarcerative penalties—have been discussed by every sentencing commission. Washington's commission did establish guidelines for prosecutors, but they are nonbinding and appear to have been without influence (Boerner 1995*b*). In 1994, Pennsylvania promulgated a new set of guidelines that set standards for noncustodial penalties (Pennsylvania Commission on Sentencing 1994), and North Carolina's similar system took effect a few months later (North Carolina Sentencing and Policy Advisory Commission 1994). In more piecemeal but still noteworthy ways, Washington and Oregon have recently set new policies for intermediate sanctions (Washington State Sentencing Guidelines Commission 1994*a*; Oregon Criminal Justice Council 1994).

Guidelines for Noncustodial Sanctions and Misdemeanors

No commission in its initial years attempted to develop guidelines for nonincarcerative sentences, in part because development of incarceration guidelines was challenge enough, in part because of a lack of community-based punishments in most jurisdictions, and in part because no one knew how to do it. Commissions today are at work in many states on proposals to integrate intermediate and noncustodial penalties into guidelines and to devise systems of interchangeability between prison and nonprison sanctions.

There has been considerable conceptual progress, but little practical policy making, since the Minnesota commission declined a legislative invitation (Laws of Minnesota for 1978, chap. 723, 9[5][2]) to devise nonincarceration guidelines: "The sentencing guidelines promulgated by the commission may also establish appropriate sentences for prisoners for whom imprisonment is not proper. Any [such] guidelines . . . shall make specific reference to noninstitutional sanctions including but not limited to the following: payment of fines, day fines, restitution, community work orders, work release programs in local facilities, community based residential and nonresidential programs, incarceration in a local correctional facility, and probation and the conditions thereof." In the event, the Minnesota commission's guidelines created presumptions as to who went to state prison (roughly 20 percent of convicted felons) and for how long, but set no presumptions for sentences for nonimprisonment sanctions for felons or for sentences of any kind for misdemeanants.

Since then, each commission has considered misdemeanor and non-imprisonment guidelines, and a few have taken small steps. Three basic approaches have been considered. The first is to create "punishment units" in which all sanctions can be expressed. If guidelines, for example, set "120 punishment units" as the presumptive sentence, a judge could impose any combination of sanctions that represented 120 units. Oregon's guidelines specify presumptive sentences for many offenders in punishment units (Bogan 1990, 1991), but do not provide for how the units are to be calculated. This has been the critical problem in every jurisdiction that has considered the punishment unit approach. Preoccupation with prison sentences as the standard punishment has so far stymied development of the concept. Jurisdictions have typically begun with prison time and then attempted to specify punitively equivalent non-prison sentences. In a number of jurisdictions, for example, one day's imprisonment has been made equivalent to one, or even three, days' community service. This limits substitution of noncustodial for custodial penalties to very short prison terms. The best-known American community service program (McDonald 1986) and the national policy in England and Wales (Pease 1985), respectively, set 70 and 240 hours as the maximum enforceable length of a community service sentence. At three days' community service to one day's incarceration, community service would be exchangeable for three to ten days' incarceration.

Besides the difficulty in reaching agreement about exchange rates between custodial and noncustodial penalties, a number of problems have impeded policy development (Morris and Tonry 1990, chap. 8). Few American jurisdictions have large numbers of well-managed, credible, noncustodial penalties in operation, which makes it difficult to promulgate guidelines premised on their availability. In an era of constrained public resources, it has been difficult obtaining new money to create new programs (even though diversion of prison-bound offenders to community penalties should in the long run conserve public funds). A related problem is that county governments in most American states pay for all or most noncustodial corrections programs. This means both that available programs differ substantially between counties within a state and that new programs must be paid for from county revenues (or from state funds, but in tight times, states are no more eager to appropriate new money than are counties).

The second approach is to create different presumptive bands within sentencing guideline grids (strong presumptive "in"; weak presumptive "in"; weak presumptive "out"; strong presumptive "out") and to allow judges to create individualized noncustodial punishments that take account of those presumptions (Morris and Tonry 1990, chap. 2). The D.C. Superior Court, Sentencing Guidelines Commission (1987) first proposed such a system, and the Pennsylvania and North Carolina guidelines in 1994 adopted this approach. The problem with this approach is that it authorizes use of noncustodial penalties for specified categories of offenders but sets no standards for their use.

The third approach is simply to specify equivalent custodial and non-custodial penalties and to authorize judges to impose them in the alternative. Washington's commission did this (Boerner 1985) and later proposed a more extensive system (Washington State Sentencing Guidelines Commission 1992*b*, pp. 19–23) that the legislature did not adopt. Like the punishment unit proposals, the equivalency approaches have so far been unable to overcome the psychological and political pressures to make "equivalent" punishments as subjectively burdensome as prison, which limits their use to the most minor offenses and offenders. Advice from academics (Wasik and von Hirsch 1988; von Hirsch, Wasik, and Greene 1989; Morris and Tonry 1990, chap. 4) has not proven enormously helpful.

Tying Sentencing Policy to Corrections Resources

The wisdom of the Minnesota-Washington-Oregon decision to tie sentencing policies to corrections resources has become ever clearer, and other states are beginning to follow suit. Pennsylvania's commission, for example, which initially chose not to take correctional resources into account in devising its guidelines, reconsidered that decision (Kramer 1992) and the 1994 guidelines amendments are premised on resource concerns. The North Carolina Sentencing and Policy Advisory Commission (1993) and the Texas Punishment Standards Commission (Reynolds 1993) proposed that their states adopt policies of tying sentencing policy to correctional resources, and North Carolina did so (North Carolina Sentencing and Policy Advisory Commission 1994). The Kansas commission proposed an "early warning system" approach in which the commissioner of corrections would certify an impending resource problem and the sentencing commission would review current practices and make recommendations for changes to the legislature (Kansas Sentencing Commission 1991).

Controlling Plea Bargaining

No jurisdiction has as yet devised an adequate system for controlling plea bargaining under a sentencing guidelines system. Washington State came closest. Aware of criticisms that guidelines for sentencing shift discretion to prosecutors, the Washington legislature authorized its sentencing commission to promulgate statewide charging and plea-bargaining standards. Because of concern that strong standards would be unenforceable (or invite judicial scrutiny of prosecutorial discretion that prosecutors adamantly opposed) and because of opposition on the merits from prosecutors, the commission developed weak aspirational standards (Boerner 1985, app. 6).

Sentence bargains, if allowed, can undermine any system of guidelines (Alschuler 1978). Charge (or "fact") bargaining in systems based on conviction offenses like Minnesota's or Oregon's enable plea-bargaining lawyers to pick the applicable guideline range and thereby greatly limit the judge's options. A number of proposals have been made for regulating plea bargaining under guidelines (Schulhofer 1980; Tonry and Coffee 1987). One is to provide an explicit percentage or other mechanical sentence discount for defendants who plead guilty (Gottfredson, Wilkins, and Hoffman 1978). The U.S. Sentencing Commission in effect does this by allowing a two- or three-level sentence reduction for "acceptance of responsibility" as evidenced by a guilty plea. The most radical proposal has been to adopt "real offense" sentencing in which penalties are based not on the defendants' conviction offense but on their "actual behavior." Only the U.S. Sentencing Commission has adopted a real offense system. The U.S. commission adopted its "relevant conduct" approach to sentencing in order to offset plea bargaining's influence (Wilkins and Steer 1990); by requiring judges at sentencing to take account of uncharged behavior, and behavior alleged in dropped or acquitted charges, the commission's approach raises difficult issues of principle (Lear 1993; Reitz 1993). In addition, that approach has not managed to avoid increased prosecutorial influence. Many judges argue that the guidelines have shifted power to the prosecutor (Federal Courts Study Committee 1990; Heaney 1991).

Evolutionary Issues

The earliest guidelines, it is easy to forget, represented a radical departure from the indeterminate sentencing systems that they displaced. Before guidelines, judges had almost complete discretion to impose any lawful sentence, and parole boards could set any release date between the minimum parole eligibility date and the maximum set by the judge (often three times the minimum). That some policy choices made by the early commissions were cautious and others in retrospect relatively crude should be no surprise. In this brief section, I identify a number of issues on which there has been gradual movement in some states toward more refined policy choices.

Scaling Offenses

In early guideline systems, commissions for the most part stayed very close to statutory definitions of offenses, however broadly defined. As time has passed, commissions have partitioned statutory offense definitions into subcategories of different severity. The Pennsylvania commission, for example, has recently reconsidered its offense severity rankings and its subdivisions of crimes. The extreme case is the U.S. commission (see table 2.5), which added numerous extrastatutory elements to its system of offense scaling.

Criminal Histories

The earliest guidelines systems used broad generic criminal history measures. In Minnesota, for example, every prior felony conviction was given one "point," every prior misdemeanor one-fourth point, and every prior gross misdemeanor one-half point. More recent systems, including revisions to Minnesota's, are subtler. Some give greater weight to prior violent than to prior property convictions. Some cross-tabulate so that a prior violent conviction weighs more heavily for a current violent conviction than for a current nonviolent conviction. Some weight prior convictions in relation to their severity under the guidelines system's offense severity scaling for current convictions. In similar fashion, guidelines commissions are becoming more subtle in their chronological weighing of past crimes, tending more often to build in "decay" provisions in which convictions prior to some date (e.g., five or ten years before the current crime) are no longer taken into account. There is no literature concerning the use of prior criminal histories in formulating sentencing policy, although Julian Roberts (1994) in a recent article on the federal guidelines has shown how policy making would be enriched were such a literature available.

There are numerous other issues, of course, on which policy thinking continues to evolve. These include such things as the handling of aggravating and mitigating circumstances, the number of offense levels in a guidelines grid, the relative location of particular crimes in offense severity rankings, and the development of special procedures and rules for regularly recurring policy issues presented by sex abuse cases, first offenders, and drug cases.

III. The Future of the Sentencing Commission

The commissions that Judge Frankel proposed have shown that they can achieve much of what he had in mind. They can attain and sustain specialized institutional competence of a variety of kinds. They can develop and implement comprehensive, jurisdiction wide standards for sentences. Their guidelines can reduce sentencing disparities, diminish racial and gender differences, and help jurisdictions link their criminal justice policies to their criminal justice budgets. That is on the bright side.

Commissions have limits as policy tools. There is evidence that, after the enthusiasms and satisfactions of innovation have passed, institutional hardening of the arteries can set in and commissions can lose their influence and lapse into passivity (e.g., Knapp 1987, pp. 127–41). Commissions are based in part on belief in norms of instrumental rationality and empirically informed policy making. When the political environment is such that elected officials insist on treating criminal justice policy making primarily as symbolic politics, as happened in New York (Griset 1991) and Kansas (Gottlieb 1993) and with Pennsylvania's first set of proposed guidelines (Martin 1984), there is little that commissions can do to resist in the long run. In the short run, as the success of Minnesota's, Oregon's, and Washington's commissions at defying the national trends toward increased use of imprisonment indicates, commissions can resist the politicization of criminal justice policy. In both Washington and Minnesota, perhaps because prison populations began to climb after get-tough guidelines amendments were enacted in the late 1980s, legislators have begun to have second thoughts and to look for ways to regain the policy rationality their guidelines systems once had (Frase 1993*b*; Lieb 1993; Boerner 1995*a*).

This overview of experience with sentencing commissions paints a partial picture and relies on literature that more often supports hypotheses than answers questions. In part, this is because so few evaluations have been carried out. With the exception of one series of outside evaluations of Minnesota's guidelines (Miethe and Moore 1985; Moore and Miethe 1986), which relied largely on the Minnesota commission's data, and the GAO's (1992) federal analysis, all of the major evaluations to date have been internal efforts carried out by permanent staff. This has two obvious consequences. The commissions have a predictable institutional self-interest in establishing the success of their policies. The extreme instance is the U.S. commission's institutional defensiveness and distortion. Its self-evaluation defined disparity in a self-serving way that was foreordained to demonstrate success, evidence was presented in the most favorable possible light, and implementation problems were attributed not to the lack of wisdom in the commission's policies but to stubborn resistance of judges (e.g., U.S. Sentencing Commission 1991*a*, pp. 419–20). The second, and more common, problem is that ongoing commission budgets tend not to be adequate to support sophisticated evaluations. The only data available for analysis are routinely collected monitoring data that are limited in coverage and may not be comprehensive (in Oregon's fifteen-month evaluation, for example, reporting forms had been filed for only 74 percent of cases sentenced under the guidelines; Ashford and Mosbaek [1991], p. x). Funds are not likely to be available to hire research consultants and supplementary staff to carry out the analysis. Minnesota's justly celebrated three-year evaluation was made possible only by one-time grants from the National Institute of Corrections and the MacArthur Foundation, which supported supplementary data collection and paid for specialist research staff (Knapp 1984).

Thus, for a number of reasons, there are severe limitations inherent in having commissions evaluate their own handiwork. To date, however, with the exception of the Miethe and Moore and GAO studies, and recent reanalyses of commission data by Frase in Minnesota (1991*a*, 1993*a*) and Boerner in Washington (1993), there have been no outside empirical assessments. With the exception of the federally funded self-evaluation by the U.S. Sentencing Commission (and the GAO follow-up), the federal government, including its research agencies, has not funded a single evaluation of sentencing commissions or their guidelines for nearly a decade, which seems a pity when so many states have tried, or are trying, to recast their sentencing policies and practices with the help of sentencing commissions.

Twenty years on, at least in an American context, sentencing commissions and their guidelines have proven themselves as the most effective prescription thus far offered for the ills of lawlessness, arbitrariness, disparity, and discrimination that were widely believed to characterize indeterminate sentencing. Perhaps in time private and public funding agencies will realize that the states' experiments with sentencing reform are continuing and will provide the financial support that is needed to help states better understand where they have been and where they are going.

3

The Federal Sentencing Guidelines

The guidelines developed by the U.S. Sentencing Commission, which took effect on November 1, 1987, are the most controversial and disliked sentencing reform initiative in U.S. history. They are commonly criticized on policy grounds (that they unduly narrow judicial discretion and shift discretion to prosecutors), on process grounds (that they foreseeably cause judges and prosecutors to circumvent them), on ethical grounds (that by forcing key decisions behind closed doors, they foster hypocrisy and undermine the integrity of federal sentencing), on technocratic grounds (that they are too complex and are hard to apply accurately), on fairness grounds (that, because only offense elements and prior criminal records are taken into account, very different defendants receive the same sentence), on outcome grounds (that they have not reduced sentencing disparities), and on normative grounds (that they are too harsh).

For all that, as chapter 2 demonstrated, in a narrow institutional sense the U.S. Sentencing Commission has been a success. As a result of the commission's guidelines and its policies, federal sentencing has overall become much harsher (as the commission wanted) than before the guidelines took effect. The commission's and the guidelines' constitutionality was upheld by the U.S. Supreme Court. Federal appellate courts have for the most part upheld the commission's interpretations of its enabling legislation and rejected trial judges' efforts to second-guess commission policies. Even widespread circumvention of commission policies by judges and lawyers is in a perverse way commentary on the commission's institutional success; were the guidelines not so rigid and the sentences they specify not so radical a departure from past practices, fewer practitioners would feel justified in circumventing them.

The commission's institutional achievement, however, is like that of a doctor whose patient died despite a successful operation. In the final judgment, no policy initiative can be said to succeed if its legitimacy is denied by the people who must implement it; evidence from a variety of sources demonstrates that most judges and defense counsel and many prosecutors resent and resist the guidelines. Nor can a policy initiative be said to have succeeded if it fails to achieve its primary goal; despite commission claims that disparities have been reduced, most informed observers disagree, and the General Accounting Office in an independent, congressionally mandated evaluation concluded that it is "impossible to determine how effective the sentencing guidelines have been in reducing overall sentencing disparity" (U.S. General Accounting Office 1992, p. 10).

Possibly the best evidence that the federal sentencing guidelines have been a policy failure comes from the experiences of other jurisdictions that have appointed sentencing commissions. As chapter 2 demonstrated, the federal example raises skepticism in many states. In Arkansas, North Carolina, Ohio, and Texas, for example (Knapp 1993; Orland and Reitz 1993; Reitz and Reitz 1995), commissions at early meetings adopted resolutions expressly repudiating the federal guidelines as a model for anything they might develop.

The U.S. Sentencing Commission's failure was not foreordained. Nor are its failed policies irreparable (although the unnecessary damage done to tens of thousands of federal defendants and their families cannot be undone). Shortly before this book was finished, four new members were appointed by President Bill Clinton to the seven-member commission and were quickly confirmed by the Senate. Should those members wish to do so, the commission's most unsuccessful and unpopular policies could be changed without any changes being made to the statutory language in the Sentencing Reform Act of 1984 that created the commission. This chapter, in its final section, explains how that could be done. First though, in sections I, II, and III, I discuss the federal guidelines experience to date, the evaluation evidence concerning the guidelines' operation, and the reasons for the commission's failures.

I.   Early Experience with Federal Guidelines

Fundamental problems with the federal guidelines were apparent soon after they took effect and were made evident by outspoken condemnation on both policy and constitutional grounds by federal district court judges. Within two years, "more than 200 district judges invalidated the guidelines and all or part of the Sentencing Reform Act" (U.S. Sentencing Commission 1990, p. 11). Those decisions were necessarily couched in constitutional terms, but the number of cases and the vehemence of the opinions suggest that the underlying problem was the judges' deep antipathy to the guidelines themselves. In *Mistretta v. United States*, 488 U.S. 361 (1989), 109 S. Ct. 647 (1989), the U.S. Supreme Court in an 8 to 1 decision upheld the commission's, the guidelines', and the Sentencing Reform Act's constitutionality.

Federal district courts declared the Sentencing Reform Act unconstitutional on three theories: that Congress's delegation of rule-making authority to the sentencing commission was excessively broad, that constitutional separation-of-powers doctrines were violated when the rule-making commission was placed in the judicial branch of government, and that the guidelines violated defendants' Fifth Amendment due process rights to individualized consideration of offense and offender characteristics at sentencing. The due process arguments were not resolved in *Mistretta*, but inasmuch as all ten circuit courts of appeals that considered them in 1989 rejected them (U.S. Sentencing Commission 1990, p. 12), they are for all practical purposes dead.

Mistretta rejected the excessive-delegation and separation-of-powers challenges. With respect to excessive delegation, the Court held that the Sentencing Reform Act contained "intelligible principles" and policy directions to guide the commission (*Mistretta v. United States,* 109 S. Ct. 647, 654–55 [1989]) and appropriately delegated authority for detailed rule-making to the commission.

There were three separate separation-of-powers arguments. On the first, the Court found no constitutional barrier to placement of the commission in the Judicial Branch. The Court noted that the commission's functions are clearly related to the historical work of the courts (*Id.* at 661–67).

The second separation-of-powers challenge concerned the commission's composition—that the statutory requirement that three federal judges serve on the commission impermissibly interfered with the functioning of the judiciary. The Court rejected that argument, observing that the nature of the commission's work "is devoted exclusively to the development of rules to rationalize a process that has been and will continue to be performed exclusively by the Judicial Branch." The Court observed that the commission was "an essentially neutral endeavor . . . in which judicial participation is peculiarly appropriate" (*Id.* at 673).

Finally, the Court rejected the third argument that presidential control of commissioners through appointment (with the advice and consent of the Senate) and removal (for cause) significantly threatened judicial independence (*Id.* at 675).

Judges' Reactions to the Federal Sentencing Guidelines

The Supreme Court's decision settled the constitutional questions, but made the guidelines no more popular. The Federal Courts Study Committee, appointed by the Chief Justice of the United States to examine and propose solutions for problems facing the U.S. courts, observed, "It became obvious from our earliest requests for comment and information from federal judges and others who work daily in the system . . . that there is a pervasive concern that the Commission's guidelines are producing fundamental and deleterious changes in the way federal courts process criminal cases" (1990, p. 135).

The committee (1990, p. 138) noted a series of practical problems with the federal guidelines. Sentencing proceedings had become much more time consuming. The guidelines were inflexible and arbitrary. They disrupted plea bargaining, threatened to increase demands for trials, and distorted the role of the probation officer. Perhaps most disturbing to judges, the committee was told "that the rigidity of the guidelines is causing a massive, though unintended, transfer of discretion and authority from the court to the prosecutor . . . the result, it appears, is that some prosecutors (and some defense counsel) have evaded and manipulated the guidelines."

The Study Committee received testimony from 270 people, including federal officials, judges, probation officers, prosecutors, defense lawyers, representatives of organized groups like the American Bar Association, and members of the U.S. Sentencing Commission. Only four of those testifying, all associated with the commission, favored the guidelines. No other witness opposed the following proposal to make the guidelines less rigid: "Congress should amend the Sentencing Reform Act to state clearly that the guidelines promulgated by the Sentencing Commission are general standards regarding the appropriate sentence in the typical case, not compulsory rules. Although the guidelines should identify the presumptive sentence, the trial judge should have general authority to select a sentence outside the range prescribed by the guidelines, subject to appellate review for abuse of discretion. The exercise of this discretion may be based upon factors such as an appropriate plea bargain or the defendant's personal characteristics and history" (Federal Courts Study Committee 1990, p. 142).

A short time later, Judge William W. Schwartzer, director of the Federal Judicial Center, the research and training agency of the federal courts, wrote of the federal guidelines: "We are paying a high price for the present sentencing system, and not only in dollars. It is a high price in terms of the integrity of the criminal justice process, in terms of human life and the moral capital of the system. The elimination of unwarranted disparities is a worthy objective but it has not been achieved. Instead a system conducive to producing arbitrary results has been created" (Schwartzer 1991, p. 341).

Judge Gerald W. Heaney, a senior judge of the Eighth Circuit Court of Appeals, in one of the first published reports of an empirical evaluation of the guidelines' operation, examined the experiences of four different federal district courts. Here are some of his major conclusions: "The roles of the prosecutor and the probation officer in the sentencing process have been enhanced and that of the district judge diminished.

While district judges are required to devote more time to sentencing, their discretion has been severely limited. . . . There is little evidence to suggest that the congressional objective of reducing unwarranted sentencing disparity has been achieved. . . . Voluminous anecdotal evidence and case law show the unfairness of the guidelines and the disparities created through their application" (Heaney 1991, pp. 163–64, 167).

The federal guidelines had been in effect for several years when the preceding criticisms were offered and they were mostly based on critics' personal experiences and on anecdotal evidence. When systematic evidence from evaluations became available, the validity of the criticisms was confirmed.

Description of Guidelines

The guidelines cover all federal crimes. These include many federal regulatory and "white-collar" crimes but also drug crimes and common law crimes coming within federal jurisdiction. Discretionary parole release was abolished. The sentence announced, less mechanically determined time-off-for-good-behavior, is the sentence that will be served. The maximum good time is 15 percent of the sentence; thus at least seventeen years must be served of a twenty-year sentence.

Judges in setting sentences are supposed first to consult a schedule for the particular offense that specifies a "base offense level." Then, on the basis of various offense characteristics, the offense level is adjusted upward or downward (almost always upward). Next, the judge must determine the offender's criminal history score. Finally, the judge is to consult a two-dimensional grid to learn the presumptive sentence for the offender, given his adjusted offense level and criminal history. (Chapter 2 contains a fuller description of the guidelines and their application; tables 2.5 and 2.6 in chapter 2 show the schedule for robbery and the forty-three-level grid.)

To this point, the federal guidelines differ from well-known and well-regarded guidelines systems in Minnesota, Washington, and Oregon only in their ornateness. The federal guidelines divide offenses into forty-three categories rather than ten (Minnesota), eleven (Oregon), or fourteen (Washington) and are considerably more detailed in differentiating offenses than are the state systems. Although these might be described as differences in degree rather than in kind, there are other, much more fundamental, differences.

Objections to Guidelines

Five features of the federal guidelines make them more restrictive than existing state guidelines, and are the source of much of their unpopularity. First, although the guidelines are in principle "presumptive," which implies that judges may "depart" from them, the grounds for departures are exceedingly limited. Under the governing statute (18 U.S.C. §3553[b]), judges may depart from the guidelines only on a finding that "there exists an aggravating or mitigating circumstance of a kind, or to a degree, *not adequately taken into consideration by the Sentencing Commission* in formulating the guidelines that should result in a sentence different from [the guidelines]" (emphasis added). Appellate courts tend to the position that the commission must have adequately considered any subject on which it adopted express policy statements.

Second, few approved bases for departures are available and most of the commonsense bases for distinguishing among offenders—for example, a sound employment record, mental abnormality or subnormality, a stable home life, effects of the sentence on dependents—are expressly forbidden. The guidelines provide that age, education and vocational skills, mental and emotional conditions, physical condition including drug dependence and alcohol abuse, employment records, family ties and responsibilities, and community ties are "not ordinarily relevant in determining whether a sentence should be outside the applicable guideline range" (U.S. Sentencing Commission 1992a, Part H, §§5H1.1–5H1.6). As a result, trial judges have considerable difficulty convincing appellate courts that the sentencing commission did not "adequately consider" offender circumstances.

The commission has claimed that its policies forbidding judges to take account of important differences between defendants are rooted in concern to prevent preferment of middle-class, white offenders. In practice those policies have mostly damaged poor and minority offenders. That this is so can be seen in two instances in which the U.S. Sentencing Commission closed "loopholes" concerning defendants' circumstances that appellate courts had opened. In *U.S. v. Big Crow,* 898 F. 2d 1326 (1990), the Eighth Circuit approved a mitigated (below-guidelines) sentence for a Native American who had overcome severe childhood adversity and achieved an exemplary work record. In response, the commission amended its guidelines to forbid mitigated sentences for "employment-related contributions and similar prior good works." When the Ninth Circuit in *U.S. v. Lopez,* 945 F. 2d 1096 (1991), approved a sentence reduction on grounds of a defendant's troubled childhood and lack of guidance as a youth, the commission amended its policies to forbid reductions for "lack of guidance as a youth and similar circumstances indicating a disadvantaged upbringing."

Third, application of the guidelines is based not on the offense to which the defendant pled guilty or of which he was convicted at trial, but on "actual offense behavior," which the commission refers to as "relevant conduct" (U.S. Sentencing Commission 1992a, §1B1.3). The rationale was that the relevant conduct approach would offset efforts by prosecutors to manipulate guidelines by dismissing charges to achieve a conviction offense that, under the guidelines, bore the preferred sentence (Wilkins and Steer 1990).

Here is how Judge Heaney, whose article was mentioned earlier, summarizes the reach of the relevant conduct rule: "Under the guidelines, however, sentencing judges are routinely required to sentence offenders for 'relevant conduct' which has not been charged in an indictment or information and which was not admitted in a guilty plea or proved at trial. Indeed, a court may also increase an offender's sentence for acts of which the offender was acquitted. Uncharged conduct need not be proved beyond a reasonable doubt, but only by a preponderance of the evidence" (Heaney 1991, p. 209).

Real offense sentencing has been unanimously rejected elsewhere for two primary reasons. Most importantly, there is the Caesar's wife problem that courts must not only do justice but be seen to do justice. Even though prosecutorial power under guidelines is widely recognized as a potential problem, adoption of a system that divorces punishment from the substantive criminal law, the law of evidence, and the requirement of proof beyond a reasonable doubt has everywhere been seen as a bigger and more important problem.

In addition, other sentencing commissions have been doubtful that real offense sentencing would be an effective counter to prosecutorial power. The federal experience to date demonstrates that it doesn't work; prosecutorial discretion is all but immune from judicial review and many tools for fine-tuning sentences besides charge bargaining are available (Schulhofer and Nagel 1989; Federal Courts Study Committee 1990; Nagel and Schulhofer 1992). Prosecutorial manipulation of guidelines, however undesirable, is less undesirable than a sentencing policy that trivializes the significance of convictions based on proof beyond a reasonable doubt or a voluntary, informed confession (Lear 1993; Reitz 1993; Yellen 1993).

Fourth, the commission took an ideological "law-and-order" approach to the setting of sentencing policy and promulgated guidelines that were intended greatly to increase the severity of federal sentencing. This took several forms. Under guidelines, sentences to probation were greatly reduced: before guidelines, for example, probation sentences were ordered for 64 percent of burglars, 60 percent of property offenders, 59 percent of fraud offenders, and 57 percent of income tax offenders; the corresponding figures under guidelines were projected respectively to be 43 percent, 33 percent, 24 percent, and 3 percent (U.S. Sentencing Commission 1987a, pp. 60–61 and table 2).

Under guidelines, sentences for several categories of offenses—crimes against persons, drug crimes, burglary, regulatory offenses, and income tax evasion—were increased. There were no significant categories of crimes for which sentences were to be reduced (U.S. Sentencing Commission 1987a, p. 61).

A final respect in which the commission chose to make sentencing more severe concerns mandatory sentencing laws and requires some explanation. The U.S. Congress has enacted many mandatory penalty laws since 1980 and the commission had to decide how to reconcile the guidelines with laws calling for two-, five-, ten-, or twenty-year minimum sentences. One possible approach would have been to establish the guidelines without regard for the mandatory penalties but subject to a policy statement that in the case of incompatibility the mandatory penalty would override the guideline; this is how state sentencing commissions handled the problem. The alternative, which the commission adopted, was to increase all drug-offense sentences across the board so that the guidelines sentences and the statutory minima for mandatory-penalty offenses would be the same. Because the guidelines system is an interlocking lattice, the former course would have permitted the center of penal gravity of the entire scheme to be lower and hence sentences for many offenses to be less severe. The latter course in effect lifts the entire lattice and increases severity overall.

Fifth, despite burgeoning interest nationally in intermediate sanctions since 1980, the guidelines do not authorize their use. The only authorized freestanding punishments are probation and imprisonment. Fines are to be imposed in every case in which the defendant possesses means to pay them, but as a supplement, not an alternative, to prison or probation. Penalties such as house arrest, intensively supervised probation, restitution, community service, and outpatient drug or sex-offender treatment, though in widespread use in many states, may be ordered only as conditions to probation. Probation for many years before the guidelines took effect was imposed on approximately half of all convicted federal offenders. In 1993, only 14.8 percent of convicted offenders received straight probation (i.e., without confinement conditions) and thus in less than one-sixth of federal convictions was it possible for a judge to sentence a defendant to an intermediate sanction (U.S. Sentencing Commission 1994, p. 67).

For these five reasons—limiting departures to matters "not adequately considered" by the commission, precluding departures for matters relating to significant offender characteristics, adoption of the "relevant conduct" standard for application of guidelines, greatly increasing the severity of federal sentencing, and allowing virtually no role for intermediate sanctions—many judges dislike the guidelines. Judge Heaney (1991), explaining the Federal Courts Study Committee's recommendation that the U.S. Judicial Conference establish a standing committee to study actual and proposed guidelines, noted: "this recommendation appears to reflect the opposition of most Article III judges to guidelines sentencing, and their belief that their views were largely ignored in the process leading to the passage of the Sentencing Reform Act of 1984 and the adoption of the guidelines in 1987."

II. Evaluations of the Guidelines

Surprisingly little systematic information on the operation of the federal
sentencing guidelines is available. In 1992, a self-evaluation by the commission and an independent evaluation by the U.S. General Accounting
Office were published; both were mandated by the U.S. Congress. The
commission publishes annual reports that contain statistical tables but
these are mostly management statistics that report numbers of cases sentenced, average sentences, percentages of defendants who plead guilty,
and demographic data on convicted offenders. The Federal Courts Study
Committee received testimony concerning the guidelines, but collected no
empirical data. There have been several modest examinations of plea
bargaining under the guidelines (Alschuler and Schulhofer 1989; Schulhofer and Nagel 1989; Nagel and Schulhofer 1992). There have been
several modest quantitative analyses of the guidelines in operation in
small numbers of district courts (e.g., Heaney 1991; Karle and Sager
1991). Finally and perhaps most interesting of all is an evaluation not of
the commission but by the commission—pursuant to a congressional
mandate that it study the operation of mandatory minimum sentencing
laws in the federal courts (U.S. Sentencing Commission 1991*b*).

No evaluation results are likely to still the controversy surrounding
the U.S. sentencing guidelines. Partly this is because many of the common
objections to the guidelines involve fundamental differences of policy and
principle. Whatever the evaluation findings, many will continue to
oppose the guidelines on grounds of their severity, their reliance on "relevant conduct," and their provisions forbidding judges to take account in
sentencing of ethically relevant differences between offenders. Thus, even
if a credible evaluation showed that the guidelines "worked" to reduce
sentencing disparities, many would continue to oppose them on the merits. That is not an important caveat, however, because the available evidence makes it clear that on policy and practical grounds the guidelines
have been a failure.

Obstacles to Evaluation

Evaluating the federal guidelines is enormously difficult, and no results
are likely to be definitive. There are four fundamental problems. First,
the research design necessarily must be a weak comparison of sentencing
patterns before and after the change. Ideally, a randomized experiment
would be used to evaluate the effects of a major legal change like the
implementation of a new sentencing system. What evaluators and policy
makers should want to know is how sentencing under the new system
differs from sentencing as it would have been had the system not been
changed. In theory, the best way to learn this is to operate the new and

old systems in parallel for some period, randomly assigning cases between them. Another way this could be done is by operating the new system in one or several circuits while continuing to impose sentences under the old system everywhere else. For a variety of practical, legal, and ethical reasons, this has never been done in evaluating a major sentencing law change, and evaluators have been forced to rely on "before-and-after" comparisons, which provide much weaker bases for drawing inferences of what might have been had things not changed.

Second, so much has changed in the federal criminal justice system since November 1987 besides effectuation of sentencing guidelines that it is difficult to attribute differences occurring after that date to the guidelines. Federal criminal justice policy has become more politicized and polemicized in the United States since the mid-1980s; this affects everything from legislation to prosecutorial policies to the decisions of individual judges and prosecutors. The governments of Presidents Ronald Reagan and George Bush openly, as a matter of declared policy, appointed only conservative lawyers to serve as federal judges. By 1992, the accumulation of unusually conservative judges, who were selected in part because of their demonstrated or presumed lack of sympathy with the interests of criminal defendants, made them a significant majority of all federal judges. The U.S. federal government launched its "War on Drugs" in the late 1980s. Beginning in 1984 and at regular intervals since, including in the Violent Crime Control and Law Enforcement Act of 1994, the U.S. Congress has enacted additional mandatory sentencing laws.

Thus even if sentencing patterns have materially changed since the guidelines took effect, it is difficult to know whether the changes result from new mandatory sentencing legislation, or from new administrative rules governing plea bargaining issued by the U.S. Department of Justice in Washington, or from "tougher" judges or harsher public attitudes toward crime and criminals, or from the federal sentencing guidelines.

Third, even if all those problems were disregarded, the complexity of the federal sentencing guidelines and their reliance on "relevant conduct" present insuperable difficulties for before-and-after comparisons. Precise information concerning drug quantity or purity or the presence of an unused firearm or the occurrence of other uncharged crimes (all important factors under the guidelines) was often not material to disposition of cases before the guidelines took effect. Consequently, there was no preguidelines reason for probation officers to seek out or record such information, and for periods before November 1987 it is not systematically and reliably available.

Fourth, there seems no doubt that the guidelines have shifted sentencing power from judges to prosecutors, and this too complicates evaluation efforts. Prosecutors have devised numerous ways to manipulate the guidelines: by bargaining with defense counsel about facts to be set out in a stipulation, by bargaining over charges to be filed or dismissed, by negotiating concessions to be made in respect of defendants giving assistance to the government. Most analyses of the guidelines' operation agree that many prosecutors, like many judges, consider the guidelines to be excessively severe and that prosecutors often manipulate the guidelines to avoid unduly harsh sentences (Schulhofer and Nagel 1989; Nagel and Schulhofer 1992).

Because of changes in plea-bargaining patterns, cases convicted under the same statutory section before the guidelines took effect, and afterward, may differ materially; conviction offenses under guidelines are sometimes referred to as "artifacts" because they result not from fact-finding but from plea bargaining. Most of these incentives to manipulate or circumvent guidelines had no precise equivalents before the guidelines were implemented and their effect is to make before-and-after comparisons all the harder.

Findings of Evaluations

Chapter 2 discusses at considerable length the evaluation literature concerning the federal guidelines' effects on sentencing disparities in general and in particular concerning racial and gender differences. This chapter does not repeat those detailed discussions; brief summaries of findings are offered instead. Readers who want to know more about the evaluations should consult chapter 2. Eight findings stand out.

First, sentencing patterns have changed in ways the commission intended: the proportion of cases receiving sentences to probation has declined greatly and average prison sentence lengths for many offenses have increased (U.S. Sentencing Commission 1991a; U.S. General Accounting Office 1992).

Second, although the U.S. commission (1991a) claims to have shown in its self-evaluation that disparities have been reduced, the General Accounting Office in its review of the commission report adopted an agnostic stance. Most sentencing evaluation specialists (Rhodes 1992; Weisburd 1992) found the commission evaluation so flawed methodologically and conceptually that no conclusions could be reached. My belief, explained at some length in chapter 2, is that disparities have worsened.

Third, guilty plea rates have remained stable, ranging from 85 to 90 percent of dispositions (U.S. Sentencing Commission 1990, fig. 6). In 1993, 88.5 percent of cases were resolved by guilty pleas (U.S. Sentencing Commission 1994, p. 66).

Fourth, judges and lawyers report that sentencing hearings take longer than before the guidelines took effect (Federal Courts Study Committee 1990; U.S. Sentencing Commission 1991a).

Fifth, the guidelines have transferred discretion and authority from judges to prosecutors (Alschuler and Schulhofer 1989; Federal Courts Study Committee 1990; Heaney 1991; Nagel and Schulhofer 1992).

Sixth, because the guidelines provide relatively little overt sentencing benefit to defendants who plead guilty, and because the guidelines are harsher than many judges and prosecutors believe reasonable, prosecutors often in collusion with defense counsel, judges, or both, engage in "hidden plea bargaining" so as to manipulate the guidelines in order to offer sentencing concessions that will induce guilty pleas, or in order to arrive at a sentence that the prosecutor and judge believe to be reasonable (Schulhofer and Nagel 1989; Federal Courts Study Committee 1990; Heaney 1991; Nagel and Schulhofer 1992).

Seventh, many judges, prosecutors, and defense counsel believe that the guidelines are too rigid and mechanical (Alschuler and Schulhofer 1989; Alschuler 1991; U.S. Sentencing Commission 1991*a*; Heaney 1991; Federal Judicial Center 1994).

Eighth, many judges, prosecutors, and defense counsel disapprove of guidelines provisions that forbid judges at sentencing to take account of personal circumstances of individual defendants (Alschuler 1991; Heaney 1991; Freed 1992).

One final mention of research on federal sentencing must be made. The commission under congressional mandate completed an ambitious and sophisticated analysis of the effects of mandatory sentencing laws on the work of the federal courts. The results are discussed at length in chapter 5. The commission concluded that mandatory penalties are unwise and unsound policy because they remove incentives to plead guilty and thereby increase trial rates, case processing times, and workloads; they foster prosecutorial manipulation in charging and plea bargaining both to induce guilty pleas and to avoid imposition of sentences prosecutors believe to be unduly harsh; they often result in imposition of sentences that are unduly harsh; they do not permit judges to take into account special circumstances concerning the defendant that might suggest some other sentence. These are, of course, the same charges that critics lay against the commission's guidelines. Capturing this point precisely, in what may initially have been a Freudian slip, the commission, on the first page of its mandatory sentencing report, refers to its own "mandatory" guidelines (U.S. Sentencing Commission 1991*b*, p. i). Since then, perhaps implicitly conceding the point, the commission has begun itself sometimes to refer to its "mandatory guidelines" (1991*c*, p. 1).

III. Why the Commission Failed

It is a bit of a mystery why the U.S. Sentencing Commission, which had ample resources, time, and personnel, failed so badly in nearly every respect. Its principal successes have been in coercing judges and lawyers into partial and grudging compliance and in gaining congressional acquiescence in the policies the commission adopted (the commission's proposed guidelines and guideline amendments take effect automatically unless rejected by Congress). The extent of the commission's failure is manifested by offhand mention in the report of the Federal Courts Study Committee (1990, p. 142) that, of several hundred persons who testified before the committee concerning the federal sentencing guidelines, only four spoke in favor of them (three current or former commissioners and Attorney General Thornburgh). Every other person testifying expressed strong reservations or outright opposition.

The guidelines' shortcomings are probably inseparable from the commission's shortcomings. The U.S. Sentencing Commission was poorly managed, its work was highly politicized from the outset, and it was riven by ideological factionalism and political intrigue. The May 1990 issue of the *Federal Sentencing Reporter* reprints critical statements from numerous agencies and spokesmen. Two members (initial commissioners Paul Robinson and Michael Block) and one ex officio member (Ronald Gainer, the attorney general's initial designee) resigned on principle over the commission's failings.

No one factor can explain why the federal commission and guidelines have been so much less successful and accepted than their state counterparts. Some observers argue that the failure was in management. With all of its resources, a better-managed commission that consulted more widely and made efforts to learn from the state experiences could have done better. Others believe the problem was inexperience; none of the initial commissioners had any prior experience with guidelines or with sentencing policy and only two—federal judges William Wilkins and George MacKinnon—had ever imposed a sentence: Wilkins had been a federal trial judge for only a short time and MacKinnon, over eighty years old and retired, had not sentenced a case for many years. Still others, more conspiracy-minded, note that a number of the initial commissioners were long known to be aspirants for higher office (two made it: Chairman William Wilkins was appointed to the Fourth Circuit Federal Court of Appeals while on the commission and Commissioner Stephen Breyer was appointed to the U.S. Supreme Court after his term expired) and suggest that the guidelines were an effort to show that the commission's policies were consonant with the views of influential congressional conservatives.

One of the commission's major problems was that it was an unpleasant place to work. This is often attributed to the personalities and political ambitions of individual commissioners. The U.S. General Accounting Office (1990*a*), when asked by the Congress to assess the commission's management and operations in its early years, described an agency in disarray.

In four years the commission had four staff directors. Kay Knapp, the first staff director, had been director of the Minnesota Sentencing Guidelines Commission and was (and is) widely acknowledged as America's foremost authority on sentencing guidelines; internal politics forced her out within a year. General counsels to the commission came and went at the same rate in the early years.

The commission was without a research director for several years (GAO 1990*a*, p. 14) during the critical start-up phase. One nationally prominent researcher joined the research staff in the face of warnings from friends; she explained that things at the commission had gotten so bad that they were bound to improve and she would be starting work as the commission rebounded. She quit within months, reporting that the environment steadily worsened during her tenure. Another nationally prominent researcher, an experienced senior civil servant, pooh-poohed friends' warnings about the commission; he explained that he was accustomed to working effectively within politicized federal agencies and was a political survivor. He survived for a year before he too was driven out by internal commission politics. More recently, one person has survived for several years as staff director, but qualified research directors proved elusive and the position was finally abolished.

Much of the U.S. General Accounting Office's scathing critique of the U.S. commission concerned individual commissioners who created a volatile and unpleasant working environment (1990*a*, pp. 3, 12–15):

1. "the extensive involvement of individual commissioners in what would normally be staff activities . . . contributes to the organizational disarray we found" (p. 12);
2. "most troublesome is the direct control by individual commissioners over major research projects" (p. 12);
3. "commissioner involvement in research . . . raises another concern. . . . the potential for the research to reflect the perspectives and interests of the commissioner conducting the project" (p. 14);
4. "according to former staff directors, it was difficult to manage in an environment where they could not maintain authority over the staff because of commissioner involvement" (p. 14);
5. "part of the problem has been finding qualified candidates who would be willing to take the [research director's] position, given perceptions that the working environment is complicated by commissioner involvement in research and other matters" (p. 15).

"Internal politics" is one way to characterize the problems described in preceding paragraphs. "Failure of management" is another. Good managers know how to recruit and motivate capable staff, how to develop and carry out a work plan, how to create and maintain a congenial working environment, how to work with and accommodate important constituencies, and—if necessary—how to control obstreperous appointees. None of those attributes characterized the processes by which the commission developed its guidelines.

With a staff in excess of seventy, a multimillion-dollar budget, and more than two years in which to develop proposed guidelines, the commission could have assembled a talented staff, learned from successful guidelines systems in the states, developed good working relations with all the agencies and constituencies that would be affected by federal guidelines, and devised and implemented a successful system of guidelines.

None of those things happened. The commission's failure to win over its most important constituency, the federal judiciary, is evident. With the exception of Kay Knapp's short-lived time as staff director, no senior commission staffer was hired from any of the several state sentencing commissions (Minnesota, Pennsylvania, Washington) that had previously established successful guidelines systems. Nor, I know from talking with the senior staff and chairmen of the state commissions, were any of them asked to serve as consultants to the U.S. commission. The U.S. commission failed to draw on the intellectual capital amassed in the states and to learn from the mistakes, successes, and policy processes of its predecessors. All of the policy and practice issues the U.S. commission faced had been addressed by its predecessors, and many of the commission's most serious blunders—reliance on "relevant conduct," the guidelines' unnecessary complexity, the daunting forty-three-level grid—could have been avoided had it drawn on their experience.

The process by which the guidelines were developed illustrates the commission's management problems. Except for the General Accounting Office's management study (1990*a*) and a few newspaper articles, there is no literature on internal commission processes. This account accordingly draws on extensive discussions with former commissioners and commission staff and my experience as a member of the commission's first research advisory board and as an occasional paid consultant (ending in 1986).

To my astonishment (then and now), the commission had no overall strategy for developing guidelines. Instead, separate teams under the leadership of professor/commissioners tried to develop incompatible guideline proposals. One team, under the direction of Commissioner Paul Robinson (before and after his time on the commission, a law professor), worked on a set of just deserts guidelines that would calibrate sentences to detailed comparative assessments of offenders' culpability. The logic came from criminal law "elements analysis," in which crimes are deconstructed into their mental and physical components. Mental states include purpose, knowledge, recklessness, negligence, and inadvertence. Physical elements include such things as the amount of property loss, the occurrence and severity of physical injury, whether a weapon was involved and what kind (handgun, other gun, knife, blunt instrument) and how it was used (carried, shown, pointed, discharged, or otherwise used). Both mental and physical elements can be scaled for seriousness. All physical elements equal, a purposeful crime can be said to be more serious than a negligent crime. A theft involving $500 is more serious than a theft involving $50. Because most definitions of crimes include four or more physical elements, separate mental elements can be specified for each. None of this is in principle surprising or unfamiliar to any criminal-law professor.

The problems with the just deserts guidelines lay in the system's sole reliance on offense elements and in its complexity. Guidelines for robbery, for example, had to distinguish not only among attempted and completed robberies and armed and unarmed robberies but had also to differentiate crimes in terms of the amount of property involved (and the amount the defendant thought was involved), the nature of any weapon and whether it was used and how and with what result, and whether any injuries were caused and how serious they were.

To deal with that complexity, a system of "punishment units" was created, into which any element could be translated. Injuries might be valued at 0 to 1,000 points, the nature of any weapon at 0 to 500, the manner of weapon use at 0 to 500, property loss at 0 to 1,000. The sentence would be determined by summing the points associated with each physical and mental element. Some elements, such as property loss, are hard to accommodate in such a scheme. (If a $500 theft equals fifty units equals ninety days in jail, what sentences should Michael Milken, Ivan Boesky, and Charles Keating receive for billion-dollar crimes?) To deal with such problems the scheme called on judges to calculate the square and cube roots of property values and to plug the answers into the sentencing calculation. Not surprisingly, perhaps, outsiders who were shown confidential drafts were incredulous and after many months the just deserts drafts were abandoned.

Unfortunately, the other guidelines drafting team by that time had given up its effort. Led by commissioners Michael Block and Ilene Nagel (at other times in their careers respectively an economics professor and a sociology professor), the goal was to devise crime-control guidelines based on research on deterrence and incapacitation. Penalties would be set that would either have optimal deterrent effects or cost-effectively incapacitate those at highest risk for future crimes. The effort soon stymied on the insuperable difficulty that existing crime-control research on deterrence and incapacitation gave no adequate answers to such questions as "What is the optimal deterrent sentence for a $5,000 theft?" or "Who among 3,000 robbery defendants has a 40 percent likelihood of committing a serious violent crime within the next five years?" The crime-control research discussed in chapter 5 is incapable of answering such questions. Utilitarian philosophers like Jeremy Bentham (1843) and economists like Gary Becker (1968) have offered theoretical answers to such questions, but there is no empirical evidence that demonstrates that their answers are valid.

Andrew von Hirsch (1988, p. 2), on the basis of extensive discussion with commission members and senior staffers, provided a similar but less detailed description of the process by which the commission developed its guidelines: "Shortly after the commissioners were appointed, however, problems began to be apparent. A first draft of the guidelines was written in the spring of 1986 by one of the commissioners [Robinson], and then jettisoned. The next two drafts emanated from the Chairman's office, were circulated for public comment, and then abandoned after an unfavorable response. It was only in the winter of 1986 that other commissioners were drawn actively into the process. The final draft was written at a late date in some haste to meet the submission deadline."

Many of the guidelines' most fundamental problems derive from the aborted Robinson guidelines. An initial set of guidelines was scheduled for release for public comment early in the fall of 1986. Because the commission's only organized guideline-drafting to that point had been the unrealistic and abandoned efforts headed by academics, the commission had nothing else to build on. When, therefore, the commission's chairman took personal charge of the drafting effort, he started from the abandoned Robinson draft and inherited that draft's daunting complexity, an enormous guidelines grid, and "real offense sentencing."

Within the logic of the Robinson draft, those features made sense. If every mental and physical element of every crime had to be translated into a punishment unit score, the guidelines necessarily had to specify what elements were material and how they were to be scored; complexity was conceptually essential. Similarly, if punishment unit totals for a robbery could range from 200 to 3,000 units, for example, the guidelines grid necessarily had to be complex and to contain many gradations of offense severity; closely scaling punishment severity to offense seriousness was also conceptually essential. Finally, in a system in which plea-bargaining is ubiquitous, "real offense sentencing" made sense. Otherwise, plea bargaining lawyers could manipulate the sentencing system at will by agreeing which offense elements would be admitted and thereby determine sentences with precision.

Chairmen of federal government agencies understandably are reluctant to admit that their agencies will not be able to meet their published schedules for release of proposals for public comment. The Robinson draft was the only draft available on which final guidelines could be built. Only weeks were available in which to adapt the Robinson draft and that is what the commission did. The punishment units concept disappeared. With it went the square and cube roots. However, the enormous guidelines grid, the complexity, and the real offense sentencing survived and were part of the first draft of guidelines that was publicly released. In later drafts, in response to adverse comment, real offense sentencing became "modified real offense sentencing." This meant that sentencing calculations begin with the offense of which the defendant was convicted; thereafter, sentences are increased on a "real offense basis," taking into account offenses that were never charged, that were dropped as a result of a plea bargain, and that resulted in an acquittal. The guidelines that took effect and that survive to this day thus reject the premises and logic of the Robinson draft but contain much of its apparatus.

The process by which the federal guidelines were devised thus explains many of their most disliked mechanical features. It does not explain, however, why they are so harsh, why the commission so narrowly limited the use of probation and virtually precluded use of intermediate sanctions, or why mandatory penalties were handled as they were. The explanation for those policies probably lies elsewhere—most likely in the changes in political climate that occurred between the time when Judge Marvin Frankel (1972) first proposed creation of a sentencing commission and the time when the federal commission began work.

Sentencing commission proposals were under congressional consideration for nearly a decade after Senate Bill 181, patterned on Judge Frankel's proposals, was introduced in 1974. In 1974, the goals of sentencing reform were idealistic: to reduce racial, gender, and other unwarranted disparities, and to bring the rule of law to sentencing so that rules governed judges' sentencing decisions and judges' decisions could be appealed to higher courts. However, by the time the Sentencing Reform Act of 1984 was enacted and the commission began its work, the political climate had changed. When Judge Frankel's rationalistic, good-government proposal took effect, the government in power did not hold those goals.

The crime-control policies of the Reagan administration in 1985 were oriented more toward toughness than toward fairness. It should not therefore be a surprise that the commissioners who were appointed sought to show that they too were tough on crime and had little sympathy for "lenient" judges. Some of the commission's unpopular policy decisions— the guidelines' overall severity, the handling of mandatory penalties, the narrowing of probation, the absence of a role for intermediate sanctions—are the product of a commission that rejected Judge Frankel's premises that sentencing should treat offenders justly and that detailed sentencing policy should to some extent be insulated from politics.

IV.   Salvaging the Federal Guidelines

The federal sentencing guidelines are salvageable, and without repeal or amendment of the Sentencing Reform Act of 1984. Many people, particularly federal judges, appear to believe that the only sentencing policy options for the federal courts are retention of the current guidelines substantially as is or repeal of the Sentencing Reform Act. This belief, which is mistaken, is encouraged by the U.S. Sentencing Commission. In its December 1991 self-evaluation, for example, the commission attributes opposition to the guidelines to "resistance . . . on the part of some federal judges and others involved in the sentencing process to the need for and wisdom of the statutory scheme for sentencing reform enacted by Congress in the 1984 Sentencing Reform Act" (U.S. Sentencing Commission 1991*a*, p. 85).

If the commission were right, if the only choices were between the current guidelines and statutory repeal, judges' despair about the guidelines would be warranted; outright repeal of the act in the foreseeable future appears unlikely. However there is a middle ground. Under the existing legislation, many of the commission's policy decisions could have been otherwise. Guidelines could have been fashioned, and still can be, that would reduce sentencing disparities but not routinely require judges to impose sentences that they consider unjust. Other sentencing commissions faced the issues that the U.S. commission faced, and arrived at different policy conclusions. If the commission were now to look at and learn from experience elsewhere, it could remedy many of the guidelines' current problems.

Many features of the current guidelines that judges find most objectionable result not from the requirements of the Sentencing Reform Act of 1984 but from the commission's policy decisions. This section discusses seven such decisions that could have been made otherwise and that together produce the combination of rigidity and harshness that has driven many judges and prosecutors to resent the guidelines and often to circumvent them:

1. giving the prosecutor sole discretion to decide when defendants are eligible for sentence reductions for substantial assistance to the government (Guidelines, Sect. 5K1.1);
2. nullifying the statutory presumption (Sect. 99[j]) against imprisonment of first offenders "not convicted of a crime of violence or an otherwise serious offense" by defining as "serious" many offenses that typically received probation before the guidelines took effect;
3. treating sentences to probation as "zero months imprisonment" and thereby triggering statutory Section 994(b)(2)'s provision that "if a sentence specified by the guidelines includes a term of imprisonment," the top of the guideline range may not exceed the bottom by the greater of 25 percent or six months;
4. adopting "relevant conduct" as the basis for applying guidelines rather than the offense of conviction;
5. providing guidelines only for imprisonment and, to a much lesser extent than before the guidelines took effect, probation; there are no guidelines for fines as stand-alone sanctions or for any intermediate punishments;
6. raising sentencing severity generally, in order to incorporate mandatory penalty provisions into the grid, rather than having the mandatories operate as trumps;

7. adopting a forty-three-level sentencing grid that inevitably looks like a sentencing machine, arbitrary, impersonal, and mechanical, and reduces the credibility of the guidelines in the eyes of judges and others.

None of these decisions was required by the act. Except for the decision to incorporate mandatory penalties into the guidelines, none of them necessarily implies greater or lesser severity in sentences. They are simply technical or technocratic decisions that the commission made, that it could have made otherwise, and that can today be changed. Of the seven decisions, the first three involve statutory interpretations; the rest involve what might be called the architecture of sentencing guidelines. Most involve issues that have confronted sentencing commissions in Canada, Kansas, Minnesota, North Carolina, Oregon, Pennsylvania, and Washington.

Substantial-Assistance Motions

Much the most common basis for open reduction of sentences below guideline ranges is that the defendant provided "substantial assistance to the government." The prosecution must request the reduction before the judge may grant it. Of all federal sentences imposed in 1993, one-sixth (16.9 percent) were downward substantial-assistance departures (U.S. Sentencing Commission 1994, tables 66 and 67).

The commission, not the Congress, conditioned sentence reductions for assistance to the government on prosecutorial motions. Statute section 994(n) directs the commission to "assure that the guidelines reflect the general appropriateness [of sentence reductions] to take into account a defendant's substantial assistance in the investigation or prosecution of another person who has committed an offense." Although the statute says nothing to suggest that the prosecutor should have sole authority to decide when and whether substantial assistance has been provided, Guidelines Section 5K1.1 provides: "upon motion of the government stating that the defendant has provided substantial assistance . . . the court may depart from the guidelines."

By amending Section 5K1.1 to substitute the word "when" for the words "upon motion of the government stating that," the commission would be acting consistently with the statute and would empower judges to exercise independent judgment when controversies arise as to whether assistance has been provided and, if so, whether it has been substantial.

The First-Offender Nonincarceration Presumption

In making a policy decision substantially to increase the use of incarceration, the commission largely overrode a statutory presumption that non-violent first offenders should receive nonincarcerative sentences. Statute Section 994(j) directs the commission to "insure that the guidelines reflect the general appropriateness of imposing a sentence other than imprisonment in cases in which the defendant is a first offender who has not been convicted of a crime of violence or an otherwise serious offense." Confronted by its own empirical research showing that many first offenders were sentenced to probation before the guidelines took effect (U.S. Sentencing Commission 1987*b*), which the commission described as a "problem," the commission devised its own definition of "serious."

Here is how the commission describes what it did: "The Commission's solution to this problem has been to write guidelines that classify as serious many offenses for which probation previously was given and provide for at least a short period of imprisonment in such cases" (U.S. Sentencing Commission 1987*b*, Guidelines Introduction, Section 4[c]).

The commission's rationale for overriding the congressional presumption was that the courts had in the past ordered probation for "inappropriately high percentages" of white-collar offenders, including such crimes as "theft, tax evasion, antitrust offenses, insider trading, fraud, and embezzlement." The weakness in this rationale is that it did not reflect the real world of the federal courts. Antitrust, insider trading, and tax evasion represent a small percentage of offenders who received probation before the guidelines took effect. The people who were hurt, swept into the commission's "white-collar" net, were people convicted of immigration offenses, minor postal thefts and property crimes, low-level bank-teller embezzlers, and others who bear no discernible resemblance to Ivan Boesky, Leona Helmsley, or Michael Milken. Thus when the commission overrode the first-offender presumption language, it did so on a false policy premise.

An easy solution, well within the authority of the commission, is available. Even if the current guidelines were changed in no other respect, the commission could add a new section to the guidelines providing: "If the defendant is a first offender who has not been convicted of a crime of violence or an otherwise serious crime, the court may depart from the guidelines in order to impose a sentence other than imprisonment." The proposed language tracks Section 994(j)'s statutory language and would allow the trial and appellate courts to determine when nonviolent first offenses are otherwise so serious that the nonincarceration presumption is overcome.

Probation as "Zero Months Imprisonment"

A third critical choice made by the commission that had radical consequences and was not required by Congress concerned the seemingly innocuous and for most purposes entirely theoretical question of whether probation is a generically different kind of sentence from imprisonment or whether a sentence to probation is a sentence of "zero months imprisonment." The commission took the second position and thereby eliminated probation as a stand-alone sentence for all but the most trifling crimes and virtually eliminated the use of intermediate sanctions (which can be ordered only as conditions of probation). This seemingly obscure conceptual point was made important by statute Section 994(b)(2), which provided: "if a sentence specified by the guidelines includes a term of imprisonment, the maximum of the range established for such a term shall not exceed the minimum of that range by more than the greater of 25 percent or six months."

If probation is not a sentence of zero months imprisonment, Section 994(b)(2) has no relevance. A guideline could, for a specific offense/criminal history combination, specify authorized sentences that include probation or, in the alternative, a range of prison sentences that satisfy the 25 percent/six months requirement (for example, probation or a sentence of six to twelve months). If, however, probation is considered a zero months prison sentence, then Section 994(b)(2) applies and a maximum range of "0 to 6 months" is the result.

Little can be said in favor of the commission's decision that probation is a form of imprisonment; it required a tortured interpretation of words whose contrary conventional meaning is clear. The common understanding is that probation is a different form of punishment, one that judges often consider as an alternative to imprisonment. The commission's interpretation is conceptually muddled; if fines were permitted by the guidelines as stand-alone punishments, the commission would presumably define a fine as a sentence of zero months incarceration. Whether that would be more forced than so regarding probation I don't know, but it is exactly the same issue. For both fines and probation, prison exists as a backup to be used when offenders fail to comply with conditions; in both cases, when obligations are met, offenders are entitled to absolute discharges. The commission's interpretation is also inconsistent with the first-offender nonimprisonment presumption because it narrows the relevance of that presumption to a tiny fraction of federal offenders.

The solution to this problem is simple: abandon the tortured interpretation that a sentence to probation is zero months imprisonment and devise separate guidelines for incarcerative and nonincarcerative penalties.

"Real Offense Sentencing"

The single feature of the federal sentencing guidelines that state officials and judges and judicial administrators outside the United States find most astonishing is the commission's policy decision to base guideline application on the defendant's "relevant conduct," including conduct alleged in charges that were dismissed or that resulted in acquittals or that were never filed. More than once when describing the relevant conduct system to government officials and judges outside the United States, I have been accused of misreporting or exaggerating. People unfamiliar with the federal guidelines have difficulty accepting that any western legal system would require judges to take conduct into account at sentencing that was the subject of charges of which a defendant was acquitted.

Every sentencing guidelines commission to date has considered whether to adopt a "relevant conduct" or "real offense" approach as a means to offset prosecutorial power to influence guideline sentencing by decisions about charges to file or drop. The potential problems posed by plea bargaining under guidelines are real. Nonetheless, the sentencing commissions in Arkansas, Canada, Delaware, Kansas, Florida, Louisiana, Minnesota, New York, North Carolina, Ohio, Oregon, Pennsylvania, Washington, and Wisconsin unanimously rejected real offense sentencing and based guidelines on conviction offenses. The reasons why—that such a policy is unjust and will not work—are discussed at length earlier in this chapter.

The commission offered three major reasons for adopting the relevant conduct approach, all demonstrably mistaken or misconceived. The first, that real offense sentencing would prevent a shift of power to the prosecutor, has been discussed earlier and shown to be false, as even commission-sponsored research shows.

The second, exemplified by *Williams v. New York,* 337 U.S. 241 (1949), is that judges have authority to look beyond the conviction offense and have always done so. The problem with this argument is that *Williams* was decided in the heyday of indeterminate sentencing when judges were expected to individualize sentences. The federal guidelines, however, are a form of determinate sentencing that is premised on the notion that judges' discretion should be more narrowly constrained than in the era of indeterminate sentencing. Thus, modern case law to the contrary notwithstanding, the rationale of *Williams* has little relevance to modern determinate sentencing. *Williams* held that judges in sentencing *may* take account of nonconviction behavior; the commission says they *must*.

The third was that the federal criminal law is incomparably more complex than are state criminal laws and that many federal offenses in their labels and elements provide no meaningful basis for measuring culpability. Mail and wire fraud and RICO (Racketeer-Influenced Corrupt Organizations) offenses are examples. If a majority of federal offenders were convicted of mail fraud, the commission's point might have been well taken. In practice, however, drug crimes make up roughly half of the federal criminal docket (18,352 of 41,838 convictions reported to the commission in 1993: U.S. Sentencing Commission 1994, table 22). Much of the rest consists of common law crimes like theft, robbery, and embezzlement (5,991 in 1993), and conceptually uncomplicated crimes like immigration (2,187 cases in 1993) and firearms offenses (3,119). By contrast, of distinctively federal regulatory offenses, there were 809 tax cases, 120 civil rights cases, 72 food and drug cases, and 39 antitrust cases. Thus modern federal criminal cases look much like state cases and there is no more need for real offense sentencing in the federal system than in the states.

There is no statutory mandate for real offense sentencing. The commission has authority to switch to an offense-of-conviction system and could do so in ways that address some of the concerns that underlay their relevant conduct approach. To deal with the problem of statutes that are too generically phrased, the commission could add additional elements (firearms use, violence) to divide broadly defined offenses into subcategories of different seriousness and by rule require that the prosecutor allege those additional elements and that they be proven beyond a reasonable doubt or admitted. That is how state sentencing commissions have handled this problem. To deal with exotic federal crimes like mail fraud and RICO, the commission could establish special rules.

Intermediate Sanctions

The federal guidelines allow no independent role for intermediate punishments like fines, house arrest, intensively supervised probation, or community service. The only freestanding sentences authorized are prison and probation (and, as noted earlier, the role allotted probation is limited).

Fines as independent sentences are conspicuously absent. Although the Congress's first charge to the commission in statute Section 9 94(a)(1) was to promulgate "guidelines for use by the court in determining the sentence to be imposed. . . . including (A) a determination whether to impose a sentence to probation, a fine, or a term of imprisonment," fines are nowhere authorized as a sole sentence for individuals. Instead, Guidelines Section 5E1.2(a) provides: "the court shall impose a fine in all cases, except [when the defendant lacks ability to pay]." Thus fines are available as add-ons to prison sentences or probation, but not as punishments in their own right.

Nor do the guidelines authorize other nonincarcerative sanctions as independent sentences. Guidelines Part F (Sections 5F1.1–3) authorizes community confinement, home detention, and community service, but only "as a condition of probation or supervised release." The guidelines make no mention of intensively supervised probation, which is widely used in American states as an alternative to imprisonment.

The absence of any provision in the guidelines for imposition of fines and other nonincarcerative intermediate punishments is remarkable (chapter 4 discusses this subject at length). Many federal crimes are especially appropriate for fines. In many Western countries, the fine is the single most often imposed punishment for many offenses, including even some violent offenses. The "day fine," calibrated both to the seriousness of the crime and to the defendant's means, provides a tested mechanism for use of fines in serious cases. Reasonable people can differ over the question whether in principle a fine is an appropriate sentence for, say, a serious assault; it is hard to see how reasonable people can disagree that there are some nontrivial crimes for which fines—which can serve both deterrent and punitive purposes—are uniquely suited. It won't do for the commission to respond that fines can be coupled with probation sentences, making a de facto stand-alone fine, because the commission restricted probation to only a small proportion of federal defendants convicted of minor crimes.

Similarly, there is much experience in the United States and Western Europe with intermediate sanctions that the commission could have drawn on in setting guidelines for such punishments. Sentencing commissions in North Carolina, Oregon, Pennsylvania, and Washington have incorporated intermediate sanctions into their guidelines. A commission task force headed by then-Commissioner Helen Corrothers offered concrete proposals for building intermediate punishments into the guidelines so that judges would have more options for better tailoring sentences to meet the circumstances of individual defendants (U.S. Sentencing Commission Alternatives to Imprisonment Project 1990). The commission did not act on the Corrothers committee's major recommendations.

Had it the will, the commission could easily incorporate fines and intermediate sanctions into the federal guidelines. The state sentencing commissions have accumulated substantial experience on this subject. There is an apposite scholarly literature (e.g., Wasik and von Hirsch 1988; Morris and Tonry 1990). Within a few months, the commission could devise guidelines for fines and other punishments scaled to offense severity that judges could use in lieu of otherwise-applicable prison sentences of up to, say, three years duration. This, of course, assumes the commission abandons the interpretation of probation as zero months imprisonment.

Mandatory Penalties as "Trumps"

The commission unnecessarily increased sentences for many crimes by the way it handled mandatory penalties. Here is the problem. Mandatory penalty provisions often call for minimum terms longer than past practice and longer than a sentencing commission as an independent body would prescribe. There are two ways to handle this. The first is to develop a comprehensive set of guidelines based on knowledge of past practices and conscious policy decisions to change past practice. If mandatory minimum statutes require longer sentences than the guidelines prescribe in individual cases, policy statements can instruct the judge that the mandatory minimum statute takes precedence and trumps the guidelines. This approach, which every state sentencing commission adopted, has the advantage that it makes clear when sentences uniquely result from application of mandatory penalty statutes.

The other approach is to incorporate the statutory minimums into the guidelines and scale all other penalties around the mandatories. This has the effect of increasing the severity of guideline sentences generally. A metaphor shows why. Imagine a sentencing guidelines grid as a lattice. Under the mandatories-as-trumps approach, long minimum sentences poke through the lattice and when they are very long, tower above it. Under the commission's approach, the entire lattice is lifted, as if the mandatory minimums were posts, and the sentences for many crimes not covered by the mandatory provisions are lifted also.

The posts and lattices metaphor understates the sentencing severity increases caused by the commission's policies concerning mandatory penalties. Under current law, a cocaine offense involving 500 grams triggers a mandatory five-year minimum prison sentence and an offense involving 5,000 grams triggers a ten-year minimum.

According to the commission, in the years immediately preceding the implementation of the guidelines, average sentences in drug cases were much shorter than subsequent mandatory minimum laws specified. The commission's policy to incorporate the statutory minimums in the guidelines raised the applicable sentences to five and ten years for all offenders convicted under the corresponding mandatory minimum statute. This, of course, would happen under a mandatories-as-trumps policy, but the commission's policies gratuitously raised sentences for drug offenders in three other ways.

First, under the "relevant conduct" policy, sentences increased substantially for defendants who were not convicted under statutory sections subject to the mandatory minimums but whose offenses involved the triggering quantities.

Second, the commission decided on policy grounds that sentences for people convicted of drug-related conspiracies and attempts—offenses not then subject to mandatory minimums—should be calculated by reference to penalties for completed offenses involving the same amount. This raised sentences for inchoate offenses substantially.

Third, the commission decided to raise sentences for many drug crimes, including inchoate offenses, more than was required by the mandatory penalty provisions. If 500 grams provoked a five-year minimum and 5,000 grams a ten-year minimum, the commission decided to fill in the gap between five and ten years by setting intermediate guideline sentences for intermediate quantities, spacing penalties at intervals between five and ten years. Thus 2,000 and 3,500 grams, respectively, were subject to seventy-eight- and ninety-seven-month minimum guideline sentences. The mandatory penalty legislation, by contrast, required five years for any quantity between 500 and 5,000 grams (U.S. Sentencing Commission 1992*a*).

Here, too, there is an easy way to salvage the federal guidelines: merely follow the lead of every other sentencing commission and shift to the mandatories-as-trumps approach. The commission could set penalties for drug crimes, subject to override by mandatory penalties. In a stroke, the unnecessary penalty increases caused by commission policies would disappear, taking with them the additional increases associated with relevant conduct, inchoate offenses, and spacing.

The Forty-Three-Level "Sentencing Machine"

One of the commission's worst blunders was promulgation of the forty-three-level sentencing grid. By being so large and giving an appearance of arbitrary sentencing by numbers, it became one of the guidelines' worst enemies.

Two major problems resulted from adoption of the sentencing grid. Both were foreseeable on the basis of evaluation research concerning parole and sentencing guidelines and on the basis of the experience of earlier sentencing commissions. First, and most important, the effectiveness of guidelines systems depends on the willingness of officials to accept and apply them. In other words, they must be credible in the eyes of the officials who must use them. If the logic of a guidelines system is not apparent on its face, if it looks mechanical and arbitrary, judges and others are likely to be alienated.

In the sentencing policy literature this is referred to as the problem of the "sentencing machine" (Blumstein et al. 1983, p. 159). Judges and lawyers believe their function in sentencing is to impose fair, deserved, and appropriate punishments. Sentencing by use of a sentencing machine is the antithesis of this. A guidelines grid that conjures up images of mechanical and arbitrary sentencing standards and processes foreseeably alienates judges and others. Judges who are alienated from a sentencing guidelines system are unlikely to invest great effort in protecting the integrity of the system from efforts of lawyers and others to circumvent it. Research discussed earlier in this chapter shows that federal judges often acquiesce in and participate in circumvention of the guidelines.

The problem of the sentencing machine is not new. Partly because of it, state guidelines systems have many fewer offense-severity levels. Minnesota's felony guidelines have ten. Pennsylvania's guidelines, which also cover misdemeanors, in 1995 have thirteen. Washington State considered adopting a twenty-six-level guidelines grid and rejected it in favor of a fourteen-level grid. The rhetorical question was asked, "Could we plausibly explain to a judge why a level sixteen crime is more serious than a level fifteen crime?" When the Washington commission realized that it could not answer that question, it realized it had a sentencing-machine problem and opted for a smaller grid.

The second problem with a complicated guidelines system with an enormous sentencing grid is that there will foreseeably be high error rates in calculating guideline sentences. A major evaluation of four parole guideline grid systems showed that even simple grids produce significant levels of inaccurate guidelines calculations (Arthur D. Little 1981). Complicated grids produce high levels of calculation errors. That this problem affects the federal guidelines is shown by a Federal Judicial Center report on a project in which forty-seven federal probation officers were asked to calculate "base offense levels" for hypothetical defendants described in sample cases used for discussion at a 1992 sentencing institute for judges from the Second and Eighth Circuits. There were enormous differences in the offense levels calculated (Lawrence and Hofer 1992).

The commission either did not know or did not care about the formidable foreseeable problems posed by creation of a sentencing machine. The Guidelines Introduction merely notes, "The Commission has established a sentencing table that for technical and practical reasons contains 43 levels." The technical reasons mentioned include a desire for overlapping guidelines ranges. No mention is made of the likely effects of the grid on judicial perceptions of the system's wisdom or desirability, or of the foreseeable problem of high rates of error in guidelines application.

The sentencing-machine problem is easy to fix. To avoid the problems of the sentencing machine, the commission will have to develop and promulgate a much smaller, facially more plausible grid.

A court could probably take judicial notice of the widespread hostility of judges and lawyers to the federal sentencing guidelines. The line that divides vehement critics from vocal proponents follows no pattern: it is not liberals versus conservatives, Republican appointees versus Democratic appointees, judicial activists versus adherents of judicial restraint. Partly this is because the guidelines have few vocal proponents outside the U.S. Sentencing Commission. Partly it is because objections to the guidelines transcend ideological and partisan differences. The core objections are that the guidelines are too rigid and too harsh, and too often force judges and lawyers to choose between imposing sentences that are widely perceived as unjust or trying to achieve just results by means of hypocritical circumventions. Judges are forced by the guidelines to choose between their obligations to do justice and their obligations to enforce the law. Many judges resent having so often to make that choice. If the commission would make the seven simple changes recommended here, it might produce a system of guidelines that could command the support of judges and prosecutors and make far likelier the achievement of the purposes of the Sentencing Reform Act of 1984.

4

Intermediate Sanctions

Three major developments in the 1960s and 1970s led to the perceived need in the 1980s and 1990s to develop intermediate sanctions that fall between prison and probation in their severity and intrusiveness. First, initially on the basis of doubts about the ethical justification of rehabilitative correctional programs (Allen 1964), and later on the basis of doubts about their effectiveness (Lipton, Martinson, and Wilks 1975; Brody 1976; Sechrest, White, and Brown 1979), rehabilitation lost credibility as a basis for sentencing. With it went the primary rationale for individualized sentences.

Second, initially in academic circles (e.g., Morris 1974; von Hirsch 1976) and later in the minds of many practitioners and policy makers, just deserts entered the penal lexicon, filled the void left by rehabilitation, and became seen as the primary rationale for sentencing. With it came a logic of punishments scaled in their severity so as to be proportionate to the seriousness of crimes committed and a movement to narrow officials' discretion by eliminating parole release, eliminating or limiting time-off-for-good-behavior, and constraining judges' discretion by use of sentencing guidelines.

Third, beginning in the 1960s and continuing into the 1990s, crime-control policy became a staple issue in election campaigns, and proponents of "law and order" persistently called for harsher penalties. With this came a widespread belief that most sentences to ordinary probation are insufficiently punitive and substantial political pressure for increased severity. Because, however, most states lack sanctions other than prison that are widely seen as credible and punitive, pressure for increased severity has been satisfied mostly by increases in the use of imprisonment.

These developments resulted in a quadrupling in the number of state and federal prisoners between 1975 (240,593) and midyear 1994

(1,012,851) and in substantial overcrowding of American prisons. At year-end 1993, the federal prisons were operating at 136 percent of rated capacity and thirty-nine state systems were operating above rated capacity. An additional 51,000 state prisoners in twenty-two jurisdictions were being held in county jails because prison space was unavailable (Bureau of Justice Statistics 1994a, 1994b).

Whatever the political and policy goals that vastly increased numbers of prisoners may have satisfied, they have also posed substantial problems for state officials. Prisons cost a great deal to build and to operate and these costs have not been lightly borne by hard-pressed state budgets in the recessionary years of the early 1990s. In 1994 and 1995, corrections budgets were the fastest rising component of state spending (National Conference of State Legislatures 1993, 1994). However, failure to deal with overcrowding attracts the attention of the federal courts, and throughout the 1990s as many as forty states have been subject to federal court orders related to overcrowding.

Intermediate sanctions have been seen as a way both to reduce the need for prison beds and to provide a continuum of sanctions that satisfies the just deserts concern for proportionality in punishment. During the mid-1980s, intermediate sanctions such as intensive supervision, house arrest, and electronic monitoring were oversold as being able simultaneously to divert offenders from incarceration, reduce recidivism rates, and save money while providing credible punishments that could be scaled in intensity to be proportionate to the severity of the offender's crime. Like most propositions that seem too good to be true, that one wasn't.

During the past decade's experimentation, we have learned that some well-run programs can achieve some of their goals, that some conventional goals are incompatible, and that the availability of new sanctions presents almost irresistible temptations to judges and corrections officials to use them for offenders other than those for whom the program was created.

The goals of diverting offenders from prison and providing tough, rigorously enforced sanctions in the community have proven largely incompatible. A major problem is that close surveillance of offenders reveals higher levels of technical violations than are discovered in less intensive sanctions. Revocations for conduct constituting new crimes are seldom higher for offenders in evaluated programs than for comparable offenders in other programs. Nor is there reason to suppose that offenders in evaluated new programs commit technical violations at higher rates. But if they do breach a curfew or stop performing community service or get drunk or violate a no-drug-use condition, the closer monitoring to which they are subject makes the chances of discovery high; once the discovery is made, many program operators believe they must take punitive action—typically revocation and resentencing to prison—to maintain the program's credibility in the eyes of judges, the media, and the community.

A second major lesson is that elected officials and practitioners often use intermediate sanctions for types of offenders other than those for whom the programs were designed. Many evaluations of intensive supervision programs and boot camps, for example, have shown that any realistic prospects of saving money or prison beds require that they be used mostly for offenders who otherwise would have served prison terms. Yet many elected officials and practitioners resist.

Elected officials resist because they are risk averse. Even in the best-run programs, offenders sometimes commit serious new crimes and officials are understandably concerned that they will be held responsible for supporting the program. The Massachusetts furlough program for prisoners serving life sentences from which Willy Horton absconded, for example, had been in operation for fifteen years and was started under Republican governor Francis Sargent in 1971, but Democratic governor Michael Dukakis was held politically accountable for Horton's 1986 rape of a Maryland woman. As a result of this and similar incidents, elected officials often support new intermediate sanctions but then take pains to limit eligibility to low-risk offenders. One illustration is the series of recent federal proposals for boot camps for nonviolent first-time youthful offenders. For reasons explained in the discussion of boot camps in section II, young, nonviolent first-offenders are among the least appropriate imaginable participants in boot camps if the aims include cost savings and reduced demand for prison beds.

Practitioners, particularly prosecutors and judges, also often resist using intermediate sanctions for the offenders for whom they were designed. Partly this is because they too are reluctant to be seen as responsible for crimes committed by participants. This is why, as the discussion of intensive supervision in section II documents, judges are often unwilling to cooperate in projects in which—as part of experimental evaluations—target categories of offenders are to be randomly assigned to a community penalty or incarceration.

Partly judges' "misuse" of intermediate sanctions occurs because they believe new community penalties are more appropriate for some offenders than either prison or probation. Forced by limited program options to choose between prison and probation, they often choose probation because prison is seen as too severe or too disruptive of the offender's and his family's lives, albeit they do so with misgivings because they believe ordinary probation too slight a sanction. Once house arrest or intensive supervision becomes available, those penalties may appear to the judge to be more appropriate than either probation or prison.

This not uncommon phenomenon is often pejoratively characterized as net-widening. That epithet oversimplifies the problem. From the perspectives of the desirability of proportionality in punishment and of availability of a continuum of sanctions, the judge's preference to divert offenders from probation to something more intrusive is understandable, perhaps admirable. From the perspective, however, of the designers of a program intended to save money and prison space by diverting offenders from prison, the judge's actions defy the program's rationale and obstruct achievement of its goals.

Probably the most important lesson learned from fifteen years' experience is that intermediate sanctions are seldom likely to achieve their goals unless means can be found to set and enforce policies governing their use. Otherwise, the combination of officials' risk aversion and practitioners' preferences to be guided solely by their own judgments is likely to undermine program goals.

Means must be found to establish policies governing the choice of sanction in individual cases. Two complementary means are available. First, discretion to select sanctions can be shifted from judges and prosecutors to corrections officials. "Back-end" programs to which offenders are diverted from prison by corrections officials, or released early, have been more successful at saving money and prison space than have "front-end" programs. Similarly, parole guidelines have been more successful and less controversial in reducing parole release disparities than have sentencing guidelines in reducing sentencing disparities (Arthur D. Little, Inc. 1981; Blumstein et al. 1983, chap. 3). Presumably these findings occur because decision processes in bureaucracies can be placed in fewer peoples' hands and more readily be regularized by use of management controls than can decisions by autonomous, politically selected judges.

Second, sentencing guidelines, which in many jurisdictions have succeeded in reducing disparities in prison sentences (Tonry 1993c), can be extended to govern choices among intermediate sanctions and between them and prison and probation. Some states have made tentative steps in this direction and many are considering doing so. Section III summarizes some of this experience and suggests how current initiatives can be advanced.

First, though, as backdrop, section I gives a brief overview of problems that make reductions in recidivism, costs, and prison use difficult to achieve. Section II summarizes experience to date with the implementation and evaluation of various intermediate sanctions, including boot camps, intensive supervision, house arrest and electronic monitoring, day reporting centers, community service, and day fines. Each discussion provides an overview of program characteristics and discusses evidence concerning various measures of effectiveness, including implementation, net-widening, and success at reducing recidivism, saving money, and diminishing demand for prison beds. The emphasis is mostly on American experience and research, but research elsewhere, especially in England and Wales, is touched on.

I. General Impediments to Effective Intermediate Sanctions

In retrospect it was naive (albeit from good intention) for promoters of new intermediate sanctions to assure skeptics that recidivism rates would fall, costs be reduced, and pressure on prison beds diminish if new programs were established. The considerable pressures for net-widening and the formidable management problems in implementation interact in complex ways to frustrate new programs. Although these challenges are now well understood, that knowledge has been hard won.

Recidivism

Consider first recidivism rates. From influential evaluations of community service (McDonald 1986), intensive supervision (Petersilia and Turner 1993), and boot camps (MacKenzie and Souryal 1994), to mention only a few, comes a robust finding that recidivism rates (for new crimes) of offenders sentenced to well-managed intermediate sanctions do not differ significantly from those of comparable offenders receiving other sentences. Recidivism and revocation rates for violation of other conditions, by contrast, are generally higher.

From different perspectives, both findings may be seen as good or bad. The finding of no effect on rates of new crime may be seen by many as good if the offenders involved have been diverted from prison and the new crimes they commit are not very serious. Sentences to prison are much more expensive to administer than sentences to house arrest, intensive supervision, or day reporting centers, and if the latter are no less effective at reducing subsequent criminality, they can potentially provide nearly comparable public safety at greatly reduced cost.

But not "comparable public safety": by definition, crimes committed in the community by people who would have been in prison would not otherwise have occurred. If diverted intermediate sanction participants commonly commit violent or sexual crimes, "no difference in recidivism rates" provides little solace. If, however, participants seldom commit violent or sexual crimes, the open-eyed choice that must be made is between avoidable minor crimes and substantial costs to hold people in prison. The suggestion that every offender be confined until he will no longer offend is impracticable. Property offenders particularly have high reoffending rates, more than 30 percent of American and English males are arrested for nontrivial crimes by age thirty (Harvey and Pease 1987; Home Office 1989), and all offenders cannot be confined forever. In effect, this trade between costs and allowing avoidable crimes to happen is made whenever community sentencing programs are established.

From the other side of the punishment continuum, the no-effect-on-new-crimes finding raises different issues. If ordinary probation is no less effective at preventing new crimes than is a new intermediate sanction at three times the cost, the case for sentencing offenders to the new program instead of probation cannot be made on cost-effectiveness terms. That does not mean that no case can be made. Joan Petersilia and Susan Turner (1993), among others, have offered the just desert argument that intermediate sanctions can deliver a punishment more intrusive and burdensome than probation and appropriately proportioned to the offender's guilt. This is a plausible argument, but it shifts the rationale from utilitarian claims about crime and cost reductions to normative claims about the quality of justice.

The equally robust finding that participants in intermediate sanctions typically have higher rates of violation of technical conditions than comparable offenders otherwise punished provokes a not-quite-parallel set of concerns. Most observers agree that the raised violation and revocation rates result from the greater likelihood that violations will be discovered in intensive programs, and not from greater underlying rates of violation. From a "the law must keep its promises" perspective, the higher failure rates are good. Offenders *should* comply with conditions, and consequences should attach when they do not.

The contrary view is that the higher failure rates expose the unreality and injustice of conditions—like prohibitions of drinking or expectations that offenders will conform to middle-class behavioral standards they have never observed before—that many offenders will foreseeably breach and that do not involve criminality. Many offenders have difficulty in achieving conventional, law-abiding patterns of living and many stumble along the way. A traditional social work approach to community corrections would expect and accept the stumbles (so long as they do not involve significant new crimes) and hope that through them, with help, the offender will learn to be law-abiding. From this perspective, it is an advantage of low-intensity programs that they uncover few violations and a disadvantage of high-intensity programs that they do.

Prison Beds

If all offenders in a community program were diverted from prison, a 30 percent revocation rate for technical violations (whatever the rate for new-crime violations, but here assuming 20 percent) would not be an insurmountable problem. The net savings in prison beds would be the number of persons diverted, multiplied by the average time they would otherwise spend in prison, less the number of persons revoked for violations (of whatever kind) multiplied by their average term to be served. Unless the gross revocation rate approached 100 percent or the average time to be served after revocation exceeded the average time that would have been served if not diverted, bed savings are inevitable.

The combination of net-widening and elevated rates of technical violations and revocations makes the calculation harder and makes prison bed savings difficult to achieve. For front-end programs, a 50 percent rate of prison diversion is commonly counted a success. Consider how the numbers work out. The 50 percent diverted from prison save prison beds, on the calculation and assumptions described in the preceding paragraph. The 50 percent diverted from probation are a different story. They would not otherwise have occupied prison beds, and if half (on 30 percent technical, 20 percent new-crime revocation assumptions) suffer revocation and imprisonment, they represent new demand for beds, and a higher demand than would otherwise exist because many more technical violations will be discovered and acted upon.

Whether a particular program characterized by 50 percent prison diversion will save or require net prison beds depends on why offenders' participation is revoked and in what percentage of cases, and whether they are sent to prison and for how long. But 50 percent is a high assumed diversion rate. If the true rate is 30 percent or 20 percent, net prison bed savings are unlikely.

Cost Savings

The third often-claimed goal of intermediate sanctions is to save money. Interaction of all the preceding difficulties makes dollar savings unlikely except in the best of cases. If a majority of program participants are diverted from probation rather than from prison, and if technical violation and revocation rates are higher in the intermediate sanction than in the ordinary probation and parole programs to which offenders would otherwise be assigned, the chances of net cost savings are slight. For boot camps, for example, assuming typical levels of participant noncompletion and typical levels of postprogram revocation, Dale Parent has calculated that "the probability of imprisonment has to be around 80 percent just to reach a break-even point—that is, to have a net impact of zero on prison bed-space" (1994, p. 9).

Cost analyses must, however, look beyond diversion rates, revocation rates, and prison beds. At least three other considerations are important. First is the issue of transaction costs. Net-widening programs that shift probationers to intensive supervision and then shift some of those to prison cost the state more because they use up additional prison space. But in addition they create new expenses for probation offices, prosecutors, courts, and corrections agencies in administering each of those transfers. Correctional cost-benefit analyses often ignore cost ramifications for other agencies, but the other agencies must either pay additional costs or refuse to cooperate. An example: community corrections officials often complain that courts sometimes do not take violations seriously and that when they do, police assign such low priority to execution of arrest warrants for program violators that they are meaningless (e.g., McDonald 1986).

Second is the problem of marginal costs. Especially in the 1980s, promoters of new programs commonly contrasted the average annual costs per offender of administering a new program (say $4,500) with the average annual cost of housing one prisoner (say $18,500) and claimed substantial potential cost savings. This ignores the complexities presented by net-widening and raised revocation rates but it also ignores a more important problem of scale.

For an innovative small program of fifty to a hundred offenders (and many were and are of this size or smaller), the valid comparison is with the marginal, not the average, costs of housing diverted offenders. Unless a prison or a housing unit will be closed or not opened because the system has fifty fewer inmates, the only savings will be incremental costs for food, laundry, supplies, and other routine items. The major costs of payroll, administration, debt service, and maintenance will be little affected. In a prison system with 5,000, 15,000, or 50,000 inmates, the costs saved by diverting a few hundred are scarcely noticeable.

Third is the issue of savings to the larger community associated with crimes avoided by incapacitating offenders. If believable values could be attached to crimes that would be averted by imprisonment but that would occur if offenders were assigned to community penalties, they would provide important data for considering policy options. Unfortunately, this is a subject that has as yet received little sustained attention. Some conservative writers (e.g., Zedlewski 1987; DiIulio 1990; DiIulio and Piehl 1991; Barr 1992) have claimed that increased use of imprisonment is highly cost-effective. Kleiman and Cavanagh (1990), for example, claimed "benefits of incarcerating that *one inmate* for a year at between $172,000 and $2,364,000" (emphasis in original).

Liberal scholars have responded by showing the implausibility of many of the assumptions made in such calculations. Franklin Zimring and Gordon Hawkins (1991), for example, showed, on the assumptions made in Edwin Zedlewski's analysis about the number of crimes prevented for each inmate confined, that the increase in the prison population of 237,000 between 1977 and 1986 should "have reduced crime to zero on incapacitation effects alone . . . on this account, crime disappeared some years ago." That is true of all the cost-benefit analyses mentioned in the preceding paragraph. If their assumptions about numbers of crimes prevented by confining offenders are correct, and are used to calculate the number of crimes prevented since prison populations began in 1976 to quadruple, we should have been living in a crime-free society since the mid-1980s.

One of the conservative contributors to this debate later recanted more extreme claims and concluded that "the truth, we find, lies . . . arguably closer to the liberal than to the conservative view" (DiIulio and Piehl 1991). These debates have, however, been more ideological than scientific and offer little guidance for thinking about intermediate sanctions. What is left is the need mentioned earlier to weigh the risks posed by particular offenders with the costs if alternate sanctioning choices are made.

No one who has worked with the criminal justice system should be surprised by the observation that the system is complex and that economic and policy ramifications ripple through it when changes are made in any one of its parts. Sometimes that truism has been overlooked, to the detriment of programs on behalf of which oversimplified claims were made. Georgia, for example, operated a pioneering front-end intensive supervision program (ISP) that was at one time claimed to have achieved remarkably low recidivism rates (for new crimes) and to have saved Georgia the cost of building two prisons (Erwin 1987; Erwin and Bennett 1987). It was later realized that many or most of those sentenced to ISP were low-risk offenders convicted of minor crimes who otherwise would have received probation. From serving initially as an exemplar of successful ISP programs that save money and reduce recidivism rates, Georgia's ISP program now serves as an exemplar of net-widening programs that increase system costs and produce higher rates of revocation for violation of technical conditions (Clear and Byrne 1992, p. 321).

II. Experience with Intermediate Sanctions

Writing about intermediate sanctions resembles shooting at a moving target. Although it typically takes at least three years from the time an evaluation is conceived until results are published, the programs themselves keep changing. Thus Doris MacKenzie (1994), describing the results of an assessment of boot camps in eight states, took pains to explain that some of them changed significantly during and after the assessment. For example, the South Carolina program, initially a front-end program with admission controlled by the judge (and thus highly vulnerable to net-widening) was reorganized as a back-end program in which participants were selected by the department of corrections from among offenders sentenced to prison. Similarly, programs in some states that had focused primarily on discipline and physical labor were reorganized to include a much larger component of drug treatment and educational opportunities.

Still, an evaluation literature has continued to accumulate, and lessons learned in some states can be useful to policy makers in other states that are designing new programs or redesigning old ones. In order, the following subsections discuss research on boot camps, ISP, house arrest and electronic monitoring, day reporting centers, community service, and day fines.

The literature for the most part raises doubts about the effectiveness of intermediate sanctions at achieving the goals their promoters have commonly set. This does not mean that there are no effective programs. Only a handful have been carefully evaluated. Many of those have since been altered. Many sophisticated and experienced practitioners believe that their programs are effective, and some no doubt are. The evaluation literature does not "prove" that programs cannot succeed but rather that many have not and that managers can learn from that past experience. Sometimes that learning produces adaptations intended to make achievement of existing goals more likely. Sometimes, it leads to reconceptualization of goals.

The evaluation literature is slight, which at first impression may seem surprising given that new programs have proliferated in every state. To anyone knowledgeable about correctional research, the relatively small amount of research will be less surprising; private foundations are conspicuously uninterested in criminal justice research, neither of the relevant specialized national funding agencies—the National Institute of Corrections and the State Justice Institute—spends much on research, and the National Institute of Justice must spread its limited research funds among a wide range of subjects.

The literature consists of a handful of fairly sophisticated evaluations funded by the National Institute of Justice, a larger number of smaller, typically less sophisticated studies of local projects, and a large number of uncritical descriptions of innovative programs. There have also been efforts to synthesize the intermediate sanctions literature, sometimes in edited collections (McCarthy 1987; Byrne, Lurigio, and Petersilia 1992; Tonry and Hamilton 1995), sometimes in unified books (Tonry and Will 1988; Morris and Tonry 1990). Given the time consumed in writing and publishing books, the collections and syntheses are current as of a year or two before their publication dates.

In order to keep this chapter to a manageable length, the discussion of each intermediate sanction is held to a few pages and emphasizes the more substantial evaluations and literature reviews. In some cases, for example concerning ISP (Petersilia and Turner 1993) and boot camps (MacKenzie 1994; MacKenzie and Piquero 1994), relatively recent and detailed literature reviews are available for readers who want more information. In other cases, for example concerning fines (Hillsman 1990) and community service (Pease 1985), the best literature reviews are more dated; there has been relatively little American research on those subjects in recent years, and those articles, despite their dates, cover most of the important research. In still other cases, notably including day reporting centers, most of the available literature is descriptive and no published literature reviews are available.

Boot Camps

The emerging consensus from assessments of boot camps (also sometimes called shock incarceration) must be discouraging to their founders and supporters. Although promoted as a means to reduce recidivism rates, corrections costs, and prison crowding, most boot camps have no discernible effect on subsequent offending and increase costs and crowding (Parent 1994; MacKenzie 1994). The reasons are those sketched in section I. Most have been front-end programs that have drawn many of their participants from among offenders who otherwise would not have been sent to prison. In many programs, a third to half of participants fail to complete the program and are sent to prison as a result. In most programs, close surveillance of offenders after completion and release produces rates of technical violations and revocations that are higher than for comparable offenders in less intensive programs.

The news is not all bad. Back-end programs to which imprisoned offenders are transferred by corrections officials for service of a 90- or 180-day boot camp sentence in lieu of a longer conventional sentence do apparently save money and prison space, although they, too, often experience high failure rates and higher than normal technical violation and revocation rates.

Boot camp prisons have spread rapidly since the first two were established in Georgia and Oklahoma in 1983. By April 1993, according to a National Institute of Justice report (MacKenzie 1993), thirty states and the U.S. Bureau of Prisons were operating boot camps. According to the results of a survey of local jurisdictions in May 1992, ten jail boot camps were then in operation and thirteen other jurisdictions were planning to open jail boot camps in 1992 or 1993 (Austin, Jones, and Bolyard 1993). The earliest were opened in 1986 in New Orleans and in 1988 in Travis County, Texas.

Boot camps vary widely in their details (MacKenzie and Parent 1992; MacKenzie and Piquero 1994). Some last 90 days, some 180. Admission in some states is controlled by judges, in others by corrections officials. Some primarily emphasize discipline and self-control; others incorporate extensive drug and other rehabilitation elements. Some eject a third to half of participants, others less than 10 percent. Most admit only males, usually under age twenty-five, and often subject to crime of conviction and criminal history limits, though there are exceptions to each of these generalizations.

The reasons for boot camps' popularity are self-evident. Many Americans have experienced life in military boot camps and remember the experience as not necessarily pleasant but as an effective way to learn self-discipline and to learn to work as part of a team. Images of offenders participating in military drill and hard physical labor make boot camps look demanding and unpleasant, characteristics that crime-conscious officials and voters find satisfying. A series of studies by the Public Agenda Foundation in Delaware, Alabama, and Pennsylvania of citizen support for intermediate sanctions, for example, found that the public is more supportive of intermediate sanctions than is widely known, but also found that they want such penalties to be burdensome and for that reason especially favored boot camps (Doble and Klein 1989; Doble, Immerwahr, and Robinson 1991; Public Agenda Foundation 1993).

Most of what we know about the effects of boot camps on participants comes from a series of studies by Doris MacKenzie and colleagues at the University of Maryland (e.g., MacKenzie and Shaw 1990, 1993; Mackenzie 1993, 1994; MacKenzie and Souryal 1994), from a General Accounting Office survey of research and experience (1993), and from an early descriptive overview of boot camps commissioned by the National Institute of Justice (Parent 1989).

The conclusions with which this subsection began are drawn from MacKenzie's work and later analyses by Dale Parent. In addition to findings on completion rates, recidivism rates, and cost and prison bed savings, MacKenzie and her colleagues looked closely in Louisiana at effects on prisoners' attitudes (MacKenzie and Shaw 1990). One early hypothesis concerning boot camps was that successful completion would increase participants' positive attitudes, which would in turn lead to more effective participation in the free community and reduced recidivism. The first half of the hypothesis was found to be correct; using psychometric measures, MacKenzie and Shaw found that successful participants developed more positive attitudes compared with comparable prisoners in conventional prisons. Unfortunately, later assessments of successful participants after release found that their improved attitudes disappeared (a plausible explanation for why the second half of the hypothesis concerning recidivism was not confirmed).

One tentative finding concerning possible positive effects of rehabilitative programs on recidivism merits emphasis. Although MacKenzie and her colleagues concluded overall that boot camps do not by themselves result in reduced recidivism rates, they found evidence in Illinois, New York, and Louisiana of "lower rates of recidivism on some measures" that they associated with strong rehabilitative emphases in those states' boot camps (MacKenzie 1994, p. 16). An earlier article describes a "somewhat more positive" finding that graduates under intensive supervision after release "appear to be involved in more positive social activities (e.g., work, attending drug treatment) than similar offenders on parole or probation" (MacKenzie and Shaw 1993, p. 465).

Boot camps illustrate most vividly of all intermediate sanctions the ways in which net-widening, rigorous enforcement of conditions, and high revocation rates can produce the unintended side effect of increased costs and prison use from programs intended to reduce both. Both MacKenzie (MacKenzie and Piquero 1994) and Parent (1994) have used a model developed by Parent for predicting the prison use implications of boot camps in light of various assumptions about net-widening, within-program failure rates, and postprogram revocation rates, including estimates of time to failure, time to revocation, and lengths of time in the boot camp, in prison if not sent to the boot camp, and in prison following failure or revocation.

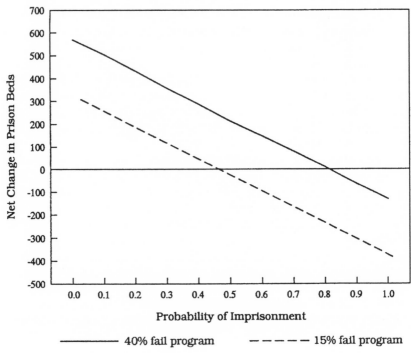

Figure 4.1. 200-Bed, 90-Day Boot Camp (9-Month Reduction). *Source:* Parent (1994).

Figure 4.1, taken from Parent's work (1994), shows the effects on prison beds of a hypothetical 90-day 200-bed facility on different assumptions of prison diversion and postprogram revocation and reincarceration. Other assumptions of failure rates within the program and lengths of confinement in lieu of boot camp and after revocation, based on averages documented in MacKenzie's eight-state assessment, are built into the model. The diagonal lines show the effects of different postprogram reincarceration rates on prison bed demand. At the lower 15 percent rate, boot camps create a net demand for additional prison beds if less than half of those in the program would otherwise have gone to prison. At the more realistic 40 percent rate, at least 80 percent of participants must have been diverted from prison before prison beds are saved.

MacKenzie (1994) developed similar estimates for states in her eight-state assessment. Figure 4.2 shows estimates based on data from New York's boot camps of bed savings given various assumptions about prison diversion. Savings occur only if at least 75 percent of participants are diverted from prison, and sizeable savings occur only if nearly all are diverted.

If a primary goal of boot camps is to reduce prison use, the policy implications of research on boot camps are straightforward. Parent

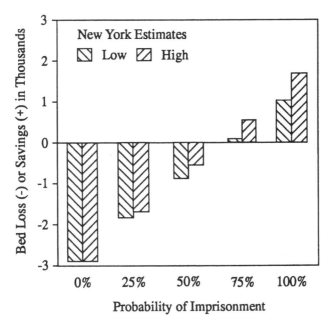

Figure 4.2. Effects on Prison Bed Needs of Prison Diversion Rates, New York. *Source:* MacKenzie (1994).

(1994, p. 10) sees at least three: "First, boot camps should recruit offenders who have a very high probability of imprisonment." This means that participants should be selected by corrections officials from among prisoners rather than by judges from among sentenced offenders. Second, boot camps should minimize failure rates by reducing in-program failures and postrelease failures. This means that misconduct within the boot camp should be punished within the boot camp whenever possible rather than by transfer to a regular prison and that misconduct after release should be dealt with within the supervision program whenever possible rather than by revocation and reincarceration. Third, participants in boot camps should be selected from among prisoners who otherwise would serve a substantial term of imprisonment. Transfer of prisoners serving nine-month terms to a 180-day boot camp is unlikely to reduce costs and system crowding. Transfer of prisoners serving two- or three-year mandatory minimum terms is likely to reduce both.

Corrections officials are aware of these findings. Some states, for example New York, already operate boot camps that draw their clientele from state prisons and that result in much shorter terms of confinement for those who complete the program (including many who thereby avoid mandatory minimums). Other states, South Carolina is an example, have shifted from judicial to correctional selection of participants. One implication is clear, however. "Boot camps for nonviolent first offenders," though often proposed in political speeches, are unlikely to accomplish any of the aims for boot camps that are generally offered.

Intensive Supervision

Intensive supervision for probationers and parolees (ISP) was initially the most popular intermediate sanction, has the longest history, and has been the most extensively and ambitiously evaluated. ISP has been the subject of the only multisite experimental evaluation involving random allocation of eligible offenders to an intermediate sanction and to whatever the otherwise appropriate sentence would have been (Petersilia and Turner 1993).

Evaluation findings parallel those for boot camps. Front-end programs in which judges control placement tend to draw more heavily from offenders who would otherwise receive less restrictive sentences than from offenders who would otherwise have gone to prison or jail. The multisite ISP evaluation by the RAND Corporation, in which jurisdictions agreed in advance to cooperate with a random assignment system for allocating offenders to sanctions, was unable to evaluate front-end ISP programs because judges refused to cooperate and would not accept the outcomes of the randomization system (Petersilia and Turner 1993). Back-end programs draw from prison populations, but even for some of these programs, suggestions have been made that their creation may lead judges to sentence more minor offenders to "a taste of prison" in the belief that they will quickly be released into ISP (Clear 1987).

Like the boot camp evaluations, the ISP evaluations have concluded that offenders sentenced to ISP do not have lower recidivism rates for new crimes than do comparable offenders receiving different sentences, but typically (because of closer surveillance) experience higher rates of violation of technical conditions and higher rates of revocation. Also, as in the case of boot camps, early proponents of ISP argued that by reducing recidivism rates and rehabilitating offenders ISP would save money and prison resources (Petersilia, Lurigio, and Byrne 1992, pp. ix–x). Evaluations, however, suggest that the combination of net-widening, high revocation rates, and related case processing costs makes the cost savings claims improbable for most programs.

One tantalizing positive finding emerges from the ISP evaluation literature, and it parallels a boot camp finding (MacKenzie and Shaw 1993): ISP did succeed in some sites in increasing participants' involvement in counseling and other treatment programs (Petersilia and Turner 1993). The drug treatment literature demonstrates that participation, whether voluntary or coerced, can reduce both drug use and crime by drug-using offenders (Anglin and Hser 1990; President's Commission on Model State Drug Laws 1993). Because Drug Use Forecasting data (e.g., National Institute of Justice 1994) indicate that half to three-fourths of arrested felons in many cities test positive for drug abuse, ISP may hold promise as a device for getting addicted offenders into treatment and keeping them there (Gendreau, Cullen, and Bonta 1994).

Few corrections programs are new in the sense that they haven't been tried before; house arrest, supervision of variable intensity, treatment conditions, community service, restitution, intermittent or partial confinement—they have all long been used on a case-by-case basis as conditions of probation. Modern ISP, however, is different in that it follows a previous generation of similar programs that was the subject of widespread programmatic adoption and evaluation.

From the 1950s through the early 1970s, probation departments experimented with caseload size in order to learn whether smaller caseloads permitting more contact between officers and probationers would enable officers to provide more and better services and thereby enhance probation's rehabilitative effectiveness. The best-known project, in California, featured caseloads ranging from "intensive" (20 offenders) to "ideal" (50), "normal" (70 to 130), and "minimum" (several hundred). Lower caseloads produced more technical violations but indistinguishable crime rates (Carter, Robinson, and Wilkins 1967).

A later survey of the experience of forty-six separate (mostly Law Enforcement Assistance Administration-funded) programs found that intensive supervision programs had no effect on recidivism rates or increased them, and diverted few offenders from prison but recruited instead mostly from people who otherwise would have received probation (Banks et al. 1977). Not surprisingly, ISP based on rehabilitative rationales withered away.

Contemporary programs, with caseloads ranging from two officers to twenty-five probationers to one officer to forty probationers, are typically based on surveillance, cost, and punishment rationales. More frequent contacts between officer and offender (in some programs, as many as twenty or thirty per month) lead to closer surveillance, which in turn enhances public safety by making it likelier that misconduct will be discovered and punished. Because of closer surveillance, low- to mid-risk offenders can be diverted from prison to less-costly ISP without jeopardizing public safety. Because of the frequency of contacts, subjection to unannounced urinalysis tests for drugs, and rigorous enforcement of restitution, community service, and other conditions, ISP is much more punitive than conventional probation.

Contemporary ISP programs are of three types, each with an exemplar that was the subject of a major National Institute of Justice-funded evaluation. Georgia established the most noted "prison diversion" program, to which convicted offenders were sentenced by judges under criteria that directed the judge to use ISP only for offenders who otherwise would have been sent to prison. An in-house evaluation concluded that most ISP participants had been diverted from prison and, on the basis of comparisons with a matched group of offenders who were imprisoned, that the program had achieved lower recidivism rates and had reduced prison use (Erwin 1987). Subsequent analyses by others concluded that most participants had not been diverted from prison, that the comparison group was not comparable, that low rates of new crimes resulted not from the program but from the low-risk character of the offenders, and that prison beds had not been saved (Morris and Tonry 1990, chap. 7; Clear and Byrne 1992).

The second form, "prison release ISP," had as its evaluated exemplar a New Jersey program to which low-risk prisoners were released after a careful seven-step screening process and then placed in low caseloads with frequent contacts and urinalyses and rigorously enforced conditions. A major evaluation, based on a post hoc comparison group, concluded that the program was effectively implemented, reduced recidivism rates, and saved public moneys (Pearson 1987, 1988). Subsequent analyses by others accepted the implementation finding but challenged the recidivism findings (because the comparison group appeared to consist of higher-risk offenders and thus was not comparable) and the cost findings (nearly half of the initial participants were sent back to prison following revocation for breach of conditions which, given the short sentences they would otherwise have served and the costs of processing the revocations, made cost-savings claims suspect) (Morris and Tonry 1990, chap. 7). Todd Clear hypothesized that judges might sentence low-risk minor offenders to prison in the belief that they would be released to ISP, and that if under 2 percent of the eligible defendants were sentenced to prison on that basis, any possible cost savings from ISP would be lost (Clear 1987).

The third form, "case management ISP," had as its evaluated exemplar a Massachusetts program designed by the state probation department in which probationers were classified on the basis of risk of offending (using a validated risk-classification instrument). The evaluation documented significant implementation problems, and concluded that offenders given intense supervision were no likelier than other comparable offenders to commit new crimes but were likelier to have their probation revoked because of technical condition violations (Byrne and Kelly 1989).

Notwithstanding the nonconfirmatory evaluation findings, ISP was adopted in most states. A General Accounting Office survey in 1989 identified programs in forty states and the District of Columbia (U.S. General Accounting Office 1990*b*; Byrne and Pattavina 1992). Probably they exist in every state; programs can be organized by state or county correctional agencies, and can be located in parole, probation, and prison departments. As a result programs are easy to miss in national mail and phone surveys.

Although ad hoc intensive supervision in individual cases presumably occurs in every probation system, no other country has adopted widespread programs of intensive probation. Small-scale pilot projects were started in the Netherlands in 1993 (Tak 1994*a*, 1994*b*). In England, as in the United States, variable caseload projects to test treatment effectiveness hypotheses were conducted in the 1960s and early 1970s, with the same discouraging results (Folkard et al. 1974, 1976), and were soon abandoned. A series of pilot projects in eight sites, linked with Home Office evaluations, has been underway in England and Wales in the 1990s with as yet inconclusive results. The programs appear to have diverted offenders from prison and to have met with approval from judges and probation officers, but in many sites they have encountered substantial implementation problems (Mair 1994; Mair et al. 1994). Findings on recidivism effects will not be available until 1996 (or later).

Two exhaustive syntheses of the American ISP literature have been published (U.S. General Accounting Office 1990*b*; Petersilia and Turner 1993) and do not differ significantly in their conclusions from those offered here. One question that naturally arises is why ISP programs have survived and continue to be created. Unlike boot camps, for which evaluation findings casting doubts on effectiveness are recent, the ISP findings have been well known and accepted since at least 1990. The answers appear to be that ISP's surveillant and punitive properties satisfy a public preference that sanctions be demanding and burdensome and that ISP is coming to be seen as an appropriate mid-level punishment. John Petersilia, Arthur Lurigio, and James Byrne (1992, p. xiv) note, "to many observers, the goal of restoring the principle of just deserts to the criminal justice system is justification enough for the continued development of intermediate sanctions."

Here, too, the policy implications are straightforward. Because recidivism rates for new crimes are no higher for ISP participants than for comparable imprisoned offenders, ISP is a cost-effective prison alternative for offenders who do not present unacceptable risks of violence. ISP may offer a promising tool for facilitating treatment for drug-using offenders and can by itself and linked with other sanctions provide credible mid-level punishments as part of a continuum of sanctions.

The challenges are to devise ways to assure that programs are used for the kinds of offenders for whom they are designed and to reduce rates of revocation for technical violations. The former problem does not exist for back-end early release programs, and sentencing guidelines systems may hold promise for reducing the extent of net-widening in front-end systems (see section III). The technical revocation problem can be addressed, as Lurigio and Petersilia (1992, p. 14) note, by imposing only conditions that relate to a particular offender's circumstances rather than imposing long lists of general standard conditions.

House Arrest and Electronic Monitoring

The lines that distinguish community penalties begin to blur after ISP. House arrest, often called home confinement, has as a precursor the curfew condition traditionally attached to many probation sentences, and may be ordered as a sanction in its own right or as a condition of ISP (Ball, Huff, and Lilly 1988). Most affected offenders, however, do not remain in their homes but instead are authorized to work or participate in treatment, education, or training programs. Finally, house arrest is sometimes, but not necessarily, backed up by electronic monitoring; Marc Renzema (1992), for example, reports that 10,549 people were on house arrest in Florida in August 1990, of whom 873 were on electronic monitoring.

House arrest comes in front- and back-end forms. In an early Oklahoma program (Meachum 1986), for example, prison inmates were released early subject to participation in a home confinement program. In Florida, which operates the largest and most diverse home confinement programs, most are front-end programs in which otherwise prison-bound offenders are supposed to be placed. In some states, especially in connection with electronic monitoring, house arrest is used in place of pretrial detention (Maxfield and Baumer 1990).

House arrest programs expanded rapidly beginning in the mid-1980s. The earliest were typically small (from thirty to fifty offenders) and often were composed mostly of driving-while-intoxicated (DWI) and minor property offenders (this was also true of most of the early electronic monitoring programs) (Morris and Tonry 1990, chap. 7).

Programs have grown and proliferated. In Florida, more than 13,000 offenders were on house arrest in 1993 (Blomberg, Bales, and Reed 1993). Programs coupled with electronic monitoring, a subset, existed nowhere in 1982, in seven states in 1986, and in all fifty states in October 1990 (Renzema 1992, p. 46).

Considered by itself, the use of electronic monitoring has grown even more from its beginnings in 1983 in the New Mexico courtroom of Judge Michael Goss and the Florida courtroom of Judge J. Allison DeFoor II (Ford and Schmidt 1985). In 1986, only ninety-five offenders were subject to monitoring (Renzema 1992, p. 41), a number that rose to 12,000 in 1990 (Baumer and Mendelsohn 1992, p. 54) and to a daily count of 30,000 to 50,000 in 1992 and 1993 (Lilly 1993, p. 4).

Manufacturers of electronic monitoring equipment no doubt expect eventually to sell their products worldwide. Within the English-speaking countries the United States is at present the major market. In early 1993, the Northern Territory of Australia was the only state operating front-end house arrest programs; Western Australia, South Australia, and Queensland operated prison-release programs. Altogether, these programs contained 330 to 400 offenders, of whom approximately half were subject to electronic monitoring (Biles 1993).

English policy makers toyed with electronic monitoring in the late 1980s and established a pilot project in three sites in 1989–90. Judges and police were skeptical about the use of electronically monitored house arrest as a custody alternative, and rates of offender noncompliance were high (Mair and Nee 1990; Mair 1993*b*). The evaluators characterized their findings as inconclusive. Although the Criminal Justice Act 1991 authorized use of electronic monitoring in conjunction with curfew orders, no monitoring equipment was in use in England and Wales in mid-1995.

No American evaluations of the scale or sophistication of the best of those on boot camps or ISP have been published. One analysis of agency data for Florida's front-end house arrest program concluded that it draws more offenders from among the prison-bound than from the probation-bound (Baird and Wagner 1990). However, this conclusion is based on two dubious analyses. The first looked to see whether offenders on house arrest should, under Florida's sentencing guidelines, have been sentenced to confinement. This seemingly straightforward calculation assumes, however, that the guidelines are taken seriously by Florida judges and significantly constrain judges' choices; the best evidence and the conclusion of a legislative study committee is that they do not (Florida Legislature 1991).

The second diversion analysis was based on statistical comparison of characteristics of samples of probationers, house arrest offenders, and prisoners, and concluded that those on house arrest more closely resembled prisoners than probationers. This is like the ISP evaluations in Georgia and New Jersey that were later challenged on the basis that seemingly comparable groups were not in fact comparable. Part of the difficulty lies in inherent limits of efforts to use statistical models to create equivalent comparison groups and part in the limited range of data about offenders that is compiled in official records.

A case study of the development, implementation, and evolution of a back-end program in Arizona cautions that house arrest programs are likely to share the prospects and problems of intermediate sanctions generally. Originally conceived as a money-saving back-end system for early release of low-risk offenders, the program—which combined house arrest with electronic monitoring—wound up costing money. One problem was that, in addition to satisfying stringent statutory criteria (no violent or sex crimes, no prior felony convictions), inmates had to be approved for release by the parole board, which proved highly risk averse and released very few eligible inmates. When the program became operational, the rate of revocation for technical violations (34 percent of participants) was twice that for ordinary parolees. Finally, many probation officers began to justify the program not as an early release system for low-risk offenders, but as a mechanism for establishing tighter controls and closer surveillance for parolees than would otherwise be possible (Palumbo, Clifford, and Snyder-Joy 1992).

There are no other large-scale evaluations. House arrest coupled with electronic monitoring has been the subject of many small studies and a linked set of three studies in Indianapolis (Baumer, Maxfield, and Mendelsohn 1993). Both of two recent literature reviews (Baumer and Mendelsohn

1992; Renzema 1992) stress the scantiness of the research evidence on prison diversion, recidivism, and cost-effectiveness. On recidivism, Renzema (1992, p. 49) notes that most of the "research is uninterpretable because of shoddy or weak research designs." Terry Baumer and Robert Mendelsohn (1992, pp. 64–65) stress that "the incapacitative and public safety potential of this sanction has probably been considerably overstated" because the technology cannot control offenders' movements. They predict that house arrest will continue primarily to be used for low-risk offenders and will play little role as a custody alternative.

Thus, while a fair amount has been learned about the operation and management of electronic monitoring systems, about technology, and about implementation of new programs (e.g., Baumer and Mendelsohn 1992; Watts and Glaser 1992), the most comprehensive review of the research observes, "we know very little about either home confinement or electronic monitoring" (Baumer and Mendelsohn 1992, p. 66). There seems little reason to believe that house arrest is any less vulnerable to net-widening than is ISP or likely to achieve different findings on recidivism.

Day Reporting Centers

Day reporting centers, like the remaining two sanctions discussed, community service and day fines, were developed earlier and much more extensively outside the United States than in. The earliest American day reporting centers—places in which offenders spend their days under surveillance and participating in treatment and training programs while sleeping elsewhere—date from the mid-1980s. The English precursors, originally called day centres and now probation centres, began operation in the early 1970s. Most of our knowledge of American day reporting centers comes from descriptive writing; no published literature as yet provides credible findings on the important empirical questions.

The English programs began with creation of four "day-training centres" established under the Criminal Justice Act 1972, charged to provide intensive training programs for persistent petty offenders whose criminality was believed rooted in general social inadequacy, and with creation of ad hoc day centers for serious offenders that were set up by local probation agencies. The training centers for a number of reasons were adjudged unsuccessful and were soon canceled.

The probation-run day centers, however, thrived, becoming the "flavor of the month" after enabling legislation was enacted in 1982. They numbered at least eighty by 1985, and served thousands of offenders by the late 1980s (Mair 1993a, p. 6). Programs vary, with some emphasizing control and surveillance more than others, some operating as a therapeutic community, and most offering a wide range of (mostly compulsory) activities. The maximum term of involvement is sixty days, and some programs have set thirty-day or forty-five-day limits.

A major Home Office study (Mair 1988) concluded that "most centres unequivocally saw their aim as diversion from custody" (Mair 1993*a*, p. 6), that more than half of the participating offenders had previously been imprisoned, and that 47 percent had six or more prior convictions. A later reconviction study (Mair and Nee 1992) found a two-year reconviction rate of 63 percent. However, George Mair writes, though "on the face of it this may look high . . . the offenders targeted by centres represent a very high-risk group in terms of probability of reconviction" (Mair 1993*a*, p. 6). In addition, the reconviction data did not distinguish between those who completed the program and those who failed. The results were seen as so promising that the Criminal Justice Act 1991 envisioned a substantial expansion in use of day reporting centers.

A 1989 survey for the National Institute of Justice identified thirteen day reporting centers in eight states (Parent 1990), though many others have since opened. Most American centers opened after 1985. The best known (at least the best documented) centers were established in Massachusetts—in Springfield (Hampton County Sheriff's Department) and in Boston (the Metropolitan Day Reporting Center)—and both were based in part on the model provided by the English day centers (Larivee 1991; McDevitt and Miliano 1992).

As with the English centers, American programs vary widely. Many are back-end programs into which offenders are released early from jail or prison. Some, however, are front-end programs to which offenders are sentenced by judges and some are used as alternatives to pretrial detention (Parent 1991). Programs range in duration from forty days to nine months and program content varies widely (Parent 1991). Most require development of hour-by-hour schedules of each participant's activities, some are highly intensive with ten or more supervision contacts per day, and a few include twenty-four-hour-per-day electronic monitoring (McDevitt and Miliano 1992). Unfortunately, no substantial evaluations have been published (a number of small in-house evaluations are discussed in Larivee [1991] and McDevitt and Miliano[1992]).

Community Service

Community service is the most underused intermediate sanction in the United States. Used in many countries as a mid-level penalty to replace short prison terms for moderately severe crimes, community service in the United States is used primarily as a probation condition or as a penalty for trifling crimes like motor vehicle offenses. This is a pity because community service is a burdensome penalty that meets with widespread public approval (e.g., Doble, Immerwahr, and Robinson 1991), that is inexpensive to administer, that produces public value, and that can to a degree be scaled to the seriousness of crimes.

Substitution of work to benefit the community for other punishments dates at least from Imperial Rome. Modern use, however, is conventionally dated from a 1960s effort by judges in Alameda County, California, to avoid having to impose fines for traffic violations on low-income women, when they knew that many would be unable to pay and would be in danger of being sent to jail as a result.

The California program attracted widespread interest and influenced the establishment of community service programs in the United States and elsewhere. The English pilot projects in the early 1970s (Young 1979), followed by Scottish pilots in the late 1970s (McIvor 1992), discussed below, both led to programs that have been fully institutionalized as a penalty that lies between probation and imprisonment in those countries' sentencing tariffs. In the United States, many millions of dollars were spent in the 1970s by the Law Enforcement Assistance Administration for programs for adults, and by the Office for Juvenile Justice and Delinquency Prevention for programs for children, but with little lasting effect (McDonald 1992).

Community service did not come into widespread use as a prison alternative in the United States (Pease [1985] and McDonald [1986] provide detailed accounts with many references). Largely as a result, there has been little substantial research on the effectiveness of community service as an intermediate punishment (Pease 1985; Morris and Tonry 1990, chap. 6; McDonald 1992).

With the exception of one major American study (McDonald 1986), the most ambitious evaluation research has been carried out elsewhere. In England and Wales, Scotland, and the Netherlands, community service orders (CSOs) were statutorily authorized with the express aim that they serve as an alternative to short-term incarceration. In each of those countries, research was undertaken to discover whether CSOs were being used as replacements for short-term prison sentences (generally, yes, in about half of the cases) and whether their use had any effect on recidivism rates for new crimes (generally, no). The American study, of a pilot community service program in New York City intended to substitute for jail terms up to six months, reached similar results (McDonald 1986).

In law and in practice, CSOs are regarded in England as more intrusive and punitive than probation and as an appropriate substitute for imprisonment (Lloyd 1991). CSOs can involve between 40 and 240 hours of work supervised by a community service officer; failure to participate or cooperate can result in revocation. It is generally estimated that half of those sentenced to community service would otherwise be sentenced to prison and half to less severe penalties (Pease 1985). Reoffending rates are believed and generally found to be neither higher nor lower than those of comparable offenders sent to prison (Pease 1985).

The Scottish experience trails several years behind the English but closely resembles it. An experimental program was established in 1977, permanent enabling legislation was enacted in 1978, and CSOs were implemented nationwide in the early 1980s. Offenders are sentenced to 40 to 240 hours work to be completed within one year. A five-year-long evaluation concluded that half of offenders sentenced to CSOs would otherwise have been confined, that both judges and offenders thought community service an appropriate penalty, and that reconviction rates after three years (63 percent) compared favorably with reconviction rates following incarceration (McIvor 1992, 1993).

The story in the Netherlands, where 10 percent of convicted offenders were sentenced to community service in 1992 and where government policy calls for successive annual 10 percent increases in the number of CSOs ordered, is similar. Pilot projects began in 1981 with the express aim of establishing a penalty that would be used in place of short terms of imprisonment. The British pattern of a maximum sentence of 240 hours to be performed within one year was followed. Evaluations reached the by-now expected conclusion that recidivism rates were no better or worse but that judges were using CSOs both for otherwise prison-bound and otherwise suspended sentence-bound offenders (with the balance as yet unknown) (van Kalmthout and Tak 1992; Tak 1995). In 1989, the Penal Code was amended to institutionalize CSOs as authorized sanctions.

The only well-documented American community service project, operated by the Vera Institute of Justice, was established in 1979 in the Bronx, one of the boroughs of New York, and eventually spread to Manhattan, Brooklyn, and Queens. The program was designed as a credible penalty for repetitive property offenders who had previously been sentenced to probation or jail and who faced a six-month or longer jail term for the current conviction. Offenders were sentenced to seventy hours community service under the supervision of Vera foremen. Participants were told that attendance would be closely monitored and that nonattendance and noncooperation would be punished. An agreement was struck with the judiciary that immediate arrest warrants would be issued and prompt revocation hearings held for noncompliant participants. The goal was to draw half of participants from the target jail-bound group and half from offenders with less extensive records; after initial judicial reluctance was overcome (when only a third were jail diversions), the 50/50 balance was achieved. An extensive and sophisticated evaluation concluded that recidivism rates were unaffected by the program, that prison diversion goals were met, and that the program saved taxpayers' money (McDonald 1986, 1992).

For offenders who do not present unacceptable risks of future violent (including sexual) crimes, a punitive sanction that costs much less than prison to implement, that promises no higher reoffending rates, and that presents negligible risks of violence by those who would otherwise be confined, has much to commend it.

Both American and European research and experience show that community service can serve as a meaningful, cost-effective sanction for offenders who would otherwise have been imprisoned. Why it has not been used in that way in the United States is a matter for conjecture, to which I return in section III.

Monetary Penalties

Monetary penalties for nontrivial crimes have yet to catch on in the United States. That is not to deny that millions of fines are imposed every year. Studies conducted as part of a fifteen-year program of fines research coordinated by the Vera Institute of Justice showed that fines are nearly the sole penalty for traffic offenses and in many courts are often imposed for misdemeanors (Hillsman, Sichel, and Mahoney 1984; Cole et al. 1987). And in many courts, most fines are collected. Although ambiguous lines of authority and absence of institutional self-interest sometimes result in haphazard and ineffective collection, courts that wish to do so can be effective collectors (Cole 1992).

Nor is it to deny that convicted offenders in some jurisdictions are routinely ordered to pay restitution and in most jurisdictions are routinely ordered to pay growing lists of fees for probation supervision, for urinalyses, and for use of electronic monitoring equipment. A survey of monetary exactions from offenders carried out in the late 1980s identified more than thirty separate charges, penalties, and fees that were imposed by courts, administrative agencies, and legislatures (Mullaney 1988). These commonly included court costs, fines, restitution, and payments to victim compensation funds. They often included a variety of supervision and monitoring fees, and in some jurisdictions (including the federal system under the Sentencing Reform Act of 1984) extended to repayment to the government of the full costs of prosecution and of carrying out any sentence imposed.

The problem is neither that monetary penalties are not imposed nor that they cannot be collected, but that, as George Cole and his colleagues reported when summarizing the results of a national survey of judges' attitudes about fines, "At present, judges do not regard the fine alone as a meaningful alternative to incarceration or probation" (Cole et al. 1987).

This American inability to see fines as serious penalties stands in marked contrast to the legal systems of other countries. In the Netherlands, the fine is legally presumed to be the preferred penalty for every crime, and Section 359(6) of the Code of Criminal Procedure requires judges to provide a statement of reasons in every case in which a fine is not imposed (Tak 1994a, 1994b). In Germany in 1986, for another example, 81 percent of all sentenced adult criminals were ordered to pay a fine, including 73 percent of those convicted of crimes of violence (Hillsman and Greene 1992, p. 125). In 1991, 83.8 percent of all sentences were fines (Albrecht 1995, p. 8). In Sweden in 1979, fines constituted 91 percent of all sentences (Casale 1981). In England in 1980, fines were imposed in 47 percent of convictions for indictable offenses (roughly equivalent to American felonies); these included 45 percent of convicted sex offenders, 24 percent of burglars, and half of those convicted of assault (Morris and Tonry 1990, chap. 4).

European monetary penalties take two forms that are seldom used in the United States. The first is the "day fine," in use in the Scandinavian countries since the turn of the century and in Germany since the 1970s, which scales fines both to the defendant's ability to pay (some measure of daily income) and to the seriousness of the crime (expressed as the number of daily income units assessed) (Grebing 1982). The second is the use of the fine as a prosecutorial diversion device; in exchange for paying the fine, often the amount that would have been imposed after conviction, the criminal charges are dismissed.

Only the day fine has attracted much American attention. Some of the efforts to establish day-fine systems are discussed below. First, though, some discussion of the remarkable success of prosecutorial diversion programs seems warranted. In Sweden, prosecutors routinely invite defendants they intend to charge to accept a fine calculated on day-fine principles in exchange for dismissal of the charges. Nearly 70 percent of fines are imposed in this way (Casale 1981; Morris and Tonry 1990, p. 144).

Under Section 153a of the German Code of Criminal Procedure, in effect since 1974, the prosecutor if "convinced of the defendant's guilt" may propose a conditional dismissal under which the defendant agrees to pay a fine. The judge must approve the arrangement (approval is seldom withheld). The defendant need not confess guilt. Two hundred forty thousand cases were resolved by conditional dismissal in 1989, constituting a 16 percent reduction in indictments that would otherwise have been filed (Weigend 1993).

In the Netherlands, the 1983 Financial Penalties Act authorized prosecutors to resolve criminal cases by means of an arrangement comparable to the German conditional dismissal. Defendants charged with crimes bearing maximum prison sentences up to six years are eligible. The prosecution is terminated but can be reinstated if the defendant commits a new crime within three years. The prosecutorial diversion program has been credited with keeping the number of criminal trials stable between 1980 and 1992, despite a 60 percent increase in recorded crime. Two-thirds of criminal cases are settled out of court by prosecutors (Tak 1994*a*).

Despite the substantial successes of fines as part of prosecutorial diversion programs in Sweden, Germany, and the Netherlands, the day fine has received principal attention as a penal import from Europe. The results to date are at best mildly promising. The initial pilot project was conducted in Staten Island, New York, in 1988–89, again under the auspices of the Vera Institute of Justice. Judges, prosecutors, and other court personnel were included in the planning, and implementation was remarkably successful. Most judges cooperated with the new voluntary scheme, the distribution of fines imposed changed in ways that showed that judges were following the system, the average fine imposed increased by 25 percent, the total amount ordered on all defendants increased by 14 percent, and 70 percent of defendants paid their fines in full (Hillsman and Greene 1992).

The Staten Island findings, while not unpromising, are subject to two important caveats. First, the participating court had limited jurisdiction and handled only misdemeanors; the use of day fines for felonies thus remains untested. Second, applicable statutes limited total fines for any charge to $250, $500, or $1,000, depending on the misdemeanor class, and thus artificially capped fines at those levels and precluded meaningful implementation of the scheme in relation to other than the lowest-income defendants.

A second modest pilot project was conducted for twelve weeks in 1989 in Milwaukee (McDonald, Greene, and Worzella 1992), and four projects funded by the Bureau of Justice Assistance operated for various periods between 1992 and 1994 in Maricopa County (Phoenix), Arizona, Bridgeport, Connecticut, Polk County, Iowa, and Coos, Josephine, Malheur, and Marion Counties in Oregon (Turner 1992). The Milwaukee project applied only to noncriminal violations, resulted in reduced total collections, and was abandoned. The Phoenix project, known as FARE (for Financial Assessments Related to Employability), was conceived as a mid-level sanction between unsupervised and supervised probation (Greene 1995b). The Iowa pilot included only misdemeanants and the Oregon projects included misdemeanants and probationable felons (excluding Marion County, the largest, which covered only misdemeanants). Only in Connecticut did the pilot cover a range of felonies and misdemeanors.

A RAND Corporation evaluation of the Arizona, Connecticut, Iowa, and Oregon projects was funded by the National Institute of Justice but no results had been released by June 1995. Given the limited reach of the projects, however, the results are unlikely to demonstrate that day fines show promise of becoming an intermediate sanction capable—as in Europe—of diverting large numbers of felony offenders from prison.

A further cautionary note comes from England and Wales which tried, unsuccessfully, to launch a day-fine system (because calculations were based on weekly rather than daily income, it was called a "unit-fine" system). Following a pattern that previous mentions of English research on electronic monitoring, ISP, and community service orders will make familiar, pilot projects to test the feasibility of unit fines were established in four magistrates' courts and evaluated by the Home Office Research and Planning Unit. The findings were positive: magistrates and other court personnel were pleased with the new system, anticipated problems about learning defendants' incomes proved soluble, low-income defendants received smaller fines, and more fines were fully paid, and earlier, than previously (Moxon, Sutton, and Hedderman 1990; Moxon 1992). As a result, the Criminal Justice Act 1991, which effected a substantial overhaul of English sentencing laws, established a national system of unit fines to take effect in October 1992.

The unit-fine system was abandoned seven months later. The immediate precipitant was a series of media stories of preposterous sentences that discredited the entire system. In one case, a defendant was fined £1,200 (late in 1995, $1,920) for throwing a potato chip bag on the ground. In another much-publicized case, a defendant was fined £500 for illegal parking after his car, worth £250, broke down on a road where parking was prohibited (Moxon 1993).

Why those (and many comparable) cases were sentenced as they were, and why the government so quickly repudiated its own innovation, is unclear. The immediate problem was over-literal application of the system. The minimum unit was set at £4 and the maximum unit at £100. To deal with the problem of defendants who do not provide income information, the policy was set in many magistrates' courts that the maximum authorized amount would be presumed to apply in such cases. What was not planned for was default cases in which the defendant does not appear. What could have been a £20 fine in the illegal parking case became instead £500. In the littering case, the £1,200 fine was reduced to £48 on appeal.

The specific problems that deprived the scheme of its credibility and led to its repeal were soluble. Some observers speculated that many magistrates disapproved in principle what were in effect sentencing guidelines for fines and used over-literal enforcement to undermine them. Some blamed the developers for setting the maximum unit amount too high (£20 was the limit in the pilot projects) and for not anticipating foreseeable problems in implementation and application. Whatever the true explanation, the system is no longer, and developers of day fine systems in the United States will ignore the English experience at their peril.

III. Is There a Future for Intermediate Sanctions?

Despite the seemingly disheartening evaluation findings that suggest that most intermediate sanctions do not reduce recidivism, corrections costs, and prison crowding while simultaneously enhancing public safety, there is a future for intermediate sanctions.

There is a need for credible, enforceable sanctions between prison and probation that can provide appropriate deserved penalties for offenders convicted of mid-level crimes, and numerous studies document the capacity of well-managed corrections departments to implement such programs. There is a need, for their sake and ours, to help offenders establish conventional, law-abiding patterns of living, and the evaluation literature suggests ways that can be facilitated. There is a need to develop intermediate sanctions that can serve as cost-effective substitutes for confinement, and the evaluation literature suggests how that can be done. Finally, there is a need to devise ways to assure that intermediate sanctions are used for the kinds of offenders for whom particular programs were created, and experience with parole and sentencing guidelines shows how that can be done.

Three major obstacles stand in the way. The first, the most difficult, is the modern American preoccupation with absolute severity of punishment and the related widespread view that only imprisonment counts. The average lengths of prison sentences in the United States are much greater than in other Western countries (Tonry 1995a, table 7.1; Killias, Kuhn, and Rônez 1995, tables 1 and 2). The ten-, twenty-, and thirty-year minimum sentences for drug crimes that are now in vogue are unimaginable in most countries. Despite a trebling in the average severity of prison sentences for violent crimes between 1976 and 1989 as documented by the National Academy of Sciences Panel on the Understanding and Control of Violence (Reiss and Roth 1993), and additional increases since 1989, federal crime legislation passed in 1994 conditions prison construction grants to states on substantial additional increases in sentences for violent offenders, using 1993 averages as a base (Wallace 1994).

This absolute severity frustrates efforts to devise intermediate sanctions for the psychological (not to mention political) reason that few other sanctions seem commensurable with a multiyear prison sentence. Data presented previously, for example, show that half or more offenders convicted of violent crimes in Sweden, Germany, and England are sentenced to fines (abandonment of unit fines in England did not result in a reduction in use of fines, which continued to be imposed on a "tariff" fixed-amount basis).

In those countries, the prison sentences thereby avoided would have involved months or at most a few years, making a burdensome financial penalty an imaginable alternative. By contrast, most of the American day-fine pilot projects would use day fines as punishments for misdemeanors or noncriminal ordinance violations or as a mid-level punishment between supervised and unsupervised probation. Likewise, with the rare exception of New York's community service project started by the Vera Institute, CSOs are generally ordered as probation conditions and not as sentences in their own right.

Data presented previously, for another example, document successful efforts to replace prison sentences of six or fewer months (moderately severe penalties in those countries) with day fines in Germany (Weigend 1992) and with community service orders in the Netherlands (Tak 1995).

In Sweden, however, less than a quarter of prison sentences are to terms of six months or longer (Jareborg 1995) and in the Netherlands less than 15 percent are for a year or longer. Equivalent crimes in the United States would be punished by terms measured in years; in 1991, 90 percent of state inmates were sentenced to terms longer than one year and 57 percent to terms longer than five years (Beck et al. 1993).

Because the modern emphasis on absolute severity of punishment is the product of partisan and ideological politics, it will not readily be changed. It does, however, stand in the way of substantial development of a continuum of punishments in which moderately punitive and intrusive sanctions serve as penalties—in place of incarceration—for moderately severe crimes.

The second, not unrelated, obstacle to fuller development of intermediate sanctions is widespread commitment to just deserts rationales for punishment and the collateral idea that the severity of punishment should vary directly with the seriousness of the crime. This has been translated in the federal and many state sentencing guidelines systems into policies that tie punishments to the offender's crime and criminal history and little else.

Such policies and their commitment to "proportionality in punishment" constitute a gross oversimplification of the cases that come before criminal courts. Crimes that share a label can be very different; robberies range from schoolyard takings of basketballs to gangland assaults on banks. Offenders committing the same crime can be very different; a thief may have been motivated by a sudden impulse, by the need to feed a hungry child, by a craving to buy drugs, or by a conscious choice to make a living as a thief.

Punishments likewise vary. Despite a common label, two years' imprisonment can be served in a maximum security prison of fear and violence, in a minimum security camp, at home under house arrest, or in some combination of these and other regimes. Even a single punishment may be differently experienced; three years' imprisonment may be a rite of passage for a young gang member, a death sentence for a frail seventy-year-old, or the ruin of the lives of an employed forty-year-old man and his wife and children.

Nonetheless, commitment to ideas of proportionality is widespread and it circumscribes the roles that intermediate sanctions can play. Although few people would disagree with the empirical observations in the preceding paragraph, sentencing policies based on ideas of proportionality somehow reify the sentencing categories into something meaningful. If guidelines specify a twenty-four-month prison term for offense X with criminal history Y, it seems unfair to sentence an offender to community service or house arrest when another like-situated (in the narrow terms of the guidelines) is sentenced to twenty-four months. It seems more unfair to sentence one offender subject to a twenty-four-month presumptive guidelines sentence to house arrest when another offender convicted of a less serious crime receives an eighteen-month prison sentence.

Commitment to proportionality interacts with the modern penchant for severe penalties. If crimes punished by months of incarceration in other countries are punished in years in the United States, comparisons between offenders are more stark. If in Sweden, two offenses are ordinarily punished by thirty- and sixty-day prison terms, imposition of a day-fine order on the offender charged with the more serious crime, out of consideration for the effects of a prison term on his family and employment, produces a contrast between a thirty-day sentence and a sixty-unit day fine. Convert the example to American presumptive sentences of two and four years, and the contrast is jarring between community service or a fine for one offender and a two-year sentence for someone convicted of a less serious crime.

Net-widening is the third obstacle to further development of intermediate sanctions. As discussed earlier, there is a natural tension between practitioners making decisions in individual cases and policy makers setting general goals for programs. In a jurisdiction that lacks well-developed community penalties, judges and prosecutors understandably want to use new programs for what seem to them suitable offenders. From the perspective of system planners, however, sentencing otherwise probation-bound offenders to a program intended for prison-bound offenders frustrates the purpose of the program.

There are two solutions to the net-widening problem. The first is to shift control over program placements from judges to corrections officials wherever possible. For some programs such as boot camps and back-end forms of ISP and house arrest, this is relatively easy and would make it likelier that such programs would achieve their goals of saving money and prison space without increasing recidivism rates.

Transfers of authority to corrections officials can, however, at best be a partial solution. No one (whom I know or can imagine) wants all sentencing authority shifted into bureaucratic hands, and judges therefore are likely to retain authority to decide who will be sent to jail or prison. A slightly more plausible alternative would be to limit judicial authority to the choice between prison and probation and to allow probation and prison authorities to decide what other sanction (house arrest, ISP, treatment participation, etc.) should be applied either as probation conditions or as custodial regimes.

Few people would want to place primary authority over questions of confinement in bureaucratic hands. Judges are after all concerned with questions of liberty and justice and most people would probably rest easier having judges make threshold decisions about confinement. In addition, it is hard to imagine any role for fines and community service in a sentencing system where judges lacked authority to order such sentences.

The alternative is to structure judges' decisions about intermediate sanctions by use of sentencing guidelines. A substantial body of evaluation and other research demonstrates that well-conceived and implemented guidelines systems can change sentencing patterns in a jurisdiction and achieve high levels of judicial compliance (sometimes as in the federal guidelines, grudging compliance) (Tonry 1993*c*).

Most state guidelines systems establish presumptions for who is sent to state prisons and for how long, but do not set presumptions concerning nonprison sentences or choices between prison and other sanctions. Two broad approaches for setting guidelines for nonprison sentences have been tried (the literature is tiny: von Hirsch, Wasik, and Greene 1989; Morris and Tonry 1990).

The first, which seems to have been a dead end, is to establish "punishment units" in which all sanctions can be expressed. Thus, a year's confinement might equal ten units, a month of house arrest three units, and a month's community service two units. A twenty-unit sentence could be satisfied by any sanction or combination of sanctions equaling twenty. This idea was taken furthest in Oregon, where sentencing guidelines, in addition to setting presumptive ranges for jail and prison sentences, specified a number of punishment units for many crime/criminal history combinations. Oregon, however, never set meaningful policies governing unit values, sometimes described as exchange rates, and neither there nor anywhere else has the idea been taken further.

The overwhelming problem lies in the idea of proportionality mentioned earlier, and can be illustrated by Washington State's more modest effort at exchange rates. Partial confinement and community service were authorized as substitutes for presumptive prison terms on the basis of one day's partial confinement or three days' community service for one day of confinement. The partial confinement/confinement exchange is probably workable (for very short sentences; house arrest, assuming that to count as partial confinement, is seldom imposed for more than a few months), but the community service exchange is not.

Starting with the idea that imprisonment is more unpleasant than community service, the Washington commission decided that the exchange must be governed by an idea of comparable intrusion in the offender's life; hence three eight-hour days' community service per day in prison. The difficulty is that for community service programs to be credible, they must be enforced, and experience in this country and elsewhere instructs that they must be short. That is why the New York program provided seventy hours' obligation and the Dutch, English, and Scottish programs establish an upper limit of 240 hours. Under Washington's policy, that range would permit community service only in place of three to ten days' confinement.

It is easy to criticize the Oregon commission for not carrying its innovation further and the Washington commission for lack of imagination, but that would be unfair. Working out exchange rates in a system predicated on strong ideas of proportionality in punishment is very difficult, if not impossible. If punitive literalism governs, the range for substitution between prison and community penalties is tiny. A system like New York's community service program—seventy hours' work in place of six months' jail—can be justified (the idea was to give repetitive property offenders some meaningful enforced penalty rather than impose a jail term that no one expected would have deterrent effects), but it requires a loosening of proportionality constraints that no sentencing commission has yet been prepared to accept. Pennsylvania's commission in 1993 gave serious consideration to a punishment unit system but abandoned it when the problem of exchange rates proved insoluble. (There are other problems with the punishment rate approach: inevitably the exchange rates are arbitrary; if conditions like treatment participation, drug testing, and electronic monitoring are given unit values, comparisons between offenders become even more implausible.)

The second approach is to establish different areas of a guidelines grid in which different presumptions about choice of sentence govern. One set of crime/criminal history combinations is presumed appropriate only for prison sentences; a second is presumed subject to a judicial choice between prison sentences or intensive community sanctions (including split sentences with elements of both); a third is presumed subject to a choice between intensive or nonintensive community sanctions (or some of both); and a fourth is presumed subject only to nonintensive community sanctions. A system like this was proposed by the District of Columbia Superior Court Sentencing Commission in 1987, but never took effect. Both North Carolina and Pennsylvania adopted such systems in 1994; how they will work in practice remains to be seen.

Readers, I hope, will draw at least six conclusions from this chapter. First, for offenders who do not present unacceptable risk of violence, well-managed intermediate sanctions offer a cost-effective way to keep them in the community at less cost than imprisonment and with no worse later prospect for criminality.

Second, boot camps, house arrest, and intensive supervision are highly vulnerable to net-widening when entry is controlled by judges. For boot camps, the solution is easy: have corrections officials select participants from among admitted prisoners. For house arrest and ISP, the solution is less easy: corrections officials can control entry to back-end programs; sentencing guidelines may be able to structure judges' decisions about admission to front-end programs.

Third, community service and monetary penalties remain woefully underdeveloped in the United States and much could be learned from Europe. Day fines remain a promising idea, but have yet to demonstrate that they can win acceptance as a penalty for nontrivial crimes. Conditional discharges, in which convictable defendants pay a substantial fine in exchange for conditional dismissal of charges, like those common in

Sweden, the Netherlands, and Germany, remain unexplored as a potentially useful European penal import.

Fourth, front-end intermediate sanctions are unlikely to come into widespread use as prison alternatives unless sentencing theories and policies become more expansive and move away from oversimplified ideas about proportionality in punishment.

Fifth, intermediate sanctions may offer promise as a way to get and keep offenders into drug and other treatment programs. With drug treatment programs, at least, there is evidence that coerced treatment programs can reduce both later drug use and later crimes, and there are suggestions in the ISP and boot camp literatures that these programs can increase treatment participation.

Sixth, there is no free lunch. Most intermediate sanctions have failed to achieve promised reductions in recidivism, cost, and prison use, but those promises were never realistic, even though they were, for the most part, offered in good faith. Intermediate sanctions can reduce costs and divert offenders from imprisonment, but those results are not easy to obtain.

5

Mandatory Penalties

The greatest gap between knowledge and policy in American sentencing concerns mandatory penalties. Experienced practitioners and social science researchers have long agreed, for practical and policy reasons discussed in this chapter, that mandatory penalties are a bad idea. That is why nearly every authoritative nonpartisan organization that has considered the subject, including the American Bar Association (1968, standard 2.3; 1994, standard18–3.21[b]), the American Law Institute (1962), and the Federal Courts Study Committee (1990), has opposed enactment, and favored repeal, of mandatory penalties. That is also why the U.S. Congress in 1970 repealed most of the mandatory penalty provisions then contained in federal law (U.S. Sentencing Commission 1991*b*).

No one who has lived in the United States in recent years, however, can be unaware that conservative politicians have consistently promoted passage of more and harsher mandatories. The widespread promotion of "three strikes and you're out" laws, following passage of Washington State's 1993 referendum, is but the latest example. There are many others. Between the mid-1970s and the mid-1980s, every American state enacted at least one new mandatory penalty law. The U.S. Congress has repeatedly since 1984 enacted new mandatory sentencing laws and increased penalties under existing ones. Although new mandatory penalties were contained in the federal crime bill enacted in 1994, Republican leaders of the U.S. Congress, immediately after learning that their party had won control of both houses, decried the "leniency" of the newly enacted law and promised to introduce more mandatory penalty provisions.

There may be no inconsistency between practitioners' and researchers' conclusions that mandatory penalties are undesirable because they achieve few of their ostensible purposes, and politicians' continued calls for more.

Most practitioners and scholars are concerned with the substance of criminal justice policies: do they achieve their goals, can they be justly administered, are they cost-effective, do they produce unwanted and unintended side effects? In our time, by contrast, many elected officials are concerned with the symbolism of criminal justice policies. (Remember Willie Horton?) Crime, along with welfare and immigration, has become a potent symbol in partisan and ideological conflicts, and the substantive as opposed to the political effectiveness of policies may be unimportant to many who propose and enact them.

This chapter's aim nonetheless is to summarize what is known about the effectiveness and effects of mandatory penalties. Sooner or later, the combination of chronic prison overcrowding, budgetary crises, and a changed professional climate will make more public officials willing to pay attention to what we have long known about mandatory penalties. Officials in some states (there seems little hope in the foreseeable future at the federal level) may in coming years be more inclined than in the recent past to make policy choices based on knowledge of how mandatory penalties operate in practice.

Evaluated in terms of their stated substantive objectives, mandatory penalties do not work. The record is clear from research in the 1950s, the 1970s, the 1980s, and the 1990s that mandatory penalty laws shift power from judges to prosecutors, meet with widespread circumvention, produce dislocations in case processing, and too often result in imposition of penalties that everyone involved believes to be unduly harsh. From research in the 1970s and 1980s, the evidence is also clear that mandatory penalties have either no demonstrable marginal deterrent effects or short-term effects that rapidly waste away.

That mandatory penalties have more costs than benefits does not mean that rational social policies might not incorporate serious penalties for serious crimes. More effective, less costly measures are available. In every era, some kinds of crime are regarded as so serious that harsh penalties appear called for. Examples in our time include aggravated forms of stranger violence, nonfamilial sexual abuse of young children, and flagrant fraudulence in the financial markets.

Assuming that legislators want to provide for severe penalties for especially serious crime, there are ways to avoid or ameliorate the foreseeable dysfunctional effects of mandatory penalties. Here are four. First, in order to establish policies calling for severe penalties for serious crimes, while allowing sufficient flexibility to avoid foreseeable unintended consequences, make penalties for especially serious crimes presumptive rather than mandatory. Prosecutors and judges both have powerful voices in sentencing; disregard of the presumption would often require that both agree either that the penalty would be too severe in a particular case or that the political climate has altered and public sensibilities no longer demand especially harsh penalties.

Second, if existing mandatory penalty laws are not repealed, legislators should add "sunset provisions" to them and include such provisions in any proposals for new mandatories. This would assure that laws passed in the passion of the moment will not endure for decades. Legislators can much more comfortably accede to the lapse of a punitive law than vote for its repeal.

Third, lengthy prison terms—whether subject to mandatories or not—should be limited to serious crimes like armed robbery, aggravated rape, and murder. The most widespread and cynical circumventions of mandatory penalty laws, and the most extreme injustices in individual cases, arise under laws requiring severe penalties for minor crimes like possession or trafficking of small amounts of drugs.

Fourth, correctional officials should be authorized to reconsider release dates of all offenders receiving prison sentences exceeding a designated length (say five or ten years). This would allow eventual release of people receiving unusually long sentences, life sentences without eligibility for parole, and sentences under "habitual offender" or three-strikes laws, without requiring extraordinary political decisions like gubernatorial pardons or commutations.

This chapter summarizes the available research on the implementation, operation, and deterrent effectiveness of mandatory sentencing laws. Section I examines research on deterrent effects. Sections II and III are chronological and survey the evolution of knowledge concerning mandatory penalties since the eighteenth century. Section II examines research before 1970. Section III examines the major recent empirical evaluations of mandatory penalties, beginning with the most ambitious, the U.S. Sentencing Commission's 1991 study of federal mandatories and the 1978 evaluation of New York's "Rockefeller Drug Laws." Section IV tries to make sense of those findings and to outline their implications for officials who want simultaneously to respond to public anxiety about serious crime and yet enact laws that waste as few public resources, foster as few hypocrisies, and do as little injustice as possible.

I. Deterrent Effects

The primary and strongest argument for mandatory penalties is that their enactment and enforcement deter would-be offenders and thereby reduce crime rates and spare victims' suffering. This claim, if true, makes a powerful case. Unfortunately, both the accumulated evidence and expert opinion agree that it is not true.

Insight into the deterrent effectiveness of mandatory penalties can be sought in two places. First, for understandable reasons, governments in many countries have asked advisory committees or national commissions to survey knowledge of the deterrent effects of criminal penalties in general, and many such reports have been completed. Second, evaluations have been conducted of the deterrent effects of newly enacted mandatory penalties.

National Advisory Bodies

No one doubts that society is safer having some penalties for crime rather than none at all, but that choice is not in issue. On the real-world question of whether increases in penalties significantly reduce the incidence of serious crimes, the consensus conclusion of governmental advisory bodies in many countries is maybe, a little, at most, but probably not.

After the most exhaustive examination of the question ever undertaken, the National Academy of Sciences Panel on Research on Deterrent and Incapacitative Effects concluded, "In summary . . . we cannot assert that the evidence warrants an affirmative conclusion regarding deterrence" (Blumstein, Cohen, and Nagin 1978). The panel's principal consultant on the subject, Professor Daniel Nagin of Carnegie-Mellon University, was less cautious: "The evidence is woefully inadequate for providing a good estimate of the magnitude of whatever effect may exist. . . . Policymakers in the criminal justice system are done a disservice if they are left with the impression that the empirical evidence . . . strongly supports the deterrence hypothesis" (Nagin 1978).

The most recent comparable examination of the evidence, by the National Academy of Sciences Panel on Understanding and Control of Violent Behavior, reached a similar conclusion in 1993. After documenting that the average prison sentence per violent crime *tripled* between 1975 and 1989, the panel asked, "What effect has increasing the prison population had on violent crime?" and answered, "Apparently very little" (Reiss and Roth 1993). That answer took account of both deterrent and incapacitative effects. It is not irrelevant that the panel's work was initiated at the request of President Reagan's Department of Justice and funded by both the Reagan and Bush administrations; the panel was an establishmentarian body bearing the imprimatur of conservative Republican administrations.

Similar bodies in other Western countries have reached similar conclusions. British Prime Minister Margaret Thatcher's government created a Home Office advisory committee on criminal penalties (the Home Office is the functional equivalent of the U.S. Department of Justice). The resulting white paper, which led to an overhaul of English sentencing laws, expressed skepticism about the deterrent effects of penalties: "Deterrence is a principle with much immediate appeal. . . . But much crime is committed on impulse, given the opportunity presented by an open window or unlocked door, and it is committed by offenders who live from moment to moment; their crimes are as impulsive as the rest of their feckless, sad, or pathetic lives. It is unrealistic to construct sentencing arrangements on the assumption that most offenders will weigh up the possibilities in advance and base their conduct on rational calculation" (Home Office 1990).

Similar conclusions were earlier reached by a Canadian national commission that was created to consider changes in Canadian sentencing laws: "Evidence does not support the notion that variations in sanctions (within a range that reasonably could be contemplated) affect the deterrent value of sentences. In other words, deterrence cannot be used, with empirical justification, to guide the imposition of sentences" (Canadian Sentencing Commission 1987).

Negative findings concerning the deterrent effects of penalties are not unique to English-speaking countries. The Finnish government made a conscious policy decision in the mid-1970s to reduce the prison population from what was seen as unacceptably high levels, and succeeded. The incarceration rate per 100,000 population fell by 40 percent between 1976 and 1992. The policy decision was based in large part on an examination of evidence on deterrence. A report issued by the Finnish National Research Institute of Legal Policy explained: "Can our long prison sentences be defended on the basis of a cost/benefit assessment of their general preventive effect? The answer of the criminological expertise was no" (Törnudd 1993).

Alfred Blumstein, chairman of National Academy of Sciences panels on deterrence and incapacitation (Blumstein, Cohen, and Nagin 1978), sentencing research (Blumstein et al. 1983), and criminal careers (Blumstein et al. 1986), and America's leading authority on crime-control research, explained why, on empirical grounds, three-strikes laws (and by implication many mandatory penalties) are misconceived: "However hard it is for rational folks to conceive of it, there are some people who simply do not respond when a threat is presented to them. The problem is that any serious three-strikes candidate probably falls into that category. For people who see no attractive options in the legitimate economy, and who are doubtful that they will live another ten years in any event, the threat of an extended prison stay is likely to be far less threatening than it would be to a well-employed person with a family" (Blumstein 1994).

Although proponents of mandatory penalties generally argue that the penalties will reduce crime rates through their deterrent effects, three-strikes laws are sometimes also premised on incapacitative rationales. Here too the clear weight of research findings is inconsistent with proponents' claims. In the 1970s, vigorous arguments were made (e.g., Wilson 1975) that crime would be reduced substantially by adoption of policies calling for incarceration of all defendants convicted of particular crimes (sometimes called "collective incapacitation"). The National Academy of Sciences Panel on Research on Deterrent and Incapacitative Effects, however, soon demonstrated that such a policy would be ineffective. Most offenders commit few or no additional offenses; the vast increase in prison populations required to implement such policies could not be justified in cost-benefit terms (Blumstein, Cohen, and Nagin 1978; Cohen 1983). Few informed calls for adoption of collective incapacitation policies have been made since the early 1980s.

In the early 1980s, however, proposals were made for "selective incapacitation" policies of incarceration of high-rate offenders (Greenwood with Abrahamse 1982). Marvin Wolfgang, Robert Figlio, and Thorsten Sellin (1972), among others, had shown that as few as 5 to 8 percent of offenders commit half or more of all offenses. Proponents of selective incapacitation, cognizant of the impracticability of collective incapacitation policies, accordingly proposed extended confinement of the small percentage of offenders who commit large numbers of crimes.

The National Academy of Sciences Panel on Criminal Careers and "Career Criminals" considered the evidence concerning selective incapacitation and concluded that it, too, was impracticable (Blumstein et al. 1986; also see Cohen 1983). The insuperable empirical problem was that no system of prediction could be developed that could identify high-rate serious offenders in advance with ethically defensible and economically affordable accuracy. Even the best prediction instruments overpredicted by 3 or 4 to 1. For each future high-rate offender incapacitated, two or three other people would also have to be confined for an extended period.

A related problem is that serious offending is highly age-specific. The highest rates of commission of violent crimes occur in the late teenage years and early twenties and of property crimes in the upper teenage years (Blumstein 1994, figs. 17.4 and 17.5). Put another way, people begin to desist from property crimes after age seventeen and from violent crimes after age twenty-two. By the time offenders have accumulated enough convictions to make it reasonable to conclude that they are high-rate serious offenders, many will have reached ages at which they will soon desist from offending in any event. Extended confinement of such people will result in relatively little but very expensive crime prevention through incapacitation. As a consequence of the problems of overprediction and the age-specific character of offending, informed proposals for selective incapacitation have seldom been made since the mid-1980s.

Deterrent Effects of Mandatory Penalties

Because few studies have attempted to examine mandatory penalty laws' deterrent effects, and because the clear weight of the evidence on the deterrent effects of marginal manipulation of penalties demonstrates few or no effects (e.g., Blumstein, Cohen, and Nagin 1978), I do not explore that literature in detail.

A number of studies were made of the crime-preventive effects of a Massachusetts law requiring a one-year minimum sentence for people convicted of possession of an unregistered firearm. The studies concluded that it had either no deterrent effect on the use of firearms in violent crimes (Beha 1977; Rossman et al. 1979; Carlson 1982) or a small short-term effect that quickly disappeared (Pierce and Bowers 1981).

Studies in other states reached similar results. An evaluation of a mandatory sentencing law for firearms offenses in Detroit, Michigan, concluded, "the mandatory sentencing law did not have a preventive effect on crime" (Loftin, Heumann, and McDowall 1983). Assessments of the deterrent effects of mandatory penalty laws in Tampa, Jacksonville, and Miami, Florida, "concluded that the results did not support a preventive effect model" (Loftin and McDowall 1984). The results of evaluations of the crime-preventive effects of mandatory penalty laws in operation in Pittsburgh and Philadelphia, Pennsylvania, "do not strongly challenge the conclusion that the statutes have no preventive effect" (McDowall, Loftin, and Wiersema 1992).

Only one major study has concluded that mandatory penalties have deterrent effects, and it did so only through statistical sleight of hand. David McDowall, Colin Loftin, and Brian Wiersema (1992), the team of researchers who conducted the Michigan, Florida, and Pennsylvania studies mentioned in the preceding paragraph, combined the data from all three states and concluded that mandatory penalties for gun crimes reduced gun homicides but not assaults or robberies involving guns. This is counterintuitive. Homicides by definition are lethal assaults and the ratios of assaults and robberies that involve guns and result in deaths should be relatively stable. If the proportions of assaults and robberies involving guns decline, gun homicides should decline commensurately, and vice versa. McDowall and his colleagues attribute the counterintuitive pattern of findings to "a lack of precision in the data."

The more likely explanation is that the homicide findings are wrong. The problem with the study is that the results were obtained only by combining the data from six separate studies, each of which had found no deterrent effects, and then analyzing the data as if they had come from one study. With that larger data set, a small but statistically significant deterrent effect was found. This happened because of the way tests of statistical significance work. The larger the data set, the smaller an effect must be to be significant. When a coin is flipped and comes up heads six times out of ten, the result is not statistically significant at the .05 level even though heads came up 50 percent more often than tails. If a coin is flipped 1,000 times and comes up heads 475 times, the result is significant at the .05 level. Put another way, a tiny absolute difference can be statistically significant if the data set is large enough.

Thus the single confirmatory study can be construed in two ways, neither of which lends much support to mandatory penalties. Either the data lacked "precision" (the authors' reason for disregarding the contrary finding concerning assaults and robberies) and the entire analysis therefore lacks credibility, or a tiny deterrent effect was found that is inconsistent with all of the other major studies to date.

Ironically, most mandatory penalty provisions enacted during the 1980s and 1990s concerned drug crimes, behaviors that both practitioners and researchers believe to be uniquely insensitive to the deterrent effects of sanctions. Despite risks of arrest, imprisonment, injury, and death, drug trafficking offers economic and other rewards to disadvantaged people that far outweigh any available in the legitimate economy. Market niches created by the arrest of dealers are as a result often filled within hours, as many studies of drug marketing by ethnographers have shown (e.g., Johnson et al. 1990; Padilla 1992; Fagan 1993). As a result, according to Alfred Blumstein: "there is no evidence that harsh drug law enforcement policies have been at all successful. Of course, that result is not surprising. Anyone who is removed from the street is likely to be replaced by someone drawn from the inevitable queue of replacement dealers ready to join the industry. It may take some time for recruitment and training, but experience shows that replacement is easy and rapid" (Blumstein 1994).

Both police officials and conservative scholars agree. James Q. Wilson (1990, p. 534) has observed that "significant reductions in drug abuse will come only from reducing demand for those drugs. . . . the marginal product of further investment in supply reduction [law enforcement] is likely to be small." He reports: "I know of no serious law-enforcement official who disagrees with this conclusion. Typically, police officials tell interviewers that they are fighting a losing war or, at best, a holding action" (p. 534). Similarly, U.S. Senator Daniel Patrick Moynihan of New York, a sometime supporter of the drug wars, has acknowledged: "'drug busts' are probably necessary symbolic acts, but nothing more" (1993).

The research on the effectiveness of mandatory penalties for drug crimes also agrees. One of the largest studies ever undertaken of the effects of mandatory penalties, an evaluation of the "Rockefeller Drug Laws," which required severe mandatory minimum sentences for drug crimes and forbade plea bargaining to avoid the laws' application, found no discernible effects on drug use or crime in New York (Joint Committee on New York Drug Law Evaluation 1978). The proliferation of mandatory penalties for drug crimes in the 1980s did not demonstrably reduce drug trafficking (Reuter and Kleiman 1986, table 5; Moore 1990, fig. 1).

No matter which body of evidence is consulted—the general literature on the deterrent effects of criminal sanctions or the evaluation literature on mandatory penalties—the conclusion is the same. There is little basis for believing that mandatory penalties have any significant effects on rates of serious crime. The list of problems with mandatory penalties, however, only begins with their crime-prevention ineffectiveness. They do great harm to the integrity of case processing and sentencing and often result in the imposition of manifestly unjust punishments.

II. Mandatory Penalties before 1970

The foreseeable problems in implementing mandatory penalties have been well known for two hundred years. Most systematic empirical research postdates 1970. This section summarizes knowledge to that date. Perhaps the best way to summarize past knowledge concerning mandatory penalties is to quote from a U.S. House of Representatives report that explained why the Congress in 1970 repealed almost all federal mandatory penalties for drug offenses. "The severity of existing penalties, involving in many instances minimum mandatory sentences, has led in many instances to reluctance on the part of prosecutors to prosecute some violations, where the penalties seem to be out of line with the seriousness of the offenses. In addition, severe penalties, which do not take into account individual circumstances, and which treat casual violators as severely as they treat hardened criminals, tend to make conviction . . . more difficult to obtain" (House of Representatives 1970, quoted in U.S. Sentencing Commission 1991*b*, pp. 6–7). Our knowledge in the 1990s concerning mandatory penalties is little different. More to the point, knowledge in the 1790s was much the same.

The least subtle way to avoid imposition of harsh penalties is to nullify them by refusing to convict offenders subject to them. "Nullification," a term in common usage for more than two centuries, encapsulates the process by which judges and juries, but particularly juries, willfully refuse to enforce laws or apply penalties that seem to them unjust. Oliver Wendell Holmes, Jr., described the jury's capacity to nullify harsh laws as its central virtue (Holmes 1889). Roscoe Pound claimed that "jury lawlessness is the great corrective of law in its actual administration" (1910, p. 18). John Baldwin and Michael McConville, in a review of jury research, observed: "The refusal of juries to convict in cases of criminal libel, the 'pious perjury' they welcomed in order to avoid conviction on a capital offense, the indulgence shown toward 'mercy killings,' and the nullification of the Prohibition laws during the 1920s are simply the most famous examples of this exercise of discretion" (1980, p. 272). The leading criminal law casebook in use in American law schools for thirty years, Jerome Michael and Herbert Wechsler's *Criminal Law and Its Administration* (1940), gave lengthy consideration to nullification.

The Death Penalty in Eighteenth-Century England

The death penalty in eighteenth- and nineteenth-century England was the subject of policy debates strikingly like late-twentieth-century American debates about mandatory penalties. In July 1991, in the face of claims that newly proposed mandatory penalty laws would overburden the courts and have little practical effect, one congressman told the *New York Times,* "Congressmen and senators are afraid to vote no" on crime and punishment bills, "even if they don't think it will accomplish anything." A senate aide suggested that "it's tough to vote against tough sentences for criminals" (Ifill 1991). At the end of the eighteenth century, Edmund Burke declared "that he could obtain the consent of the House of Commons to any Bill imposing the punishment of death" (Select Committee on Capital Punishment 1930, paras. 10, 11). Samuel Romilly, England's most celebrated contemporary prison reformer, by contrast, repeatedly called for repeal of capital punishment provisions because the laws were applied erratically and unfairly and because the erratic application inevitably undermined the laws' deterrent effects (Romilly 1820). During the reigns of the four British Kings George, between 1714 and 1830, the British Parliament created 156 new capital offenses. By 1819, British law recognized 220 capital offenses, most of them property crimes.

During the same period, however, the number of executions carried out not only failed to increase commensurately with the passage of new laws but declined. Executions were four times more common in the early 1600s than in the mid-1700s (Hay 1975, p. 22). According to Sir Leon Radzinowicz, executions in the late eighteenth century varied between a low of twenty-one per year during the 1780s and a high of fifty-three in the 1790s (Radzinowicz 1948–68, vol. 1, pp. 141, 147).

Douglas Hay (1975), in a famous essay "Property, Authority, and the Criminal Law," explained the contrast between continuous extension of the reach of the death penalty and steady decline in the incidence of its use. He argued that the explanation can be found in the efforts of propertied classes in the early years of the Industrial Revolution to protect their class interests through passage of laws that symbolically emphasized the importance of private property (by making numerous property crimes punishable by death). At the same time these propertied classes operated a legal system that both provided exemplary punishments and, by making frequent merciful exceptions and observing procedural rules, supported its own public legitimacy. In this period before the creation of professional police departments and widespread use of prisons for punishment, the civil peace depended on general acceptance of the legitimacy of the existing social order.

More important, however, are the methods used in practice to avoid carrying out death sentences. First, and most important, juries often refused to convict offenders; an acquittal is a simple but effective way to avoid a mandatory penalty (Baldwin and McConville 1980, p. 272). A variant, which has twentieth-century echoes, was for the jury to convict of a lesser offense. According to a 1930 report of the British Select Committee on Capital Punishment describing eighteenth-century practices: "In vast numbers of cases, the sentence of death was not passed, or if passed was not carried into effect. For one thing, juries in increasing numbers refused to convict. A jury would assess the amount taken from a shop at £4. 10d. so as to avoid the capital penalty which fell on a theft of £5. In the case of a dwelling, where the theft of 40s. was a capital offense, even when a woman confessed that she had stolen £5, the jury notwithstanding found that the amount was only 39s. And when . . . the legislature raised the capital indictment to £5, the juries at the same time raised their verdicts to £4 19s" (Select Committee on Capital Punishment 1930, para. 17).

Second, as more capital offenses were created, the courts adopted increasingly narrow interpretations of procedural, pleading, and evidentiary rules. Prosecutions seemingly well founded as a factual matter would fall because a name or a date was incorrect or a defendant's occupation was wrongly described as "farmer" rather than "yeoman" (Radzinowicz 1948–68, vol. 1, pp. 25–28, 83–91, 97–103; Hay 1980, pp. 32–34).

Third, increasing numbers of offenders were accorded protection from death under the doctrine of "benefit of clergy." A doctrine that initially protected clergymen from execution following convictions at civil (as opposed to religious) courts, benefit of clergy was extended to literate layman in the medieval period and to all accused in 1706. Its effect was to exempt first offenders convicted of lesser felonies from execution (Baker 1977, p. 41).

Fourth, among those who were sentenced to death, the proportion executed declined steadily. According to the Select Committee on Capital Punishment, "the Prerogative of the Crown [pardon] was increasingly exercised. Down to 1756 about two thirds of those condemned were actually brought to the scaffold; from 1756 to 1772 the proportion sank to one-half. Between 1802 and 1808 it was no more than one-eighth" (1930, para. 21). Most of those pardoned received substituted punishments of a term of imprisonment or transportation (Stephen 1883, vol. 1, chap. 13).

Briefly to summarize, experience with "mandatory" capital punishment in eighteenth-century England instructed all who would pay attention that mandatory penalties, especially for crimes other than homicide, elicited a variety of adaptive responses from those charged to enforce the law, including juries' refusals to convict "guilty" offenders and decisions to bring in convictions for less serious charges not subject to the penalty, development of technical procedural devices used by judges to discharge cases, and extensive use of pardons and other postconviction devices to avoid carrying out executions.

American Mandatory Penalties in the 1950s

Our best source of information on criminal court processes in the 1950s, the various reports emanating from the American Bar Foundation's Survey of the Administration of Criminal Justice in the United States, confirms the lessons from eighteenth-century England. Frank Remington, director of the eighteen-year project, in the foreword to the sentencing volume, noted, "Legislative prescription of a high mandatory sentence for certain offenders is likely to result in a reduction in charges at the prosecution stage, or if this is not done, in a refusal of the judge to convict at the adjudication stage. The issue . . . thus is not solely whether certain offenders should be dealt with severely, but also how the criminal justice system will accommodate to the legislative charge" (Dawson 1969, p. xvii).

The American Bar Foundation survey was conceived as an empirical investigation and description of the administration of criminal justice in the United States. "Pilot studies" were undertaken in several states in the mid-1950s. As the enormity of the project became apparent, the pilot studies became the survey and led to the publication of five volumes based on extensive reviews of files, interviews, and participant observation (including *Conviction* [Newman 1966], *Prosecution* [Miller 1969], and *Sentencing* [Dawson 1969]). Several volumes deal with charging, case processing, and sentencing aspects of mandatory penalties.

The survey's findings on mandatories are exemplified by three processes the reports describe. First, Donald Newman describes how Michigan judges dealt with a lengthy mandatory minimum for drug sales: "Mandatory minimums are almost universally disliked by trial judges. . . . The clearest illustration of routine reductions is provided by reduction of sale of narcotics to possession or addiction. . . . Judges . . . actively participated in the charge reduction process to the extent of refusing to accept guilty pleas to sale and liberally assigning counsel to work out reduced charges. . . . To demonstrate its infrequent application, from the effective date of the revised law (May 8, 1952) to the date of tabulation four years later (June 30, 1956), only twelve sale-of-narcotics convictions were recorded in Detroit out of 476 defendants originally charged with sale. The remainder (except a handful acquitted altogether) pleaded guilty to reduced charges" (1966, p. 179).

Second, on a related subject (avoidance of long statutory maximum sentences), Newman (1966, p. 182) describes efforts to avoid fifteen-year mandatory maximum sentences for breaking-and-entering and armed robbery: "In Michigan conviction of armed robbery or breaking and entering in the nighttime (fifteen-year maximum compared to five years for daytime breaking) is rare. The pattern of downgrading is such that it becomes virtually routine, and the bargaining session becomes a ritual. The real issue in such negotiations is not whether the charge will be reduced but how far, that is, to what lesser offense. As has been pointed out, armed robbery is so often downgraded that the Michigan parole board tends to treat a conviction for unarmed robbery as prima facie proof that the defendant had a weapon. And the frequency of altering nighttime burglary to breaking and entering in the daytime led one prosecutor to remark: 'You'd think all our burglaries occur at high noon.'"

Third, Robert Dawson (1969, p. 201) describes "very strong" judicial resistance to a twenty-year mandatory minimum for sale of narcotics: "All of the judges of Recorder's Court, in registering their dislike for the provision, cited the hypothetical case of a young man having no criminal record being given a twenty-year minimum sentence for selling a single marijuana cigarette. Charge reductions to possession or use are routine. Indeed, in some cases, judges have refused to accept guilty pleas to sale of narcotics, but have continued the case and appointed counsel with instructions to negotiate a charge reduction."

These findings from the American Bar Foundation survey differ in detail from those of eighteenth-century England, but only in detail. When the U.S. Congress repealed most mandatory penalties for drug offenses in 1970, it was merely acknowledging enforcement problems that had been recognized for centuries.

III.   Mandatory Penalties in the 1970s, 1980s, and 1990s

Despite earlier generations' understanding of why mandatory penalties are unsound policy, mandatory sentencing laws since 1975 have been America's most popular sentencing innovation. By 1983, forty-nine of the fifty states (Wisconsin was the holdout) had adopted mandatory sentencing laws for offenses other than murder or drunk driving (Shane-DuBow, Brown, and Olsen 1985, table 30). By 1994, every state had adopted mandatory penalties; most had several (Austin et al. 1994). Most mandatories apply to murder or aggravated rape, drug offenses, felonies involving firearms, or felonies committed by persons who have previous felony convictions. Between 1985 and mid-1991, the U.S. Congress enacted at least twenty new mandatory penalty provisions; by 1991, more than sixty federal statutes defined more than one hundred crimes subject to mandatories (U.S. Sentencing Commission 1991b, pp. 8–10).

The experience in most states in the late 1980s and early 1990s was similar. In Florida, for example, seven new mandatory sentencing bills were enacted between 1988 and 1990 (Austin 1991, p. 4). In Arizona, for another example, mandatory sentencing laws were so common that 57 percent of felony offenders in fiscal year 1990 were subject to mandatory sentencing enhancements (Knapp 1991, p. 10).

The political attractiveness of mandatory sentencing laws is not difficult to understand. During the 1980s many political figures of both parties campaigned on "tough on crime" platforms and few elected officials dared risk being seen as "soft." A *New York Times* story captures the climate in its title: "Senate's Rule for Its Anti-crime Bill: The Tougher the Provision, the Better" (Ifill 1991). Mandatories are often targeted on especially disturbing behaviors, such as large-scale drug sales, murder, or rape, or especially unattractive characters, such as repeat violent offenders or people who use guns in violent crimes. In the case of firearms offenses, mandatory laws allow the state, like Janus, to frown on law-defying villains who use firearms for criminal purposes and to smile on law-abiding citizens who use firearms for legitimate purposes. In a nation in which most sensible approaches to control of gun use are politically impracticable, mandatory sentencing laws are a mechanism for attempting to deter illegal gun use and encourage offenders to use less lethal weapons.

Although the uninitiated citizen might reasonably believe that, under a mandatory sentencing law, anyone who commits the target offense will receive the mandated sentence, the reality is more complicated. Sentencing policy can only be as mandatory as police, prosecutors, and judges choose to make it. The people who operate the criminal justice system generally find mandatory sentencing laws too inflexible for their taste and take steps to avoid what they consider unduly harsh, and therefore unjust, sentences. And, frequently, the mandatory sentencing law is simply ignored. For example, in Minnesota in 1981, of persons convicted of weapons offenses to which a mandatory minimum applied, only 76.5 percent actually received prison sentences (Knapp 1984, p. 28).[1]

Research on mandatory sentencing laws during the 1970s and 1980s reveals a number of avoidance strategies. Boston police avoided application of a 1975 Massachusetts law calling for mandatory one-year sentences for persons convicted of carrying a gun by decreasing the number of arrests made for that offense and increasing (by 120 percent between 1974 and 1976) the number of weapons seizures without arrest (Carlson 1982). Prosecutors often avoid application of mandatory sentencing laws simply by filing charges for different, but roughly comparable, offenses that are not subject to mandatory sentences. Judges too can circumvent such laws. Detroit judges sidestepped a 1977 law requiring a two-year sentence for persons convicted of possession of a firearm in the commission of a felony by acquitting defendants of the gun charge (even though the evidence would support a conviction) or by decreasing the sentence they would otherwise impose by two years to offset the mandatory two-year term (Heumann and Loftin 1979).

Considerable recent research taken together, like the work of earlier generations, supports the following generalizations:

1. lawyers and judges will take steps to avoid application of laws they consider unduly harsh;
2. dismissal rates typically increase at early stages of the criminal

---

1. One striking form of plea bargaining around mandatory penalties occurs in Arizona, where Knapp (1991, pp. 10–11) found that 3,739 (24 percent) of 15,720 felony convictions in 1990 were for the inchoate offenses of attempt and conspiracy. Inchoate offenses are not subject to mandatory penalties. Defendants charged with completed felonies subject to mandatories are routinely allowed to bargain down to inchoate offenses.

justice process after effectuation of a mandatory penalty as practitioners attempt to shield some defendants from the law's reach;

3. defendants whose cases are not dismissed or diverted make more
vigorous efforts to avoid conviction and to delay sentencing,
which results in increased trial rates and case processing times
increase;

4. defendants who are convicted of the target offense are often sentenced more severely than they would have been in the absence of
the mandatory penalty provision; and

5. because declines in conviction rates for those arrested tend to
offset increases in imprisonment rates for those convicted, often
the overall probability that defendants will be incarcerated
remains about the same after enactment of a mandatory sentence
law.[2]

The empirical evidence concerning the operation of mandatory sentencing laws comes primarily from five major studies. One is the U.S.
Sentencing Commission's 1991 study of mandatory penalties in the U.S.
federal courts (U.S. Sentencing Commission 1991*b*). The second concerns the Rockefeller Drug Laws, which required mandatory prison sentences for persons convicted of a variety of drug felonies (Joint Committee on New York Drug Law Evaluation 1978). One concerns the
operation of a 1977 Michigan law requiring imposition of a two-year
mandatory prison sentence on persons convicted of possession of a gun
during commission of a felony (Loftin and McDowall 1981; Loftin,
Heumann, and McDowall 1983). Two concern a Massachusetts law
requiring a one-year prison sentence for persons convicted of carrying a
firearm unlawfully (Beha 1977; Rossman et al. 1979).

U.S. Sentencing Commission Report

Were federal officials more interested in rational policy making than in
political posturing, the U.S. Sentencing Commission report, *Mandatory
Minimum Penalties in the Federal Criminal Justice System,* would result
in repeal of all mandatory penalties.

The commission's report demonstrates that mandatory minimum
sentencing laws unwarrantedly shift discretion from judges to prosecutors, result in higher trial rates and lengthened case processing times,
arbitrarily fail to acknowledge salient differences between cases, and

---

2. This finding recurs in research on mandatories in the 1970s. Whether it will be
found in the 1990s is unknown. The U.S. Sentencing Commission study of mandatory
penalties, like earlier research, revealed longer case processing times and lower guilty plea
rates than for non-mandatory-penalty crimes but does not consider whether incarceration
probabilities, given an arrest, have changed.

often punish minor offenders much more harshly than anyone involved believes is warranted. Interviews with judges, lawyers, and probation officers at twelve sites showed that heavy majorities of judges, defense counsel, and probation officers disliked mandatory penalties; prosecutors were about evenly divided. Finally, and perhaps not surprisingly given the other findings, the report shows that judges and lawyers not uncommonly circumvent mandatories.

The commission's study was prompted by a congressional mandate. The congressional charge had eight parts, including an assessment of the effects of mandatories on sentencing disparities, a description of the interaction between mandatories and plea bargaining, and "a detailed empirical research study of the effect of mandatory minimum penalties in the Federal system."

The commission's research design effectively combined methods and data sources for investigating charging, bargaining, and sentencing patterns. The combination of quantitative analyses of 1984–90 sentencing patterns, a detailed quantitative analysis of case processing in 1990, and various interviews and surveys aimed at capturing officials' opinions provide complementary sources of information. In presenting and discussing findings, the report carefully notes the limits of the claims it can make and describes alternative interpretations of findings.

The commission analyzed three data sets describing federal sentencing and two sources of data concerning the opinions of judges, assistant U.S. attorneys, and others. The three sentencing data sets were FPSSIS,[3] U.S. Sentencing Commission monitoring data for fiscal year 1990, and a 12.5 percent random sample from the commission's file of defendants sentenced in fiscal year 1990.[4] Data for the random sample were augmented by examining computerized and paper case files to identify cases (there proved to be 1,165 defendants) that met statutory criteria for receipt of a mandatory minimum drug or weapon sentence.

The two sources of data on practitioners' opinions were structured interviews in twelve sites of 234 practitioners (forty-eight judges, seventy-two assistant U.S. attorneys, forty-eight defense attorneys, sixty-six probation officers), and a May 1991 mail survey of 2,998 practitioners (the same groups as were interviewed; 1,261 had responded by the time the report was written).

---

3. FPSSIS, pronounced "fipsiss," is an acronym for "Federal Probation Sentencing and Supervision Information System," the administrative office of the U.S. courts' automated information system for federal sentencing.

4. The FPSSIS and monitoring data are insufficiently detailed to permit the fine-grained factual analyses of actual offense behavior that are required to determine whether facts alleged in specific cases might warrant filing of mandatory-bearing charges. As a result, those data sources are used to provide more general portraits of sentencing patterns over time and in 1990.

Results of the Sentencing Analyses

The sentencing data revealed a number of patterns that the commission found disturbing. First, there were clear indications that prosecutors often did not file charges carrying mandatory minimums when the evidence supported such charges. For one example, prosecutors failed to file charges for mandatory weapons enhancements against 45 percent of drug defendants for whom they would have been appropriate. For another, prosecutors failed to seek mandatory sentencing enhancements for prior felony convictions in 63 percent of cases in which they could have been sought. For a third, defendants were charged with the offense carrying the highest applicable mandatory minimum in only 74 percent of cases.

Second, there were clear indications that prosecutors used mandatory provisions tactically to induce guilty pleas. For one example, among defendants who were fully charged with applicable mandatory sentence charges and who were convicted at trial, 96 percent received the full mandatory minimum sentence; by contrast, 27 percent of those who pled guilty pled to charges bearing no mandatory minimum or a lower one. For another example, of all defendants who pled guilty (whether or not initially charged with all the applicable mandatory-bearing charges), 32 percent had no mandatory minimum at conviction and 53 percent were sentenced below the minimum that the evidence would have justified. For a third example, among those defendants against whom mandatory weapons enhancements were filed, the weapons charges were later dismissed in 26 percent of cases.

Third, mandatories increased trial rates and presumably also increased workloads and case processing times. Nearly 30 percent of those convicted of offenses bearing mandatory minimums were convicted at trial, a rate two-and-one-half times the overall trial rate for federal criminal defendants.

Fourth, there were indications that judges (often presumably with the assent of prosecutors) imposed sentences less severe than applicable mandatory provisions would appear to require. Before examples are given, it bears mention that the U.S. Sentencing Commission's "modified real offense" policies direct judges, especially in drug cases, to sentence on the basis of actual offense behavior and not simply the offense of conviction.

A number of the commission's findings suggest that judges are often willing to work around, and under, the mandatories. Forty percent of all defendants whose cases the commission believed warranted specific mandatory minimums received shorter sentences than the applicable statutes would have specified. Mandatory minimum defendants received downward departures 22 percent of the time. The commission observes that "the increased departure rate may reflect a greater tendency to exercise prosecutorial or judicial discretion as the severity of the penalties increases" (U.S. Sentencing Commission 1991*b*, p. 53). To like effect, "The prosecutors' reasons for reducing or dismissing mandatory charges . . . may be attributable to . . . satisfaction with the punishment received" (U.S. Sentencing Commission 1991*b*, p. 58).

Taken together, these findings suggested to the commission that mandatory minimums were not working. They were shifting too much discretion to the prosecutor. They were provoking judges and prosecutors willfully to circumvent their application (U.S. Sentencing Commission 1991*b*, pp. ii, 76). They were producing high trial rates and unacceptable sentencing disparities.

Two studies confirm some of the commission's principal findings. First, a series of analyses of plea bargaining under the federal guidelines conducted under the direction of University of Chicago law professor Stephen Schulhofer showed that prosecutors and defense counsel, in nearly a third of cases examined, manipulated the guidelines, often with tacit judicial approval, to permit sentence reductions (Schulhofer and Nagel 1989; Nagel and Schulhofer 1992). This finding may not surprise readers who are familiar with criminal courts; plea bargaining is common everywhere and sentence reductions are directly or indirectly what defendants want in exchange for guilty pleas. The federal courts, however, according to U.S. Sentencing Commission policies, are supposed to work differently. To prevent prosecutorial sentencing concessions, the federal guidelines provide that sentencing is to be based on the defendant's "actual offense behavior," including behavior that was the subject of dismissed charges (or even of charges as to which juries have found the defendant not guilty). For prosecutors to reduce sentences through plea bargaining, they must take very deliberate actions (such as accepting pleas only to offenses with maximum authorized sentences less than guidelines specify or conspiring with defense counsel, and sometimes the judge to ignore aspects of the crime or the defendant's criminal record that would require a harsher sentence).

Schulhofer's conclusion that sentences in a third of cases are reduced by prosecutorial manipulation is probably an underestimate. The manipulations are in violation of commission (and often Department of Justice) policies and sometimes involve judicial acquiescence. Neither assistant U.S. attorneys nor judges have an interest in announcing their willful evasion of sentencing guidelines and mandatory penalties. It seems likely that some surreptitious sentencing concessions went undiscovered by Schulhofer and his colleagues.

The second more recent relevant study of federal sentencing illustrates why practitioners would work so hard to avoid mandatories. A 1994 analysis of the federal prison population showed that 16,316 federal prisoners (36.1 percent of drug offenders and 21.2 percent of the prison population) were "low-level drug law violators . . . non-violent offenders with minimal or no prior criminal history whose offense did not involve sophisticated criminal activity" (U.S. Department of Justice 1994, pp. 2102–2103). The average sentence for these prisoners, two-thirds of whom had been sentenced under mandatory minimum laws, was 81.5 months. It is not surprising that many practitioners are willing to be hypocritical to avoid imposition of seven-year prison sentences on minor nonviolent offenders.

Results of the Opinion Surveys

No category of federal court practitioners, including prosecutors, much likes mandatory minimum sentencing laws (U.S. Sentencing Commission 1991*b*, chap. 6). In one-hour structured interviews, thirty-eight of forty-eight federal district court judges offered unfavorable comments. The most common were that the mandatory sentences are too harsh and that they eliminate judicial discretion. Among forty-eight defense counsel, only one had anything positive to say about the mandatory penalties, and he also had negative comments. The most common complaints were that the mandatories are too harsh, that they result in too many trials, and that they eliminate judicial discretion. Probation officers were also overwhelmingly hostile to the mandatories; their most common complaints were that the mandatories are too harsh, result in prison overcrowding, and eliminate judicial discretion. Only among prosecutors was sentiment more favorable to mandatories, and even then thirty-four of sixty-one interviewed who expressed a view were wholly (twenty-three) or partly (eleven) negative.

Consistent with the interview data, the mail survey showed that 62 percent of judges, 52 percent of private counsel, and 89 percent of federal defenders want mandatories for drug crimes eliminated, compared to only 10 percent of prosecutors and 22 percent of probation officers. In a similar vein, a 1993 Gallup Poll survey of judges who are members of the American Bar Association found that 82 percent of state judges and 94 percent of federal judges disapproved of mandatory minimums (*ABA Journal* 1994). A 1994 Federal Judicial Center survey reported that 72 percent of circuit court judges and 86 percent of district court judges moderately or strongly support changes in "current sentencing rules to increase the discretion of the judge" (Federal Judicial Center 1994).

The Rockefeller Drug Laws in New York

Perhaps the most exhaustive examination of mandatory sentencing laws before the commission's work was an evaluation of the later repealed Rockefeller Drug Laws in New York. These laws took effect in New York on September 1, 1973. They prescribed severe mandatory prison sentences for narcotics offenses and included statutory limits on plea bargaining. A major evaluation (Joint Committee on New York Drug Law Evaluation 1978) focused primarily on the effects of the drug laws on drug use and drug-related crime and only to a lesser extent on case processing. The study was based primarily on analyses of official record data routinely collected by public agencies. The key findings were these:

1. Drug felony arrests, indictment rates, and conviction rates all declined after the law took effect.
2. For those who were convicted, however, the likelihood of being imprisoned and the average length of prison term increased.
3. The two preceding patterns canceled each other out and the likelihood that a person arrested for a drug felony would be imprisoned was the same—11 percent—after the law took effect as before.
4. Because defendants struggled to avoid the mandatory sentences, the proportion of drug felony dispositions resulting from trials tripled between 1973 and 1976, and the average time required for processing of a single case doubled.

Table 5.1 shows case processing patterns for drug felony cases in New York during the period 1972–76. The percentage of drug felony arrests resulting in indictments declined steadily from 39.1 percent in 1972, before the law took effect, to 25.4 percent in the first half of 1976. Similarly, the likelihood of conviction, given indictment, declined from 87.3 percent in 1972 to 79.3 percent in the first half of 1976. Of those defendants, however, who were not winnowed out earlier, the likelihood

Table 5.1. Drug Felony Processing in New York State

Stage	1972	1973*	1974	1975	1976 (January–June)
Arrests	19,269	15,594	17,670	15,941	8,166
Indictments					
N	7,528	5,969	5,791	4,283	2,073
Percent of arrests	39.1	38.3	32.8	26.9	25.4
Indictments disposed	6,911	5,580	3,939	3,989	2,173
Convictions					
N	6,033	4,739	3,085	3,147	1,724
Percent of dispositions	87.3	84.9	78.3	78.9	79.3
Prison and jail sentences					
N	2,039	1,555	1,074	1,369	945
Percentage of convictions	33.8	32.8	34.8	43.5	54.8
Percentage of arrests	10.6	10.0	6.1	8.6	11.6

Source: Joint Committee (1978), tables 19, 24, 27, 29.

*The drug law went into effect September 1, 1973.

that a person convicted of a drug felony would be incarcerated increased from 33.8 percent in 1972 to 54.8 percent in 1976.

The usual explanation for those findings is that practitioners made vigorous efforts to avoid application of the mandatory sentences in cases in which they viewed those sentences as being too harsh, and that the remaining cases were dealt with harshly as the law dictated (Blumstein et al. 1983, pp. 188–89). Thus, the percentage of drug felonies in New York City disposed of after a trial rose from 6 percent in 1972 to 17 percent in the first six months of 1976 (Joint Committee on New York Drug Law Evaluation 1978, p. 104). In other words, many fewer defendants pled guilty, and the trial rate tripled. No doubt as a consequence of the increased trial rates, it "took between ten and fifteen times as much court time to dispose of a case by trial as by plea," and the average case processing time for disposed cases increased from 172 days in the last four months of 1973 to 351 days in the first six months of 1976. Backlogs rose commensurately notwithstanding the creation of thirty-one additional criminal courts in New York City for handling of drug prosecutions (Joint Committee on New York Drug Law Evaluation 1978, tables 33–35, p. 105).

Sentencing severity increased substantially for defendants who were eventually convicted. Only 3 percent of sentenced drug felons received minimum sentences of more than three years between 1972 and 1974 under the old law. Under the new law, the percentage of convicted drug felons receiving sentences of three years or longer increased to 22 percent. The likelihood that a person convicted of a drug felony would receive an incarcerative sentence increased in New York State from 33.8 percent in 1972, before the new law took effect, to 54.8 percent in the first six months of 1976 (Joint Committee on New York Drug Law Evaluation 1978, pp. 99–103).

The broad pattern of findings in the New York study, while more stark in New York than in other mandatory sentencing jurisdictions that have been evaluated, recurs throughout the impact evaluations. The Rockefeller Drug Laws' effects were more than the system could absorb, and many key features were repealed in mid-1976.

Massachusetts's Bartley-Fox Amendment

Massachusetts's Bartley-Fox Amendment required imposition of a one-year mandatory minimum prison sentence, without suspension, furlough, or parole, for anyone convicted of unlawful carrying of an unlicensed firearm. An offender need not have committed any other crime; the Massachusetts law thus was different from many mandatory sentencing firearms laws that require imposition of a minimum prison sentence for the use or possession of a firearm in the commission of a felony.

Two major evaluations of the Massachusetts gun law were conducted (Beha 1977; Rossman et al. 1979). Some background on the Boston courts may make the following discussion of their findings more intelligible. The Boston Municipal Court is both a trial court and a preliminary hearing court. If defendants are dissatisfied with either their conviction or their sentence, they may appeal to the Suffolk County Superior Court where they are entitled to a trial de novo.

James Beha's analysis (1977) is based primarily on comparisons of police and court records for the periods six months before and six months after the effective date of the mandatory sentencing law. David Rossman and his colleagues (1979) dealt with official records from 1974, 1975, and 1976 supplemented by interviews with police, lawyers, and court personnel.

The primary findings:

1. Police altered their behavior in a variety of ways aimed at limiting the law's reach. They became more selective about whom to frisk; the absolute number of reports of gun incidents taking place out-of-doors decreased, which meant a concomitant decrease in arrests, and the number of weapons seized without arrest increased by 120 percent from 1974 to 1976 (Carlson 1982, p. 6, relying on Rossman et al. 1979).

2. The number of persons "absconding" increased substantially between the period before the law took effect and the period after (both studies).

3. Outcomes favorable to defendants, including both dismissals and acquittals, increased significantly between the before-and-after periods (both studies).

4. Of persons convicted of firearms-carrying charges in Boston Municipal Court, appeal rates increased radically (Beha 1977, table 2). In 1974, 21 percent of Municipal Court convictions were appealed to the Superior Court. By 1976 that rate had increased to 94 percent (Rossman et al. 1979).

5. The percentage of defendants who entirely avoided a conviction rose from 53.5 percent in 1974 to 80 percent in 1976 (Carlson 1982, p. 10, relying on Rossman et al. 1979).

6. Of that residuum of offenders who were finally convicted, the probability of receiving an incarcerative sentence increased from 23 percent to 100 percent (Carlson 1982, p. 8, relying on Rossman et al. 1979).

Thus the broad patterns of findings from the U.S. Sentencing Commission and Rockefeller Drug Law evaluations carry over to Massachusetts: more early dismissals, more protracted proceedings, and increased sentencing severity for those finally convicted.

The Michigan Felony Firearms Statute

The Michigan Felony Firearms Statute created a new offense of possessing a firearm while engaging in a felony and specified a two-year mandatory prison sentence that could not be suspended or shortened by release on parole and that had to be served consecutively to a sentence imposed for the underlying felony. The law took effect on January 1, 1977. The Wayne County prosecutor banned charge bargaining in firearms cases and took measures to enforce the ban, suggesting that the likelihood of circumvention should have been less than was experienced in New York and Massachusetts.

There has been one major evaluation of the Michigan law that gave rise to a number of related publications (Heumann and Loftin 1979; Loftin and McDowall 1981; Loftin, Heumann, and McDowall 1983). Several other articles concerning the Michigan gun law have been published, and one of these (Bynum 1982) also discusses empirical data.

Timothy Bynum's study (1982) demonstrates how prosecutors control the use of mandatory sentencing laws. Drawing on a sample of cases from a statewide data set collected during the course of a sentencing guidelines project, Bynum identified 426 cases that, from records, involved robberies with firearms that were committed after January 1, 1977, and were therefore eligible for prosecution under the felony firearms statute. In only 65 percent of the eligible cases was the firearms charge filed.[5] More indicative, however, of prosecutorial control of mandatory sentencing laws was the finding that in some courts firearms charges were filed in 100 percent of the eligible cases and in other courts firearms charges were filed in none of the eligible cases (Bynum 1982, table 4.1).

Milton Heumann and Colin Loftin observed a strong tendency in Wayne County toward early dismissal of charges other than on the merits, which they interpret as evidence of efforts to avoid applying the mandatory penalties. Their inquiry focused on three offenses that were relatively common: felonious assault, "other assault," and armed robbery. Armed robbery means in Wayne County what it means most places. "Felonious assaults" tend to arise from "disputes among acquaintances or relatives and are, by conventional standards, less predatory than armed robbery." "Other assaults" is an intermediate category of "assault with intent to . . ." offenses. The three offense categories offered a severity continuum. Most armed robberies would generally be perceived as serious crimes. Many felonious assaults would commonly be regarded as

---

5. Milton Heumann and Colin Loftin in their examination of case records to determine the existence and extent of undercharging found that the gun law charge had been made in 96 percent of the eligible cases in Wayne County (1979, p. 407).

impulsive and expressive and less serious than armed robbery. Other assaults are more heterogeneous.

Case processing patterns for felonious assault did not change after the mandatory penalty provision took effect. There was some increase in early dismissal of armed robbery charges and a substantial increase in the rate of early dismissals of "other assault" charges. These findings are consistent with the hypothesis that efforts will be made to avoid application of harsh sentencing laws to defendants for whom lawyers and judges feel that they are inappropriately severe: "other assault" was the offense category in which the greatest ambiguities about culpability were likely to exist.

The probabilities of conviction differed after implementation depending on the offense. Consistent with the Massachusetts findings that mandatory sentences reduce the probability of convictions, Loftin and his colleagues concluded that conviction probabilities declined for felonious assault and armed robbery (Loftin, Heumann, and McDowall 1983, p. 295).

Loftin and his colleagues assessed the impacts of the Felony Firearms Statute on sentencing severity in two ways. Using quantitative methods, they concluded that the statute did not generally increase the probability that prison sentences would be imposed but that, for those receiving prison sentences, it did increase the expected lengths of sentences for some offenses (Loftin, Heumann, and McDowall 1983, pp. 297–98). Using simpler tabular analyses in an earlier article, they concluded that, overall, the percentage of defendants vulnerable to the firearms law who were incarcerated did not change markedly in Wayne County after implementation of the new law (Heumann and Loftin 1979).

As table 5.2 indicates, the probability of receiving a prison sentence, given filing of the charge, increased slightly for felonious assault and other assault and decreased slightly for armed robbery. The probability of incarceration given conviction also did not change markedly for felonious assault or armed robbery but did change for other assault and increased from 57 percent of convictions prior to implementation of the firearms law to 82 percent afterward. This resulted in part from the substantial shift toward early dismissal of other assault charges, reducing the residuum of cases to be sentenced from 65 percent of all cases to 50 percent.

Finally, trial rates remained roughly comparable before and after implementation except for the least serious category of offenses, felonious assaults, for which the percentage of cases resolved at trial increased from 16 percent of cases to 41 percent of cases (Heumann and Loftin 1979, table 4). This is explained by Heumann and Loftin in terms of an innovative adaptive response, the "waiver trial." Either by agreement or by expectation, the judge would convict the defendant of a misdemeanor rather than the charged felony (which made the firearm law

Table 5.2. Disposition of Original Charges in Wayne County, Michigan by Offense Type and Time Period

Original charges	N	Dismissed at/before Pretrial (%)	Dismissed or Acquitted after Pretrial (%)	Convicted/ No Prison (%)	Some Prison (%)	Total (%)
Felonious assault						
Before*	145	24	31	31	14	100
After†	39	26	26	31	18	101
Other assault						
Before	240	12	24	28	37	101
After	53	26	24	9	41	100
Armed robbery						
Before	471	13	19	4	64	100
After	136	22	17	2	60	101

Source: Cohen and Tonry (1983), tables 7–10; adapted from Heumann and Loftin (1979), table 3.

Note: The totals do not always sum to 100 percent because of rounding.

*Offense committed before January 1, 1977, and case disposed between July 1, 1976, and June 30, 1977.

†Offense committed and case disposed between January 1, 1977, and June 30, 1977.

inapplicable because it specified a two-year add-on following conviction of a felony) or would simply, with the prosecutor's acquiescence, acquit the defendant on the firearms charge. Either approach eliminated the mandatory sentence threat and both are consistent with processes described in the American Bar Foundation Survey twenty years earlier to avoid imposition of twenty-year minimum sentences for drug sales (Dawson 1969, p. 201). A third mechanism for nullifying the mandatory sentencing law in cases in which imprisonment would be ordered in any case was to decrease by two years the sentence that otherwise would have been imposed in respect of the underlying felony and then add the two years back on the basis of the firearms law (Heumann and Loftin 1979, pp. 416–24).

Observations on New York, Massachusetts, and Michigan Studies

For a variety of reasons, the Massachusetts, Michigan, and New York laws ought to be especially good illustrations of the operation of mandatory sentencing laws. For differing reasons, vigorous and highly publicized efforts were made to make the mandatory sentencing laws stick. In New York, amidst enormous publicity and massive media attention, the legislature established thirty-one new courts, including creation of additional judges, construction of new courtrooms, and provision of supporting personnel and resources, and expressly forbade some kinds of plea bargaining in an effort to assure that the mandatory sentences were imposed. In Massachusetts, while the statute did not address plea bargaining, it expressly forbade "diversion in the form of continuance without a finding or filing of cases," both devices used in the Boston Municipal Court for disposition of cases other than on the merits. (Filing is a practice in which cases are left open with no expectation that they will ever be closed; continuance without finding leaves the case open in anticipation of eventual dismissal if the defendant avoids further trouble.) In Michigan, while the statute did not address plea bargaining, the Wayne County prosecutor established and enforced a ban on plea bargaining in cases coming within the operation of the mandatory sentencing law. He also launched a major publicity campaign, promising on billboards and bumper stickers that "One with a Gun Gets You Two."

Thus, in all three states, the new laws were accompanied by evidence of seriousness of purpose. If mandatory sentencing laws are to operate as their supporters hope they will, the experience in these three states should provide a good test of the realism of those hopes.

Those hopes are unrealistic. Findings from all three states suggest that mandatory sentencing laws are not an especially effective way to achieve certainty and predictability in sentencing. To the extent that they prescribe sanctions more severe than lawyers and judges believe appropriate, they can be, and are, circumvented. For serious criminal charges, the mandatory sentence laws are often redundant in that offenders are, in any case, likely to receive prison sentences longer than those mandated by statute. For less serious cases, mandatory sentencing laws tend to be arbitrary; they result in either increased rates of dismissal or diversion of some defendants to avoid application of the statute, or occasionally result in sentencing of "marginal" offenders in ways that most parties involved consider unduly harsh.

IV.   Mandatory Penalties as Instruments and Symbols

Officials who support mandatory penalties often do not much care about problems of implementation, foreseeable patterns of circumvention, or the certainty of excessively and unjustly severe penalties for some offenders. Their interests are different, as recent policy debates demonstrate. According to a *New York Times* article about mandatory proposals offered by U.S. Senator Alfonse D'Amato of New York, "Mr. D'Amato conceded that his two successful amendments, which Justice Department officials say would have little practical effect on prosecution of crimes, might not solve the problem. 'But,' he said, 'it does bring about a sense that we are serious'" (Ifill 1991).

Supporters of mandatory penalties in anxious times are concerned with political and symbolic goals. Put positively, elected officials want to reassure the public generally that their fears have been noted and that the causes of their fears have been acted on. Put negatively, officials want to curry public favor and electoral support by pandering, by making promises that the law can at best imperfectly and incompletely deliver.

However their motives are portrayed, for many legislators, their primary purpose has been achieved when their vote is cast. They have been seen to be tough on crime. Calls for enactment of mandatory penalties, or introductions of bills, or castings of votes are symbolic statements. Instrumental arguments about effectiveness or normative arguments about injustice to offenders, whether by Sir Samuel Romilly in eighteenth-century England or by Senator Edward Kennedy in our own place and time, fall on deaf ears.

The dilemma is that the public officials who enact mandatory sentencing laws support them for symbolic and political reasons while the public officials who administer mandatory sentencing laws oppose them for instrumental and normative reasons. The instrumental argument against mandatory penalties is clear. First, they increase public expense by increasing trial rates and case processing times. The U.S. Sentencing Commission study found that trial rates were two-and-one-half times greater (30 percent of dispositions) for offenses bearing mandatory penalties than for other offenses (12 percent of dispositions). Disposition by trial tripled under the Rockefeller Drug Laws (17 percent of dispositions after taking effect versus 6 percent before). In Michigan, dispositions by trial for felonious assaults involving firearms increased from 16 percent to 41 percent after mandatory penalties became applicable.

Second, in every published evaluation, judges and prosecutors were shown to have devised ways to circumvent application of the mandatories. Sometimes prosecutors simply refused to file mandatory-bearing charges. Sometimes plea bargaining was used. Sometimes judges refused to convict. Sometimes judges ignored the statute and imposed sentences inconsistent with it.

The normative arguments against mandatories are also straightforward. First, simple justice: because of their inflexibility, such laws sometimes result in imposition of penalties in individual cases that everyone involved believes to be unjustly severe. Second, perhaps more important, mandatory penalties encourage hypocrisy on the part of prosecutors and judges. To avoid injustices in individual cases, officials engage in the adaptive responses and circumventions described throughout this chapter.

The hypocrisies that mandatory penalties engender are what most troubles prosecutors and judges with whom I speak. Plea bargaining may be a necessary evil, an essential lubricant without which the machinery of justice would break down, but it is typically routinized. Armed robbery is pled down to robbery, aggravated assault to assault, theft 1 to theft 2. Prosecutors, defense counsel, judges, probation officers—all who are involved—know what is happening, understand why, and acknowledge the legitimacy of the reasons.

Mandatory penalties elicit more devious forms of adaptation. When Michigan judges in the 1950s or the 1970s acquit factually guilty defendants, or when Arizona prosecutors in the 1980s permit people who have committed serious crimes to avoid mandatories by pleading guilty to attempt or conspiracy, or when prosecutors and judges fashion new patterns of plea bargaining solely to sidestep mandatories, important values are being sacrificed. Many practitioners find these practices dishonest and tawdry.

Legislators, whatever their purposes for supporting mandatory sentencing laws, once the vote is cast move on to other issues. For judges, prosecutors, and defense counsel, it is another story. They must live with their own consciences and with their shared views of the bounds of fair treatment of offenders. They must also keep the courts functioning. That they sometimes devise ways to avoid application of laws they believe to be uncommonly harsh should come as no surprise.

If the findings of empirical evaluations of mandatory sentencing laws were heeded, there would be no mandatory penalties. Given the American political climate of the 1990s, wholesale repeals are unlikely. A more modest hope is that elected officials will become slightly more responsible about crime-control policy and balance their felt need to make symbolic and rhetorical statements through passage of legislation with well-established knowledge of how mandatories operate in practice. Four suggestions for how that might be done follow.

Making Mandatory Penalties Presumptive

Much of what legislators hope to accomplish with mandatory sentencing laws could be achieved by making such laws presumptive. In a few states, Minnesota is an example, judges are given authority to disregard mandatory penalties and impose some other sentence if reasons are given. Converting all mandatory penalties to presumptive penalties would sacrifice few of the values sought to be achieved by such laws but would avoid many of the undesirable side effects.

By enacting a mandatory (presumptive) penalty law, the legislature would be expressing its policy judgment that, say, people who commit robberies with firearms deserve at least a three-year minimum prison term. Most prosecutors and judges would accept that such policy decisions are the legislature's to make and that that one is not patently unreasonable. The law's facial legitimacy would presumably cause many prosecutors and judges to deal in good faith with it. The law's presumptive character, however, would let judges take account of mitigating circumstances (the defendant was an underage, bullied, unarmed participant who remained in the car) without resort to subterfuge. That the judge possessed authority to decide that special circumstances rebutted the presumption would signal that prosecutors also could legitimately take special circumstances into account in plea bargaining.

If official circumvention of mandatory penalties in cases where they seem unduly harsh is foreseeable, and it is, conversion to mandatory (presumptive) penalties is likely to result in no less systematic enforcement but to avoid hypocritical efforts at avoidance.

Mandatory Penalties and "Sunset" Clauses

Our understandings of the politics and empirical experience of mandatories could be married by including sunset clauses in all future mandatory penalty laws and adding them to existing ones. Sunset clauses provide for automatic repeal of a statute at a fixed time unless a new vote is taken to extend its life. This proposal, first made to my knowledge by Alfred Blumstein of Carnegie-Mellon University at a "presidential crime summit" in 1991, would both acknowledge felt political imperatives and limit the damage mandatory penalties do.

Any honest politician will concede two points: that it is often difficult to resist political pressures to vote for tough penalties, and that it is always difficult to vote to make penalties more "lenient." Blumstein's proposal addresses both propositions. If a charged political climate or campaign, or a series of notorious crimes, makes it difficult to resist "tough-on-crime" proposals, such laws will continue to be enacted. Statute books are cluttered with provisions passed on the passions of moments. Often, however, passions subside with time and competing values and calmer consideration makes the wisdom of such laws less clear. Sunset clauses would permit laws to lapse without the need for legislators to vote for repeal and thereby expose themselves to "soft-on-crime" attacks.

Narrowing Mandatories' Scope

If the bases for passing sentencing laws were concerns for justice and institutional effectiveness, most mandatories would be repealed and few others would be enacted to take their places. That is unlikely. Horrible, senseless crimes do occur, public fears and anxieties are heightened, and elected officials want to respond. There being in practice little that officials can do about crime, the attractions of mandatory penalties as a rhetorical demonstration of concern are great.

If a call for repeal of all mandatories is likely to pass unheard, conceivably a call for a narrowing of their scope to serious violent crimes might be credible. The most extreme versions of nullification and circumvention involve laws that mandate severe penalties for minor crimes. In eighteenth-century England, juries often refused to convict of capital offenses those who were charged with property crimes. In Michigan in the 1950s, judges refused to impose mandatory minimum twenty-year sentences for drug sales. Modern federal prosecutors often work to avoid imposition of lengthy minimum sentences on minor offenders.

Similar instances of imbalance between the gravities of crimes and the severity of penalties are common. In Alabama, for example, any sale of narcotics within three miles of a school provokes a mandatory minimum. While the goal of protecting children from drugs has obvious appeal, the three-mile radius encompasses the entire area of most cities and towns.

One way, therefore, better to balance the symbolic goals of legislators and the instrumental and normative concerns of practitioners would be to confine mandatory penalties to patently serious crimes like homicide and aggravated rape and to maintain a realistic balance between gravity of crimes and severity of punishments.

Correctional Review of Sentences

Little public harm would accrue, and considerable private benefit obtain, if correctional or parole authorities were accorded routine discretion to release prisoners serving mandatory terms after some decent interval (say, five or ten years). Increasing numbers of prisoners are now being held under ten-, twenty-, and thirty-year mandatory minimum terms or under sentences of life without parole. In many states, the steady accumulation of such prisoners promises sizeable long-term increases in prison populations and budgets. More important, many such long-term prisoners continue to be held long after they present any threat to anyone, and long after any clamor for their continuing incarceration has subsided. Under present laws of most states, such prisoners can be released only by pardon or commutation. In our era, these powers are seldom exercised, in part because they expose public officials to "soft-on-crime" attacks.

The argument for administrative reconsideration of lengthy mandatory sentences parallels the argument for sunset clauses in mandatory penalty statutes: some decisions present such excruciating political problems for elected officials that it is better to eliminate the need to make them. Whatever the desirability of repealing a mandatory penalty, or releasing old and harmless prisoners from prison, political vulnerability prevents decisions that on their merits ought to be made. Permitting corrections or parole officials to decide when a prisoner under mandatory sentence has served long enough would remove those decisions from the public eye.

Mandatory penalties is not a subject on which research counts for much in modern America. Policy debates are likely neither to wait for nor depend much on research results. We now know what we are likely to know, and what our predecessors knew, about mandatory penalties. As instruments of public policy, they do little good and much harm. If America does sometime become a "kinder, gentler place," there will be little need for mandatory penalties and academics will have no need to propose "reforms" premised on the inability of elected officials to make sensible decisions. As yet, however, America is neither completely kind nor universally gentle, and proposals such as those offered here might provide mechanisms for reconciling the symbolic and rhetorical needs of elected officials with the legal system's needs for integrity in process and justice in punishment.

6

Judges and Sentencing Policy

Proposals for major changes in sentencing laws or procedures pose a dilemma for judges. Because many such proposals are or appear to be premised on criticism of judges, it is not unnatural for judges to oppose them. If judicial opposition succeeds, the proposed change is forestalled; if it fails, the change goes forward and judges have little influence in its shaping.

Similarly, the judge's centrality poses a dilemma for sentencing policy makers. If substantial deference is given to judicial views and sensibilities, major policy shifts are seldom likely to occur. However, if major policy initiatives are imposed on judges who oppose them in substance and are alienated from the process that produced them, the changes are likely to fail. In principle, the underlying differences in institutional interests and policy preferences should be reconcilable. In practice, at least in the United States, reconciliation has proven difficult. Amidst a few successful sentencing "reforms," the American legal landscape is littered with failed and unpopular innovations.

With only a few exceptions, American judges have been seen as part of the sentencing problem and have played relatively little role in the fashioning of sentencing policy. This is unfortunate from the perspectives both of judges and of justice. The role and authority of the judge is diminished when discretion is ostensibly eliminated, as happens when now ubiquitous mandatory sentencing laws are enacted, or when discretion is rigidly regulated, as happens when complex and mechanical sentencing schemes like the federal guidelines are promulgated.

The quality of justice is impoverished when sentencing laws or guidelines, in the interest of treating like cases alike, make it difficult or impossible for judges to treat different cases differently. The quality of justice and public respect for legal institutions likewise are diminished

165

when judges, forced to choose between their oaths to do justice and to enforce the law, participate in disingenuous circumvention of mandatory minimum sentence laws and rigid guidelines in order to do justice.

American judges are themselves largely to blame for their exclusion from a central role in fashioning sentencing policy. In many jurisdictions, judges refused to acknowledge that unwarranted sentencing disparities were real and unjust (or that many influential people believed disparities to be real and unjust, which for practical purposes is the same thing) and opposed sentencing reform efforts. In some states—Maine, Connecticut, New York, and South Carolina in the 1980s offer examples—judges managed to derail proposed sentencing guidelines that would have structured judicial sentencing discretion (von Hirsch, Knapp, and Tonry 1987). In a second set of states—Florida and Maryland offer examples—judges attempted to co-opt sentencing reform by devising their own "voluntary" sentencing guidelines that provided the appearance but not the substance of change (Carrow 1984; Carrow et al. 1985). These strategies of resistance and co-optation, though successful in the short term, because they forestalled more substantial changes, in the longer term are likely to have won Pyrrhic victories.

In some jurisdictions—Minnesota, Oregon, and Washington offer examples—judges, though hostile to sentencing changes, were less obstructionist than passive. Many judges believe it inappropriate and possibly unethical to take an active part in policy making or policy debates. Where that belief is predominant, judges tend to be poorly organized and politically weak, which lessens their ability to obstruct change but also lessens their ability to shape change and to introduce the benefits of judicial experience and insight into the policy process.

In the federal sentencing guidelines system, for example, judges had little influence on the development of the guidelines, which are much the most detailed and mechanical now in use, and leave little role for judicial discretion. In Minnesota, Oregon, Pennsylvania, and Washington, where many trial judges are today reasonably satisfied with guidelines, judges had relatively little collective influence on sentencing policy as a result of organized political influence, but individual judges were influential participants in the development process.

This chapter examines judicial participation in development and implementation of sentencing policies in the United States. There is, to my knowledge, no literature on the subject. There are, however, evaluation literatures on the operation of sentencing guidelines, mandatory sentencing laws, and other sentencing policy changes, and a number of reports and resolutions issued by judicial bodies shed some light. Drawing on these sources and on my own interviews of people who were centrally involved in the development and implementation of sentencing guidelines in Minnesota, Pennsylvania, Oregon, Washington, and the

U.S. federal system, I suggest lessons about the role of the judiciary in sentencing policy making that might be drawn from recent experience.[1]

A major change in sentencing laws is likely to succeed if judges are convinced that they should, or must, make it work. Thus in thinking about judges and sentencing policy, it may be useful to distinguish two processes. Before or during the policy development phase, efforts must be made to involve the judiciary in the process so that they will at least understand and respect the underlying rationales or aims of the changes. Before implementation and continuously afterward, efforts must be made to persuade judges of the new scheme's merits and to help judges and others understand new rules and processes.

I.   Eliciting Judicial Participation and Support

To my knowledge, no developers of presumptive sentencing guidelines have managed to make the organized judiciary or the preponderance of judges into enthusiastic supporters, either while guidelines were being developed or afterward. In several states, though, the personal persuasiveness of individual judges who were involved in the policy development process has served to neutralize judges as opponents of change.

Legislators and others involved in passage of guidelines enabling legislation probably believe that they have addressed legitimate concerns of judges by providing that specific numbers of sentencing commission members be judges. On the U.S. Sentencing Commission, for example, three of the seven positions are by statute reserved for judges. It is probably reasonable to assume that judicial members of commissions will bring judicial sensibilities to the policy process and also, later, serve as commission ambassadors to the judiciary. In practice, part of the explanation for successful implementation of the Oregon, Minnesota, and Washington guidelines can probably be found in the personalities and persuasiveness of the individual judges who were members of those commissions. Nonetheless, in retrospect, as the experience of the U.S. Sentencing Commission demonstrates, including judges on a commission does not by itself assure that guidelines will be palatable to the mass of judges.

Both policy developers and judges share blame for the relatively limited judicial role in policy development. Partly the problem lies in limited efforts to reach out to judges: a few regional information meetings are held; presentations are given at judges' annual conferences; judges are told that they can be added to mailing lists to receive minutes of meetings

---

1. Unattributed quotations in this chapter are from personal interviews and correspondence.

and other materials; judges are invited to testify at hearings. Every sentencing commission of which I am aware did all these things.

In Pennsylvania, for example, staff of the Commission on Sentencing gave presentations at the midsummer and midwinter meetings of the Pennsylvania judiciary in 1979, 1980, and 1981; held special-purpose regional and county-level meetings to discuss guideline development; submitted questionnaires to all judges soliciting their opinions on alternate ways to handle particular issues; and invited judges to testify at public hearings on draft guidelines.

In Washington, sentencing commission members gave presentations at regularly scheduled judicial conferences, convened six sessions at individual county courthouses with groups of judges, and invited judges to submit comments and suggestions to the sentencing commission.

In Minnesota, much less effort was devoted to developing judicial support than was expended on prosecutors, law enforcement officials, and defense counsel. The strategy was to maximize support for the guidelines and minimize opposition; prosecutors and law enforcement officials were seen as politically organized and effective; defense counsel as volatile, unpredictable, and therefore politically dangerous; judges as poorly organized and politically ineffectual. Relationships with the judiciary were left to the judicial members of the commission who served as ambassadors to their peers.

Even less attention was lavished on judges in Oregon. The guidelines were motivated in large part by fiscal pressures resulting from sizeable increases in prison and jail populations, and by perceived threats of federal court intervention if state officials could not resolve crowding problems (Bogan 1990, 1991). A primary objective was to link sentencing policy to correctional resources. Guidelines were going to happen and selling the concept to judges was not seen as a high priority.

According to Kathleen Bogan, director of the Oregon Criminal Justice Council when it developed the guidelines, the goal was to persuade judges to adopt a stance of neutrality when the proposed guidelines were presented to the legislature. This was done partly by using research on past sentencing and paroling patterns to show judges how extensive sentencing disparities were and how little influence judges had over sentence lengths in a state with an active parole board. In addition, five unofficial judicial members were appointed by the state chief justice to the Oregon Criminal Justice Council's sentencing guidelines committee (two judges were official members) in hopes that they would serve as liaison to the organized judiciary. In the event, the organized judiciary neither supported nor opposed the proposed guidelines.

If sentencing commissions were less assiduous at courting judges than they might have been, many judges did little to attract courting. In Pennsylvania when commission staff attended judicial conferences, according to long-time staff director John Kramer, "the discussions were often intense and sometimes heated." Dale Parent, the first director of Minnesota's commission, describes open and intense hostility from judges at an annual judicial conference during the period when the guidelines were being developed. Douglas Amdahl, then a trial judge and later chief justice of the Minnesota Supreme Court, interceded and insisted that the judges at least listen to how and why the guidelines were formulated. By meeting's end, Parent reports, the judges' reactions demonstrated a "mild and highly qualified endorsement."

Righteous indignation to the very idea of guidelines, sanctimonious claims that sentencing is a judicial prerogative, denials that sentencing disparities exist—all of these commonly observed judicial postures may be entirely understandable reactions of judges accustomed to complete (and typically in the United States, lacking appellate sentence review, unreviewable) discretion, but they run head-on into the cliché that "either you are part of the solution or you are part of the problem." Judges often did not look like part of the solution. Instead, they, and demonstrated patterns of sentencing disparity, in general and particularly in relation to sentencing of black and other minority offenders, have widely been seen as the problem.

From sheer institutional self-interest, judges cannot afford to be absent from the give and take of policy development. Contemplated legal changes can be fought from an insider's position, through the processes of negotiation, or from the outside by means of sheer political power. In most American jurisdictions, only the insider's strategy is likely to work. In Washington, one observer writes, a successful group "must be willing to entertain and contend with the views of other interest groups and involve themselves in 'give and take.' The culture for judges in our state is not to do that, to hold themselves at a distance. Thus, they are weak and easy to defeat." In Minnesota, Dale Parent writes, judges were not regarded as sufficiently politically powerful to worry about: "Minnesota judges were politically non-powerful, tending to present a united legislative front only on issues of salary. . . . Judges, we assumed, would go along with change (they were after all sworn to uphold the law and guidelines were soon to be the law)."

Thus, while some sentencing commissions were more thoroughgoing than others in their approaches to the judiciary, and while judicial members of some commissions simultaneously represented judicial values in the policy-making process and worked to sell guidelines to judges, future sentencing commissions and the judges in those states can do better.

II. Training

Jurisdictions that have sentencing guidelines tend to convene training sessions for judges more frequently than do other jurisdictions. The Pennsylvania Commission on Sentencing holds upwards of twenty training sessions per year. The U.S. Sentencing Commission in 1993 held seventy training sessions for 4,700 individuals, including sentencing institutes for judges from six of the twelve federal circuits (U.S. Sentencing Commission 1994). However, these are ongoing adult education programs and are not unlike judicial education on other subjects.

New sentencing policies ought ideally to result from a process in which judges were central participants, in which all the affected officials, agencies, and public interest groups felt that their points of view had been given fair consideration, and in which the decisions made were believed by all involved to be sound, principled, and workable. Under those happy circumstances, judicial training would be relatively straightforward. Judicial training staff would develop easy-to-understand manuals that explain and illustrate the operation of the new policies. Before the new policies took effect, sessions for judges, probation officers, prosecutors, and defense lawyers would be held in which the aims and justifications of the new scheme would be discussed and in which changes in procedures would be explained. If the new policies included sentencing guidelines, substantial time and attention would be devoted to the mechanics of the new system in order to demystify what may otherwise to many court personnel appear alien and mysterious.

After the new system took effect, judicial staff would maintain a "hot line" to answer judges' and probation officers' questions, "refresher" training would become a part of regular judicial conferences, and periodic training courses would be held for new judges and other court personnel. In practice, what I have described has been done, at varying levels of competence and sophistication, by most American states and by the federal government when new guidelines or statutory determinate sentencing laws have taken effect.

The problem, however, has been that the ideal conditions described in the previous two paragraphs above have never existed. Typically, instead, most judges have felt excluded from the policy-making process and have been hostile to the new system. This means that effective training must pursue two objectives: it must socialize judges into acceptance of the normative premises of new sentencing arrangements *and* convey information on procedures and mechanics.

Research discussed in chapters 2, 3, and 5 shows that judges and prosecutors who want to circumvent mandatory or determinate sentencing statutes or presumptive guidelines can generally find ways to do so. The less sympathetic judges are with a new sentencing system, the likelier they are to find ways to work around it. Thus a necessary condition to smooth operation of a new system is that judges be persuaded of its merits.

People who believe in what they are doing are likely to do it better than people who merely go through the motions. From that trite but true proposition, one might assume that sentencing commissions would devote considerable efforts to persuading judges to accept the goals and normative premises of the guidelines before they were formally approved. Instead most American commissions made few such efforts and now believe they erred in not doing more.

Convincing judges that a new system makes sense and is preferable to whatever preceded it is inherently difficult. Most people are more comfortable with the old than with the new, with the familiarity of comfortable routines than with promised "improvements" that may not be better at all. This is expressed in the declamation often attributed by Norval Morris to an unnamed, possibly apocryphal, Victorian penal administrator, "Reform, reform, don't speak to me of reform; things are bad enough as it is."

There is no reason to assume that judges are more sympathetic to innovation than are the rest of us, particularly to the kinds of radical changes that occurred in the U.S. federal system when a familiar system of indeterminate sentencing that had changed little for fifty years was replaced by detailed sentencing guidelines that greatly limited judicial discretion. In chapter 3, I quoted the Federal Courts Study Committee (1990), the U.S. Sentencing Commission (1991*a*), the General Accounting Office (1992), the director of the Federal Judicial Center (Schwartzer 1991), and a senior federal appeals court judge (Heaney 1991) on the proposition that the vast majority of federal judges are deeply dissatisfied with the federal guidelines.

Anecdotal evidence confirms that dissatisfaction. In talking with a number of federal officials about judicial training, I was repeatedly told that federal judges at sentencing institutes often are openly hostile to members of the U.S. Sentencing Commission and to anyone else who speaks to them about the merits of the existing guidelines, but they are respectful and often complimentary to probation officers and others who speak to them about mechanics. That description is consistent with my personal observations at recent federal sentencing institutes.

The explanation is that judges grudgingly accept that the guidelines are law, whether they like them or not, and as responsible professionals they appreciate technical information that helps them better understand the system, but most are so alienated from the guidelines that they simply do not wish to listen to anyone try to justify them. If we step back from the particularities of the federal guidelines, what this suggests is that the strategy for eliciting judicial cooperation with a new sentencing policy must be developed before the policy takes shape; afterward may be too late.

Many judges in each presumptive guidelines jurisdiction disliked the guidelines. John Kramer notes that in Pennsylvania "not all judges like to have their discretion restricted, nor do they like having a state agency enacting such guidelines." In Oregon, Kathleen Bogan reports that little was done in Oregon to persuade the judges of the wisdom of the guidelines approach but reports "there was some effort to explain to judges the stated values of the legislation, which many of them nevertheless rejected while grudgingly agreeing they were bound to apply the law."

Dale Parent says of Minnesota training, "We tried during training to convey a sense that the guidelines were a fundamental shift in rules, that there was a noble and uplifting element. . . . It was clear in retrospect that we focused too much on the mechanical aspects of guideline application, and not enough on the principles that undergirded them, so maybe we should have tried to socialize them more."

In Washington, David Boerner, a former Seattle prosecutor and one of the guidelines architects, argues both that more should have been done to "socialize" judges, to convince them that guidelines were a desirable innovation, and that the Washington guidelines' success results in large part from appellate judges' beliefs that the guidelines were "a responsible and principled reform that was well within the range of reasonable legislative choice."

Efforts were made in Washington to persuade judges that guidelines were preferable to indeterminate sentencing on grounds of fairness and effectiveness. Nonetheless, Boerner, like Roxanne Lieb (the commission's first director), believes that "if the judges had their way, the [guidelines] would be either repealed or radically altered," and that the general pattern of compliance results more from Washington judges' commitment to the rule of law than to their support for the guidelines.

All of the American commissions were thorough and conscientious in training judges on the mechanics and procedures of sentencing guidelines. The Pennsylvania Commission on Sentencing, for example, held numerous training conferences for judges when the guidelines were implemented. The Oregon, Washington, Minnesota, and U.S. commissions have been comparably conscientious through their own activities or by working with judicial educators. In each jurisdiction, substantial efforts were devoted to developing training materials and guidelines forms and manuals that are clearly written and easy to understand and use. The U.S. commission published a "questions-and-answers" guide and operates an information office to answer questions about guidelines application. The Minnesota, Oregon, and Washington commissions made it a practice to examine every sentencing disposition information sheet and to contact judges or their probation officers every time an apparent error in calculation of offense or criminal history scores was observed, or any time when guidelines appeared to have been misapplied.

III. Implications

This chapter may seem to suggest that the politics of law reform, the content of sentencing policies, the processes of sentencing commissions, the cultivation of support, and the implementation of policy make up a seamless web, and of course they do. There is no ideal way to remake or refashion the web.

It does seem wise, however, from the perspective of judicial sensibilities and institutional self-interest, and from the perspective of sound and balanced sentencing policies, to hope that judges will participate in the policy process and that resulting policies will reflect judicial experience without being trammeled by judicial parochialism or judicial hubris.

Judges will seldom have their own way in these matters, even when they participate in the policy process. Too many other institutional interests and political points of view are involved. To name but a few, law enforcement officials, judges, the private defense bar, public defenders, and probation and correctional officials all want to influence policy. So do the media, victims' advocacy groups, and civil liberties groups. And, not unimportantly, so do legislators and elected executive branch officials who are variously concerned about substantive matters, finances, and political symbolism.

Although judges can hardly expect to dominate so complex and multifaceted a political process, the process needs to take heed of legitimate and deep-seated judicial concerns, both in the substance of policy and in training efforts. Evaluations of American sentencing innovations make it clear that judges can and often will, by themselves or in collaboration with prosecutors and defense counsel, circumvent sentencing guidelines or sentencing laws that they disapprove. Mandatory sentencing laws everywhere seem to stimulate energetic efforts by judges and lawyers to avoid doing injustice. Eight years after the implementation of the U.S. Sentencing Commission's guidelines, something like judicial guerrilla warfare continues. Even in law-abiding Minnesota where judicial acceptance of sentencing guidelines was common, though not universal, as Richard Frase (1991*b*) has shown, judges have crafted doctrines to justify departures from guidelines on rehabilitative grounds that the commission expressly rejected.

If judges, in truculent rejection of the premise that sentencing needs reform, become seen as part of the problem, they will probably play no part in crafting the solution. Yet if judges are not part of and dislike the solution, they will be a continuing problem. That is a conundrum. The answer appears to be for the judiciary to recognize that sentencing raises issues within the judicial province, but also within others' legitimate provinces, and for others to recognize the inexorably central role of the judge in sentencing. In some cases, for example, the U.S. federal sentencing reform, the political setting may be so contentious that no acceptable reconciliation of interests may be possible. In most times and places, however, honorable people of good motive should be able to formulate and implement improved sentencing policies that are both workable and just.

7

Sentencing Reform in Comparative Perspective

Sentencing looks much the same in most Western countries. In circumstances of some formality, after a process that signals the symbolic importance of the state's taking of a citizen's liberty or property, an impartial judicial official soberly announces the penalty the offender will suffer. It seems quite simple, almost universal. Without acceptable excuse or justification, an individual has done something that the law forbids, and the state has declared him blameworthy and deserving of punishment. The problems that can arise—that the fact-finding process is unfair or unreliable, that judges are capricious or biased or idiosyncratic, that penalties are ineffective or cruel or inconsistently applied—also are universal. Different legal systems should, it would appear, want and be able to learn from one another about such elemental problems. In recent decades, however, there has been relatively little international transfer of sentencing technology and learning between legal systems. That's understandable, but a pity.

As a small but accumulating empirical literature on sentencing research and policy demonstrates (e.g., Clarkson and Morgan 1995), there are lessons to be learned across national and subnational boundaries that can help individual jurisdictions improve their systems while avoiding foreseeable mistakes. "Improve," of course, is a loaded term. Champions of reduced sentencing disparities or greater control over officials' decisions count as improvements legal and policy changes that many officials find abhorrent. No doubt the proponents of England's Criminal Justice Act 1991 saw its passage as a harbinger of improved sentencing (Wasik and Taylor 1991; Ashworth 1992a); judicial opponents saw the repeal of key provisions in 1993 as an appropriate rejection of benighted legislation (Wasik 1993; Thomas 1995). In the United States, sentencing reform had been on congressional agendas for ten years when the Sentencing Reform Act of 1984 was enacted; after guidelines were implemented, most of the act's initial proponents and most federal judges saw it as a disastrous mistake (Stith and Koh 1993; Miller 1995).

Nonetheless, many sentencing policy initiatives in many countries have resulted in positive changes. What was then West Germany successfully implemented 1960s legislation intended to substitute financial penalties for prison sentences of six months or less (Weigend 1992). In the 1970s West Germany successfully introduced a system of day fines and a conditional dismissal program under which prosecutors dismissed charges in exchange for defendants' agreements to pay fines that would have been imposed had they been convicted (Weigend 1992; Albrecht 1995). In the 1980s and 1990s, the Netherlands successfully implemented a conditional dismissal program and a system of community service sentences (Tak 1994*a*). The Swedish government in the 1980s successfully implemented a system to structure sentencing discretion that relies on the establishment of guiding principles for sentences rather than on American-style numerical guidelines (Jareborg 1995). The government of England and Wales successfully established an extensive community service program in the 1970s (Pease 1985), followed a few years later by the government of Scotland (McIvor 1992). In the 1980s, England and Wales established a successful network of day reporting centers (Mair 1993*a*). The Australian State of Victoria in the 1990s successfully implemented a new "Truth in Sentencing" system (Freiberg 1992, 1993, 1995). The states of Delaware, Minnesota, Oregon, and Washington implemented well-regarded systems of sentencing guidelines in the 1980s (see chap. 2) and new widely approved intermediate sanctions have been introduced in many states (see chap. 4).

For each of these successes, there have been corresponding failures that shed at least as much light on sentencing policy development as do the successes. Where Germany managed to make day fines an integral and widely used sentencing option, England's unit-fine system (based on a week's income rather than a day's) was a widely touted part of the Criminal Justice Act 1991 but was abandoned within a year after it took effect (Moxon 1993). Day-fine projects have been conducted in at least five American states but nowhere have day fines come into widespread use for nontrivial crimes. Likewise, no American jurisdiction has managed, like the Dutch, the English, and the Scots, to establish the community service order as a widely used free standing sanction. Where Victoria implemented a "Truth in Sentencing" law that abolished remission (good time in the United States) without increasing its prison population, the neighboring Australian state of New South Wales enacted a similar law that produced a substantial unintended rise in the number of prisoners

(Gorta 1992, 1993). Finally, in contrast to the successful institution of new sentencing regimes in Sweden and a number of American states, the English government, within months after they took effect, repealed major provisions of the more modest sentencing policy changes contained in the Criminal Justice Act 1991, and the American federal sentencing guidelines have been a conspicuous failure. (There have been others: see Tonry 1991 and chaps. 1 and 2).

This chapter distills from the empirical literature on sentencing policy a number of observations that seem relevant to any Western legal system. They relate to the simple, elemental nature of sentencing that can be seen behind the obscuring mechanical and procedural details of different legal systems. Three points stand out. First, just as real estate brokers cite "location, location, location" as the key to property values, "planning, planning, planning" is the key to effective implementation of new sentencing schemes. Second, well-planned and executed innovations can alter judges' behavior and sentencing outcomes. Third, while "one size fits all" may work for bathrobes and synthetic socks, it will not work for sentencing policy. Different jurisdictions have different problems.

The preceding claims at their most exciting are prosaic. Anyone should know that solutions must be tailored to problems, that successful implementation of anything is facilitated by careful planning, and that well-conceived, well-executed changes should have some effect.

In practice, few sentencing policy changes are well planned or well implemented. Jurisdictions contemplating changes can learn from the occasional successes and frequent failures of others. This chapter offers an overview of the current scant English-language literature on sentencing policy changes. Because chapters 2, 3, and 4 of this book discuss American research in some detail, this chapter emphasizes developments outside the United States. Section I discusses discretion and disparity as common backdrops of sentencing policy in every country. Section II sets out a number of generalizations from past documented sentencing policy changes that can illuminate paths for other jurisdictions to follow. Section III discusses the implicit goals of all modern efforts to reduce sentencing disparities and argues that fairness, not "desert" is the common theme. Section IV examines interactions between concern about disparities and for desert, and their implications for sentencing policy.

I. Discretion and Disparity

Proposals for sentencing change come from many quarters. Penal abolitionists, humanitarians, and political liberals typically want reduced severity. Law enforcement officials, victims groups, and political conservatives want penalties made tougher. Academics and civil libertarians want them made fairer. Utilitarians and crime-control spokesmen want them made more effective. Nearly all want sentencing made more consistent, whether in the name of justice, efficiency, effectiveness, or economy.

Whoever wants what, however, must confront the antipodean twins of discretion and disparity. Someone must in every case decide what to do. In most common law jurisdictions, at least until recently, judges have been accorded great latitude to decide what will happen to individual offenders who come before them. The difficulty is that sentences sometimes reveal more about judges than about offenders, just as book reviews sometimes reveal more about reviewers than about books.

If sentencing is, at least substantially, about offenders' blameworthiness, systems in which judges have wide discretion are troublesome. Equally principled and thoughtful judges, call them Plato and Aristotle, Jeremy Bentham and Immanuel Kant, or William O. Douglas and Felix Frankfurter, are sometimes going to impose different penalties on seemingly similar offenders. Unintelligent or unprincipled or unscrupulous or partial or egoistic or bigoted judges are often going to impose very different penalties on comparable wrongdoers. Research in many countries documents the existence of disparities in sentencing that cannot be accounted for by reference to the characteristics of offenders or the circumstances of offenses. Even concerning the Netherlands, long the possessor of the developed world's lowest incarceration rates, a recent overview of Dutch sentencing noted, "The absence of mandatory rules for sentencing and sentencing guidelines may contribute to the present mild penal climate but may also result in greater disparity in sentencing, as recent research has shown" (Tak 1994a, p. 8).

The association of unwarranted disparities with unstructured discretion seems inevitable to many observers and a self-evident problem. Curiously, however, that problem is not at all self-evident to many judges. In most English-speaking countries, at least, the prevailing judicial ethos rejects both the need to structure sentencing discretion and the appropriateness of doing so. By American standards, for example, the sentencing policy innovations represented by the Criminal Justice Act 1991 in England and Wales were modest; they principally established a number of statutory presumptions for the handling of prior record and the relation between crime seriousness and incarceration. Much closer to the Scandinavian declaration of general principles to guide discretion than to detailed American sentencing guidelines, the Criminal Justice Act's most controversial provisions left substantial opportunity for judicial construction of important but undefined and elastic words like "serious" (see Thomas 1995; Jareborg 1995). Yet the Lord Chief Justice of England, in a widely reported speech, was moved to say that its provisions forced sentencers into a straitjacket and that the new law, fashioned by "penologists, criminologists, and bureaucrats," had created a system that was "incomprehensible to right thinking people generally." That key provisions of the 1991 act were repealed in 1993 is attributable at least in part to judicial hostility (Wasik 1993, p. 1; Moxon 1993).

Australian judges appear to be committed at least as strongly as their English brethren to the notion that judges in some sense own sentencing and that legislative encumbrances on that ownership are inherently inappropriate. Arie Freiberg traces the genesis of Victoria's Sentencing Act 1991, which abolished remission of sentence, to *Yates*, [1985] V.R. 41, a decision of the Supreme Court of Victoria. The central issue was whether sentencing judges should take the likely effect of remission (good time) into account when setting sentence. The answer was an emphatic "no." The court observed that the very existence of remission communicated to observers either that "the court had no authority because little notice was taken of the sentence imposed" or that the court was engaged in a charade designed to mislead the public about the severity of sentences. The most telling bit of rhetoric, "The authority of the court is eroded whenever the executive is authorized to interfere with its orders," intimates that the central issue is acknowledgment of the authority of the court rather than justice to the offender or achievement of the policy aims of government.

If there were grounds for believing that legal doctrine, court rules, or tariff case law assured that sentences were justly imposed, and that they were reasonably consistent and proportionate, the primary emphasis on acknowledging the court's authority might seem less anomalous. At least in Victoria, however, there is little reason to believe this. Freiberg cites *Williscroft*, [1975] V.R. 292, 300, a decision of the Court of Criminal Appeal, on the sentencing process: "Now, ultimately every sentence imposed represents the sentencing judge's intuitive synthesis of all the various aspects involved in the punitive process. Moreover, in our view, it is profitless . . . to attempt to allot to the various considerations their proper part in the assessment of the particular punishments presently under examination. We are aware that such a conclusion [about appropriate punishments] rests upon what is essentially a subjective judgment largely intuitively reached."

This belief in the "intuitive synthesis," that judges are uniquely qualified to set sentences and, presumably, despite the different experiences, values, and personalities of individual judges, that the sentences imposed are just ones, is not unique to Victoria. In New South Wales, in an important decision concerning the Sentencing Act 1989, the Court of Criminal Appeal in *R. v. McClay*, [1990] 19 N.S.W.L.R. 112, acknowledged a new approach but insisted that judges give "appropriate weight to well-established principles of sentencing." To like effect, the High Court of Australia, in *Veen* (no. 2), [1988] 164 C.L.R. 465, 476, averred that "sentencing is not a purely logical exercise. . . . The purposes overlap and none of them can be considered in isolation. . . . They are guideposts to the appropriate sentence."

Nor is belief in the judges' capacity for "intuitive synthesis" unique to England and Wales and Australia. At the Colston Symposium on comparative studies of sentencing in Bristol, England, in 1993, Manfred Burgstaller of the University of Vienna described the "existential conversation" that is used in Austria as a metaphor to describe judges' mental processes when deciding sentences, and noted that observers of Austrian courts, like observers of courts everywhere, worry about the unwarranted disparities that appear to be common (Clarkson and Morgan 1995).

In many American jurisdictions, judges long denied the existence of sentencing disparities. Many still do. Disparity research is faulted as misleading because it fails to take all the relevant factors into account. At least a dozen times, while discussing seemingly anomalous sentences, judges have told me, "if we were present at the sentencing, we would understand why the judge imposed that sentence." I suspect that many judges in Western countries would dispute the findings of disparity research in similar terms, without acknowledging the assertion's inherent ambiguity.

Understood one way, the claim is about measurement. The model has not been adequately specified and more variables, especially qualitative variables, should be taken into account. This can always be true, but it is not a claim that disparity does not exist, merely that it has not convincingly been demonstrated. Understood another way, the claim is about judges. Had we been there, we would understand why *that* judge imposed that sentence. This will often be true, but it recasts the question from "Has this defendant received a sentence that is reasonably consistent with those imposed on other like-situated offenders sentenced by other judges?" to "Has this judge, in light of his or her environment, beliefs, and experience, imposed an unreasonable sentence?" Understood in this latter way, the refutation of the existence of disparity is instead a reassertion of judicial ownership of sentencing, an assertion that an "understandable" or "not unreasonable" sentence is a just one.

Belief in judicial ownership of sentencing has in England and Wales been remarkably influential. I have many times asked English colleagues about their experiences as members of the English Parole Board and several times have been told of prisoners coming before the board who were serving what appeared to all involved to be aberrantly long sentences. Each time, the stories go, someone observed that the judge must have had a good reason to impose such a long sentence, although nothing in the files revealed what that reason might have been, and as a result the board decided not to recommend release.

It is unclear how much of the opposition of American federal judges to the U.S. Sentencing Commission's guidelines (Doob 1995) derives from objections to their severity and rigidity and how much from the guidelines' explicit rejection of the notion that judges own sentencing. The more than two hundred federal district court opinions declaring the entire system unconstitutional, a conclusion with which the U.S. Supreme Court in *United States v. Mistretta*, 488 U.S. 361 (1989), disagreed, suggests that intrusion on judicial discretion was a major and emotional consideration.

There is, unfortunately, no way around the dilemma that sentencing is inherently discretionary and that discretion leads to disparities. In the United States, serious attempts have been made to objectify sentencing by establishing explicit standards to guide decisions in individual cases. At the extreme, as Anthony Doob (1995) details, the guidelines adopted by the U.S. Sentencing Commission for use in the federal courts purport to be mandatory. They are all but universally criticized for their rigidity and their consequent inability to draw distinctions between cases that most observers believe should be distinguished.

Three major substantive lessons can be drawn from the sizeable American evaluation literature on the effects of major efforts to reduce disparities by changes in sentencing laws and practices (see chap. 2). First, newly established standards for sentencing can effect changes in the patterns of sentences judges impose and can reduce sentencing disparities. Second, insofar as standards direct judges to impose sentences they consider unjust or otherwise inappropriate, they will often devise ways, sometimes in concert with counsel, to do something else. Third, standards that aggressively try to eliminate disparities and to achieve uniformity in sentencing, like the federal guidelines, often violate the second half of the equality injunction (". . . and treat different cases differently") and are especially likely therefore to drive discretion underground as judges and lawyers try to achieve sentences that those involved agree are reasonable.

Artifices in the federal system to circumvent guidelines that the judge and counsel consider unjust are legion (U.S. Sentencing Commission 1991*a*, pp. A-1–A-90; Nagel and Schulhofer 1992). Judges sometimes simply refuse to find facts (for example, a larger quantity of drugs or use of a firearm) that, if found, would require a much harsher sentence. Judges sometimes consent to plea bargains that, because of the authorized maximum sentences they entail, make it impossible to impose the sentence specified by the guidelines. Sometimes judges defer to proposed stipulated findings of fact that omit incontrovertible details requiring a harsher sentence; other times judges order probation officers to omit key facts from their presentence investigation reports; both these practices are expressly forbidden by U.S. Sentencing Commission policies. Sometimes judges ignore the applicable guideline or an applicable statutory mandatory minimum sentence; unless one of the parties objects and appeals, that is the end of the matter.

There is some irony in this causal chain: to reduce disparities that the visible exercise of discretion makes evident, standards are set that operate to make the exercise of discretion surreptitious, which makes disparities all but invisible and nearly impossible to monitor. In the federal system, some judges feel ethically bound to observe their oath to enforce the law and apply guidelines they believe to be unjust, and others feel ethically bound to observe their oath to do justice and circumvent the guidelines; aggregate disparities probably exceed those in the system the guidelines displaced.

The preceding paragraphs should not be construed as counsel of despair. Some American states, as for example Minnesota, Oregon, and Washington, have found a middle ground on which presumptive guidelines set standards that most practitioners find reasonable and in which there is sufficient flexibility to allow meaningful differences between cases to be taken into account openly (Tonry 1993c). That balance has been hard to strike, however, and many more states have failed than have succeeded (though at the time of writing, promising new guidelines systems have recently taken effect in Kansas, North Carolina, and Arkansas [Gottlieb 1993; Proband 1993; Knapp 1993; Wright 1995]).

As a policy matter, it is hard to imagine a persuasive argument why celebration of judicial ownership of sentencing is a more important policy goal than reduction of unwarranted sentencing disparities. The best I can devise would be a slippery slope argument that an independent judiciary is essential to preservation of an ordered democracy and that any intrusion on the existing scope of judicial authority threatens the concept of judicial independence. This would be a silly argument, although some judges may believe it. Were it valid, it would apply as readily to codification of bodies of law like contracts, property, and torts that evolved under the common law as to establishment of rules for sentencing where formerly there were none.

Andrew Ashworth (1992b) has demonstrated why it is a confusion to conflate protection of the judge's authority, within applicable law, to decide the facts of individual disputes and apply the law to them, a process at the core of judicial independence, with protection of the judge's preference to set sentences free from standards that might constrain his exercise of discretion, a claim that ultimately is incompatible with the premises of democratic self-government. Discussions of this subject are difficult because the conflation is common and the suggestion that legislatures have the same legal and constitutional authority to set standards for sentencing as for the law of contracts is often met with an emotional defense of judicial independence.

American efforts at sentencing reform offer some insights into the discretion-disparity nexus. First, judges are educable. From a beginning in the 1970s, when indeterminate sentencing was ubiquitous and judges were as opposed to constraints on their sentencing discretion as are English and Australian judges today, most American judges today are prepared to agree that sentencing should be guided by rules. That one of the earliest and most influential books calling for sentencing reform, *Criminal Sentences: Law without Order*, was written by a federal trial judge who decried "lawlessness" in sentencing, may have helped legitimize sentencing reform in judicial eyes (Frankel 1972). As a result, and as chapters 1 and 2 document, more and more states are moving to adopt sentencing guidelines.

Second, intransigent opposition by judges to efforts to reduce disparities is a dangerous strategy. Sometimes, as in England and Wales in regard to the Criminal Justice Act 1991, or as in Victoria and New South Wales generally, intransigence wins out. Other times, as in the American federal system, intransigence excludes judges from the policy process and the standards adopted in their absence are the worse for it.

In England and Wales, although the judges appear to have won the day in 1993, passage of the 1991 act in the face of judicial dubiety suggests that judicial obstructionism may yet be swept away when a future reform wave rolls in. That is in effect what happened in the American federal system. Bills calling for a sentencing commission and sentencing guidelines were first introduced in 1974, first passed in the Senate in 1979, and passed by both houses of Congress in 1984, always over the opposition of most federal judges (Stith and Koh 1993). America's federal sentencing guidelines should be a lesson to judges everywhere that oppositionism can carry a high price.

II.   Learning Across Jurisdictional Boundaries

Sentencing policy changes in the English-speaking countries have seldom been the subjects of sophisticated impact evaluations. A dozen or two studies in the United States, a handful in England and Wales (mostly of the use of community service orders; see Pease 1985), and a few in Australia (e.g., Freiberg 1992, 1995; Gorta 1992, 1993) make up the evaluation literature. Such studies are rare if not nonexistent in Canada because, as Anthony Doob (1995) engagingly puts it, Canada has gotten nowhere with its sentencing reform efforts, but has taken a very long time to get there.

There are nonetheless things to be learned by looking at sentencing policy changes across jurisdictional boundaries. Drawing on the American, Australian, and English literatures and experience, I offer a number of generalizations about efforts to change sentencing policies and practices. Much of what I say may seem and be self-evident. My defense is that, self-evident observations or not, many jurisdictions have failed to take account of them.

First, among ambitious innovations, more fail than succeed, and the explanations often can be found in the carefulness and thoroughness of planning and implementation. Unit fines in England and Wales, a continental import, were repealed in part because of opposition from magistrates and partly because of design failures such as their application only to magistrates' (but not Crown) courts, their application to venial offenses like motoring violations and littering, and a default policy in many courts that offenders for whom income information was unavailable received the highest possible unit-fine (Moxon 1993). Restriction to the magistrates' courts meant that any defendant could appeal to the Crown Court and petition to have the fine reassessed by a judge who was not subject to the unit-fine rules. The interaction between application of unit fines to trivial offenses and the presumption that defendants whose income is unknown have means to pay the highest allowable unit fine produced £500 and £1,000 fines for littering and traffic offenses that undermined the unit fine's credibility. By contrast, a modest day-fine pilot project in Staten Island, New York, won judicial support and was later implemented, in part because judges who would apply the system were integrally involved in its planning and in part because methods for calculation and collection of fines were investigated and tested in excruciating detail (Hillsman and Greene 1992).

There are other examples. Abolition of remission in Victoria was sufficiently well advertised and implemented that prison populations held steady because judges adjusted their sentences downward accordingly (Freiberg 1992, 1993). Abolition of remission in New South Wales produced rising prison populations when judges failed to make the necessary adjustments (Gorta 1992, 1993).

In the United States, planners in Minnesota, Washington, and Oregon worked to win judicial support for sentencing guidelines (see chap. 6). The support won oftentimes may have been grudging, but it was won and most of the goals of sentencing reform were realized. In Pennsylvania, the judges were not successfully won over and many simply ignored the guidelines. In the federal system, judges were excluded from the policy development process and treated as opponents rather than as collaborators. As a result, widespread judicial defiance and opposition continues many years after the guidelines took effect.

Second, sentencing policy changes can alter sentencing practices. Examples include Victoria's successful abolition of remission, several American states' guidelines' effects on racial and other unwarranted disparities, and the American federal guidelines. Despite widespread dislike of the federal guidelines, no one disagrees that the guidelines, vigorously policed by probation officers, the U.S. Sentencing Commission, and the federal appellate courts, have changed sentencing patterns and practices (see chap. 2). Whether disparities have been reduced is at best unclear. With sufficient vigor, however, even the most unpopular sentencing changes can achieve high levels of nominal compliance.

The lessons to be drawn from the American, Australian, and English experiences involve process and can be found in any introductory textbook on public management. Include all affected agencies and constituencies in the planning and design work. Make the planning process open and accessible so that affected constituencies can voice their concerns early, and so that policy fights, and necessary resulting compromises, can be made before plans have become firm rather than afterward. Anticipate and develop contingency plans for all foreseeable problems. Cultivate support from the mass media. Conduct extensive public relations and outreach programs. Hold training sessions for officials and practitioners who must work with the new regime, so that its goals and rationales are at least understood and respected (even if they are not agreed with). Before implementation, establish monitoring programs so that patterns and pockets of noncompliance will be apparent. Establish technical support facilities so that answers are available for questions about policies and procedures.

None of this is glamorous, but it holds the key to whether policy initiatives succeed. No laws are self-executing. Sentencing laws and rules, because they impinge on self-perceived judicial ownership of sentencing, may be even less likely than others to achieve widespread acceptance. The evaluation literatures have shown what can go wrong and suggest ways that the past's problems can be avoided in the future.

III. Proportionality with a Human Face

Anthony Bottoms in a recent essay (1995) suggests that desert, managerialism, and community are the key ideas that underlie modern policy debates about the criminal justice system. From them can be triangulated "proportionality with a human face" as a widely accepted goal of sentencing policy in most jurisdictions. Desert captures the widely shared intuition that just penalties should be proportioned to the offender's blameworthiness. Managerialism provides the means to achieve compliance with sentencing policy. Community expresses the recognition that questions of justice are generally best decided in local settings.

Desert does not have widespread appeal, I believe, because all reasonable people believe that retribution rather that general prevention is the general justification of punishment, but instead because there is a widely shared intuition that justice is inexorably linked with fairness and that fairness consists in treating like cases alike. Even in an incapacitative or rehabilitative scheme of punishment, most people would find it appropriate that cases be dealt with consistently within applicable criteria and inappropriate that they be dealt with inconsistently. Fairness, not desert, is the key idea. Because desert implies a comprehensive approach to setting sentencing standards that can then be consistently or inconsistently applied, desert often serves as a proxy concept for fairness.

If fairness is a major goal of policy, managerialism with its interest in inputs, outputs, and throughputs, impact projections, accountability, and cost-effectiveness provides the tools to deploy in its pursuit. Managerialism is often used pejoratively as a code word to express dissatisfaction with dehumanized technocracy, management as an end in itself, and evolution toward a Foucauldian future of discipline and surveillance. No doubt those are legitimate concerns but they overstate. Thought of another way, managerialism is a metaphor for bureaucratic rationality and the simple idea that policies worth setting are worth achieving, and that there are more and less effective ways to do that.

Bottoms's third idea, community, is the most important and the least acknowledged of the three. Notions of community abound in relation to sentencing—the movement for community-based sanctions, interest in devolving power to local levels, concern in an avowedly pluralist world that communities vary widely in their composition and in their predominant values and traditions. All these are important ideas and together they reveal a powerful constraint on national, provincial, or state sentencing policies—justice is local.

Tensions arise when sentencing policies direct judges to impose sentences that are discordant with local notions of justice. Many illustrations can be offered (e.g., Blumstein et al. 1983, chaps. 2 and 3). In American jurisdictions, for example, research nearly always shows that sentences for many crimes are harsher in rural areas than in cities. Sentencing policy makers invariably decide that the new standards should apply throughout the state. Not surprisingly, rural judges often resist and not uncommonly disregard the new "too-lenient" sentences. Mandatory minimum sentence laws often require judges to impose sentences that they, the prosecutor, and the defense lawyer believe are too harsh. Sometimes the sentences are imposed and all concerned believe that injustice has been done. More often the lawyers or the judge figure out a way to avoid imposing an "unjust" sentence, thereby frustrating state policy goals.

Bottoms might object that I am not describing community variations but differences in the views of individual judges and the court work groups of which they are a part. That is at least partly true, though it is likely that the views and values of court functionaries are at least partly shaped by the predominant views and values of the communities from which they come. The key points, however, are that no one, presumably particularly including judges, is comfortable behaving in ways that they believe are unjust, and that dissonance between official policies and decision makers' sense of injustice will often be resolved in favor of the latter.

Bottoms's analysis leads, I believe, to a notion of proportionality with a human face as the overall goal of sentencing policy. This means that there should be standards for sentences and tools of public management should be used to develop, implement, promote, monitor, and enforce those standards. They should be sufficiently flexible, however, that local officials can adapt them to local notions of justice and meaningful differences between cases.

Like all calls for just the right amount of anything, not too much and not too little, a proposal for sentencing standards that are constraining enough to assure that like cases are treated alike and flexible enough to assure that different cases are treated differently is a counsel of unattainable perfection. Nonetheless, that is probably what most people would want to see in a just system of sentencing, and we know some things about how a jurisdiction can move closer toward that goal.

IV. Desert and Disparity

The maxim "treat like cases alike" has as its complement "treat different cases differently." For jurisdictions in which unwarranted sentencing disparities are believed to be common, experience with sentencing and parole guidelines in the American federal system and in some states shows that disparities can be reduced (Arthur D. Little 1981; Blumstein, et al. 1983, chap. 3; Tonry 1988). American experience with parole and sentencing guidelines, Swedish experience with enactment of statutory principles to guide sentencing, German experience with day fines and prosecutorial fines, Dutch experience with conditional dismissal and community service orders, English and Scottish experience with community service orders, and Victorian experience with abolition of remission instruct that well-implemented sentencing policy changes can successfully change decision-making patterns. The American federal experience, however, also shows that sentencing standards and policies can be so detailed and inflexible that they risk violating the equality complement's adjuration to treat different cases differently.

What David Thomas in a recent essay (1995) calls "the newly fashionable desert theory" provides the calipers by which most people measure the extent of unwarranted disparity. "Disparity" is an empty category that can be filled only by reference to some standard. In principle, the standard could be set by any criteria. In practice, both the empirical grounding and the normative consensus are lacking for sentencing standards based on deterrence, rehabilitation, or incapacitation. By default, most people appear to believe that fairness means "treating like cases alike," which in turn means, at least, "alike in respect to the crime they committed."

Even the American federal guidelines, which are avowedly not based on a desert rationale, or any other explicit rationale, in practice look like a desert system. The guidelines grid sets out forty-three levels of offense severity ranked from lowest to highest, much as desert-premised guidelines might do, and six levels of prior record seriousness, also much as desert-premised guidelines might do.

A considerable literature on proportionality in punishment argues that punishment is an exercise in blaming and that punishments must be commensurate to the offender's relative blameworthiness (e.g., von Hirsch 1992). More serious crimes are more blameworthy and warrant harsher penalties than less serious crimes and crimes of comparable seriousness are equally blameworthy and warrant comparable penalties. Although spirited debates center on the precise role proportionality should play in setting sentencing policy or imposing sentences in individual cases (see, for example, Frase [1994] and von Hirsch [1994]), no one argues that desert has no relevance to justice in sentencing.

For most people in most places, as a normative matter, "unwarranted" disparities exist when sentences in general are disproportionate to the relative severities of the offenses for which they are imposed. Systems in which judges are not subject to established and enforceable standards are presumably those in which the likelihood of unwarranted disparities is greatest.

Not every jurisdiction should attempt to learn from the American experience and establish sentencing guidelines to structure sentencing discretion. The cure may be worse than the ailment. In effect, the question is, when is an American cure the right prescription for another country's sentencing ailments? The answer is, it depends on the distribution and severity of sentences that characterize a legal system. Where few offenders receive prison sentences, and those are typically short, the human costs of unwarranted disparities may be relatively slight and the iatrogenic risk that a structured sentencing system will fail to treat different cases differently may be unacceptably high. Where prison sentences are often severe, the burdens borne by the victims of unwarrantedly severe or otherwise disparate sentences may be unacceptably high and the risks of inflexibility worth taking.

Table 7.1 shows the distribution of prison sentences imposed in selected recent years in Sweden (Jareborg 1995) and Victoria (Freiberg

Table 7.1. Distribution of Prison Sentences Imposed in Sweden, Victoria (Higher Courts), and United States (State Prisons)

Duration	Sweden (%)	Victoria (%)	American State Prisons (%)	
			(1986)	(1991)
10+ years	0	3.6	39	43
4–10 years	1.7	19.6	25[a]	24[a]
2–4 years	3.8	36.0	25[b]	23[b]
1–2 years	5.0	23.2	↓	↓
6 mo.–1 year	12.0	↓		
2 mo.–6 mo.	28.0	13.4	10	10
under 2 mo.	50.0	↑	↑	↑

Sources: Beck et al. (1993); Freiberg (1995); Jareborg (1995).

[a] = 5–10 years.

[b] = 2–5 years.

1995), and being served in American state prisons in 1986 and 1991. The data are from secondary sources and for a variety of reasons are not fully comparable; nonetheless, because each represents the distribution of dispositions within a single jurisdictional system, their noncomparability is not a problem for my purposes. In Sweden, Jareborg (1995) reports that 41 percent of convicted offenders in 1991 received prison sentences and that 95 percent of those were for two years or less. In Germany in 1993, only 6 percent of all criminal penalties involve prison sentences more than one year. In 1991, only 1 percent of all sentences were to prison terms of two years or longer (Albrecht 1995). Similarly, in The Netherlands in 1991, only 14 percent of all prison sentences exceeded one year and less than 1 percent exceeded six years (Tak 1994a). Where relatively few offenders are incarcerated, and the vast majority of those for very short periods, the human costs for individuals of unwarranted disparities are seldom likely to be great. If two like-situated offenders receive one-and three-month prison sentences, or even one- and two-year sentences, the absolute difference, while still a cause for concern, will not drastically alter the offender's life. In Victorian High Courts, Freiberg (1995) reports that 47.9 percent of offenders received prison sentences in 1991. Nearly a quarter of those received terms exceeding four years and nearly three-fifths received terms longer than two years. Where many offenders are incarcerated for long terms, the potential range of disparity is great and the case for standards is much stronger. In American states in 1986 and 1991, respectively 39 and 43 percent of prisoners held in state prisons were serving terms of ten years or longer; because the U.S. prison population by the end of 1995 had increased by nearly 300,000 over the 1991 figure, the proportion is probably now higher.

Table 7.1 is only a starting point. Despite the dispersion of sentences in Victoria, for example, it is possible that a case law tariff policed by appellate sentence review suffices to reduce the risk of unacceptable disparities. Or conceivably local or national norms about punishment are so well established and so widespread that injustice from disparity is unlikely to be substantial.

For myself, I am skeptical that appellate sentence review anywhere is rigorous in the absence of reasonably precise standards whose appropriate application in individual cases can be assessed on appeal. The American federal appellate courts have aggressively policed judicial compliance with the federal guidelines, but they are very mechanical and detailed, much more like income tax regulations than a general sentencing tariff. The Minnesota appellate courts have been moderately aggressive in enforcing Minnesota's guidelines but have created case law doctrines of amenability and nonamenability to probation (Frase 1991b) that give judges considerable latitude to individualize sentences. The few evaluations of appellate sentence review in American states that lack detailed sentencing standards have concluded that without standards, appellate courts can do little more than make ad hoc decisions in individual cases and that typically only aberrantly severe sentences are overturned (e.g., Zeisel and Diamond 1977). Even in England, where the publication and analysis of appellate sentencing decisions is more extensive than in any other English-speaking country, David Thomas (1995), unquestionably the leading authority on the subject, acknowledges that statutory and policy changes in the late 1970s "effectively brought to an end the hopes for a more ambitious review of judicial sentencing practice."

Although few sentencing reforms that affect judges' discretion have leaped across national boundaries, there is an available body of evidence on the effects of sentencing policy changes that should be transferable. In the United States, the Washington Sentencing Guidelines Commission built on Minnesota's experience, as did Oregon's commission on Washington's, and later commissions on their predecessors'. The federal commission for a variety of reasons made no effort to learn from its state predecessors; federal courts and defendants will for many more years suffer the consequences. In Australia, Victoria has shown how to implement the abolition of remission while avoiding the unintended consequence of increased prison populations and crowding. New South Wales has shown how not to do it. The Germans in the early 1970s showed that a country can successfully adopt day fines; the English recently showed how not to. Minnesota and Washington showed that judges can be persuaded to accept substantial diminutions in the scope of their discretion over sentencing; the recent English and American federal experiences offer alternate scenarios of how things can go wrong when judges are not persuaded of the legitimacy of the new regime.

When I first began to examine sentencing policy literatures outside the United States, I was skeptical whether we know much about sentencing policy that has cross-national relevance. I was mistaken. National and subnational jurisdictions can learn a great deal by looking outside their boundaries to the documented experiences of earlier innovators. There are positive and negative lessons to be learned. George Santayana observed that those who cannot remember the past are condemned to repeat it. Adapted to sentencing policy the aphorism might go, those jurisdictions that refuse to learn from the experiences of others are condemned to repeat their mistakes.

8

"What Is to Be Done?"

The ways in which Americans think about punishment of offenders have fundamentally changed since 1970. No doubt they will keep changing. A book like this one written twenty-five years from now may describe a return to the values of indeterminate sentencing, the emergence of a Brave New World of aversive conditioning and chemical controls on behavior, or something I cannot imagine.

In our time, it is clear that the paradigm that governed indeterminate sentencing, with its rehabilitative rationales, broad unstructured discretions, and disregard of fairness to offenders is dead. It is less clear whether any generally supported paradigm has appeared in its place.

Many recent policy initiatives have been distinct less for what they were than for what they were not. Rehabilitation, on normative and technological grounds, no longer commands support as an overriding rationale for punishment, but neither does anything else. Utilitarian crime-control approaches based on deterrence and incapacitation have champions, especially among elected officials. So do sentencing strategies premised on the desirability of imposing retributively deserved punishment, especially among academics but also among large numbers of public officials. Even rehabilitative strategies, especially for sex offenders and drug-dependent offenders, still have many adherents.

Likewise, determinate sentencing systems are united in rejection of the broad unaccountable discretions once possessed by judges, but are highly diverse in their approaches to regulating decision making. Mandatory sentencing laws and the federal sentencing guidelines give the important powers to legislatures and sentencing commissions and try to coerce judges to follow detailed policies set by others. Presumptive sentencing guidelines like those in Minnesota, Washington, and Oregon set moderately detailed standards for sentencing, but then allow judges to decide whether and how to apply them in individual cases, subject to the right of the defendant or the state to challenge by appeal the validity of the judge's reasons for disregarding applicable standards. Voluntary guidelines like those in Delaware and Arkansas set standards for sentences that provide benchmarks, but defer entirely to the judge's decision whether to apply sentences recommended in the guidelines and do not give rise to appeal rights when judges do something else.

Similar diversity afflicts parole. Few people any longer claim that parole board members have special capacities to know when prisoners have been rehabilitated and therefore merit release. The idea that prisoners' releases should be the outcome of gestalt decisions by parole boards has in many states been discredited. There is, however, no unanimity on what to do next. Some states and the federal government have abolished parole release. Some states have retained parole release, but adopted guidelines (coupled with inmates' rights to file administrative appeals of adverse decisions) to govern release decisions. Other states that have retained parole have shifted its primary function from setting release dates for worthy prisoners to controlling prison populations by means of changing release policies. Still other states, more from inertia than anything else, retain parole boards that operate in ways indistinguishable from those of the 1950s.

A just sentencing system would be simultaneously respectful of the public interests in safety and crime prevention and in parsimonious expenditure of public funds. It would also assure that convicted offenders are treated fairly and consistently and that judges are subject to rules that guide their decisions and are accountable for those decisions. Twenty-five years of research and experience concerning sentencing "reforms" have shown how better sentencing systems can be fashioned. We know what works and what doesn't, and by what criteria. We can with confidence predict both intended and undesirable unintended consequences of policy changes. We know now that, along with well-charted deficiencies, there was much that was good in indeterminate sentencing.

A sentencing system that incorporated the following eight elements, the best of existing determinate sentencing systems and past indeterminate ones, would be far better than any now in operation.

First, legislatures would repeal all mandatory minimum penalties, including three-strikes laws. They do little that is good and much that is bad, both to the integrity of the legal system and to offenders who are often punished more severely than anyone directly involved believes is appropriate. The research evidence makes it clear that enactment of mandatory penalties has either no or at best modest and short-term deterrent effects, and authoritative government-sponsored commissions in many countries, including the United States, England, and Canada, agree. Lengthy mandatory penalties often keep offenders in prison long after it makes incapacitative sense—because crime, especially violent crime, is a young man's game and older prisoners age out of their violent proclivities. Finally, judges and prosecutors often resist imposing penalties that they believe are unjustly severe, sometimes by deception. Specifying presumptive minimum sentences for especially serious crimes in guidelines will give guidance to judges, and for serious crimes and typical offenders, judges are likely to heed that guidance. When they do not, it is better to allow them openly to impose a less harsh sentence and explain why than surreptitiously to impose a less harsh sentence.

Second, legislatures would invest the funds needed to establish credible, well-managed noncustodial penalties that can serve as sanctions intermediate between prison and probation. Research on intensive supervision probation, house arrest, and community service consistently shows that offenders sentenced to those sanctions have no worse recidivism rates than comparable offenders sentenced to prison, but at substantially less cost to taxpayers. In many countries, including Germany and the Netherlands, fines are legally presumed to be the appropriate sentence in most cases, and as a result are often imposed for many crimes that result in prison sentences in the United States. In many countries, including England, Scotland, and the Netherlands, community service orders are commonly imposed as a free standing sentence more severe than probation and are imposed for many crimes that in the United States result in prison sentences. Unfortunately, comparatively few intermediate sanctions are adequately funded. As a result they lack credibility in the eyes of justice system officials and are insufficiently available to be incorporated into sentencing guidelines.

Third, authority for creation of rules for sentencing would be delegated to an administrative agency, often but not necessarily called a sentencing commission. In the 1970s, some of the states that first rejected indeterminate sentencing established detailed statutory rules for sentencing, and others established sentencing commissions and directed them to promulgate sentencing rules. The statutory rules typically had little effect on sentencing patterns. The very existence, however, of statutory provisions made them irresistible targets for politicians who wanted to increase penalties to demonstrate their concern about crime. The difficulty with that is not that the penalties they sought were necessarily wrong—few people claim on absolute metaphysical or other grounds to know precisely what penalties are right for what crimes—but that the process was wrong. It created pressures only for penalty increases and made it impossible to develop balanced, comprehensive policies that took account of cost ramifications, correctional resources, and the relations between penalties for different crimes.

Sentencing commissions, by contrast, showed that they were able to some degree to insulate policy development from political whimsy and that they were able to adopt comprehensive, system wide policies. As a result, though no additional states adopted detailed statutory sentencing schemes after the early 1980s, many created sentencing commissions. In 1994 alone, new commissions began work in Massachusetts, Missouri, and Oklahoma (Greene 1995*a*).

Fourth, the sentencing commission would be directed to develop, promulgate, and monitor systems of sentencing rules, usually but not necessarily called sentencing guidelines. The rules would be presumptive, neither merely voluntary nor mandatory, and judges would be expected either to impose a presumptively appropriate sentence or to impose some other sentence and explain why. Experience with presumptive guidelines in a number of states shows that judges apply them in a substantial majority of cases and that racial, sexual, and other unwarranted disparities are thereby reduced. By contrast, experience with voluntary guidelines in a number of states (excluding Delaware, which is a special case) shows that judges seldom follow them and that disparities are unaffected. And experience with mandatory guidelines in the federal system shows that judges and prosecutors often resent and resist them and devise ways to circumvent them, with the result that disparities are not reduced.

Fifth, the sentencing commission would be directed to take account of existing and planned corrections resources, both community based and institutional, and to devise guidelines that are compatible in their projected impact with the facilities and resources that are or will become available. This does not mean that penalties cannot be increased, merely that responsible public officials should be prepared to find the funds required to pay for facilities that they believe public safety concerns require. Too often, legislators vote to increase penalties this year and leave to their successors the problem of paying for the facilities needed to carry them out. The requirement that policies be matched with resources has a salutary effect; policy makers can increase penalties and funding, or increase penalties for some crimes while reducing them for others and holding funding constant, or not increase penalties at all. A number of state sentencing commissions have tied their guidelines to available and planned resources—Minnesota and Washington in the 1980s, Oregon and Kansas in the 1990s—and thereby controlled their prison populations and corrections spending when most states experienced record increases in both.

Sixth, sentencing commissions would be directed to devise guidelines for custodial penalties that set maximum presumptive terms of confinement for all cases and minimum terms for the most serious crimes. Evidence concerning every guidelines system on which data are available shows that judges seldom impose sentences longer than those presumed to be appropriate. Guidelines thus have been shown drastically to reduce risks of aberrantly long sentences. At the same time, evidence concerning guidelines systems shows that judges often believe that offenders' individual circumstances and characteristics justify sentences less severe than guidelines direct. When guidelines so permit, they "depart downward." When guidelines do not so permit, judges often (with prosecutors' cooperation) find a way to circumvent the guidelines. Specifying presumptive minimum terms for especially serious crimes expresses the judgment that any penalty less than a designated term of confinement will depreciate the seriousness of the crime or the importance of the behavioral norm violated. For all other crimes, allowing judges to tailor noncustodial and short custodial sanctions to the circumstances of individual cases will bring into the open processes that are often now surreptitious and will make noncustodial penalties more widely available.

Seventh, guidelines for noncustodial penalties would permit judges to choose among noncustodial penalties for minor crimes and between them and periods of full or partial confinement for more serious crimes. Whether a particular noncustodial penalty is appropriate for an offender often depends on the offender's characteristics. For crimes of comparable severity but different character, noncustodial penalties are variously appropriate: for a drug-dependent shoplifter or burglar or drug dealer, compulsory drug treatment (outpatient or residential, depending on the offender's drug problem and prior treatment experience); for a bank teller embezzler, restitution and community service; for the perpetrator of a commercial fraud, restitution and a substantial fine; for an employed head of family who has committed a serious assault while intoxicated, a substantial fine and nighttime and weekend confinement, thereby permitting him to continue to work and support his family. Similar differences between cases will sometimes make a prison sentence appropriate for one offender convicted of offense X with criminal history Y, and a noncustodial penalty appropriate for another.

Eighth, enabling legislation and sentencing commission policy would establish a presumption that, within the range of sanctions set out in applicable guidelines, judges should impose the least punitive and intrusive appropriate sentence. This may to some seem a radical shift from contemporary policy, but that is only because Americans have over the past fifteen years become accustomed to mechanical application of standardized penalties, whether or not in individual cases they make sense or are just or effective.

Partly this recent one-penalty-fits-all approach resulted from the politicization of crime-control policy and indifference by some political figures to the effects of policies on individuals. To justify human suffering caused by the Bolshevik takeover of the Russian government in 1917, Trotsky observed that omelets cannot be made without breaking eggs. Many of the more cynical recent proponents of harsh crime-control policies have apparently decided that elections cannot be won without breaking people.

Acceptance of mechanistic sentencing policies has also been influenced by just deserts theories of punishment. In the interest of reducing disparities, policy makers tried to establish objective criteria for sentencing. Crimes can readily be scaled by seriousness and records of past criminality by their seriousness and extent. That is because both are linear scales that start from zero and increase in intuitively plausible ways.

Other considerations that are relevant to sentencing are not linear and their relevance depends on the circumstances of individual cases. Take employment, family status, or mental abnormality. The relevance of each to sentencing varies with circumstances and cannot be expressed in a linear scale or in a single statement as can, for example, offense seriousness or gratuitous infliction of violence in a robbery or rape.

Because crimes and criminal records can be scaled in intuitively plausible ways, and most other ethically relevant factors cannot, guidelines systems tend to scale sentences solely to current and past criminality. Other circumstances are simply ignored, not because they are irrelevant, but because they cannot be encapsulated in a guidelines matrix. In many systems, judges are discouraged from taking an offender's personal circumstances into account. In the federal guidelines, judges are forbidden to depart from guidelines because of case-specific considerations such as employment and education, family status, a disadvantaged background, and mental abnormality or subnormality. Yet most people, and most judges, find these kinds of considerations highly relevant, but in different ways in different cases.

Creation of least restrictive appropriate alternative presumptions would be a return to what was long widely deemed good practice. The American Law Institute's *Model Penal Code* (1962) has such a presumption. So does the model criminal code proposed by the National Commission on Reform of Federal Criminal Laws (1968). So do all three editions of the American Bar Association's Sentencing Standards. The most recent provides: "The sentence imposed should be no more severe than necessary to achieve the social purpose or purposes for which it is authorized" (1994, Standard 18–6.1[a]).

No sentencing system will ever be perfect or free from risks of injustice in individual cases. Systems that incorporated the eight propositions set out here would, however, represent an amalgam of the best features of both indeterminate and determinate sentencing. From the former come the ideas that sentencing should take account of all ethically relevant differences between cases, that unnecessary suffering should not be imposed or public monies wasted, and that mandatory penalties are virtually never sound public policy. From the latter come the ideas that sentencing disparities matter, that safeguards should be created against aberrant and invidious exercises of discretion, that sentencing—like any legal proceeding involving property or liberty interests—should be subject to rules, and that judges should be accountable for their correct application of sentencing rules by means of appeals to higher judicial authority.

Policy makers seldom pay much attention to academics' proposals, especially in relation to crime control and sentencing, and especially in our time. Should there be policy makers who want to make sentencing fairer, more cost-effective, and no less protective of public safety, research findings and experience from a quarter century's sentencing ferment show the path to be followed.

References

ABA Journal. 1994. "The Verdict Is In: Throw Out Mandatory Sentences: Introduction." *ABA Journal* 79:78.

Albrecht, Hans-Jörg. 1995. "Sentencing Reform in Germany." *Overcrowded
Times* 6(1):1, 6–10.

Allen, Francis A. 1964. *The Borderland of Criminal Justice.* Chicago: University
of Chicago Press.

Alschuler, Albert W. 1978. "Sentencing Reform and Prosecutorial Power." *University of Pennsylvania Law Review* 126:550–77.

———. 1991. "The Failure of Sentencing Guidelines: A Plea for Less Aggrega-
tion." *University of Chicago Law Review* 58:901–51.

Alschuler, Albert W., and Stephen J. Schulhofer. 1989. "Judicial Impressions of
the Sentencing Guidelines." *Federal Sentencing Reporter* 2:94–99.

American Bar Association. 1968. *Sentencing Alternatives and Procedures.*
Chicago: American Bar Association.

———. 1994. *American Bar Association Standards for Criminal Justice: Sentencing Alternatives and Procedures.* 3d ed. Washington, D.C.: American
Bar Association.

American Friends Service Committee. 1971. *Struggle for Justice.* New York: Hill
& Wang.

American Law Institute. 1962. *Model Penal Code (Proposed Official Draft).*
Philadelphia: American Law Institute.

Anglin, Douglas, and Yih-Ing Hser. 1990. "Treatment of Drug Abuse." In *Drugs
and Crime,* edited by Michael Tonry and James Q. Wilson. Vol. 13 of
Crime and Justice: A Review of Research, edited by Michael Tonry and
Norval Morris. Chicago: University of Chicago Press.

Arthur D. Little, Inc. 1981. *An Evaluation of Parole Guidelines in Four Jurisdictions.* Report prepared for the National Institute of Corrections. Washington, D.C. and Cambridge, Mass.: Arthur D. Little, Inc.

Ashford, Kathryn, and Craig Mosbaek. 1991. *First Year Report on Implementation of Sentencing Guidelines: November 1989 to January 1991.* Portland: Oregon Criminal Justice Council.

Ashworth, Andrew. 1992*a*. "The Criminal Justice Act 1991." In *Sentencing, Judicial Discretion, and Training,* edited by Colin Munro and Martin Wasik. London: Sweet & Maxwell.

———. 1992*b*. "Sentencing Reform Structures." In *Crime and Justice: A Review of Research,* vol. 16, edited by Michael Tonry. Chicago: University of Chicago Press.

Austin, James. 1991. *The Consequences of Escalating the Use of Imprisonment: The Case Study of Florida.* San Francisco, Calif.: National Council on Crime and Delinquency.

Austin, James, Michael Jones, and Melissa Bolyard. 1993. *The Growing Use of Jail Boot Camps: The Current State of the Art.* Research in Brief. Washington, D.C.: National Institute of Justice.

Austin, James, Charles Jones, John Kramer, and Phil Renninger. 1994. *National Assessment of Structured Sentencing.* Final report to the Bureau of Justice Assistance. San Francisco, Calif.: National Council on Crime and Delinquency.

Australia Law Reform Commission. 1980. *Sentencing of Federal Offenders.* Canberra: Australian Government Publishing Service.

Baird, S. C., and D. Wagner. 1990. "Measuring Diversion: The Florida Community Control Program." *Crime and Delinquency* 36:112–25.

Baker, J. H. 1977. "Criminal Courts and Procedure at Common Law, 1550–1800." In *Crime in England, 1550–1800,* edited by J. S. Cockburn. Princeton, N.J.: Princeton University Press.

Baldwin, John, and Michael McConville. 1980. "Criminal Juries." In *Crime and Justice: An Annual Review of Research,* vol. 2, edited by Norval Morris and Michael Tonry. Chicago: University of Chicago Press.

Ball, R. A., C. R. Huff, and J. R. Lilly. 1988. *House Arrest and Correctional Policy.* Newbury Park, Calif.: Sage.

Banks, J., A. L. Porter, R. L. Rardin, T. R. Silver, and V. E. Unger. 1977. *Phase I Evaluation of Intensive Special Probation Projects.* Washington, D.C.: Law Enforcement Assistance Administration, National Institute of Law Enforcement and Criminal Justice.

Barr, William. 1992. *The Case for More Incarceration.* Washington, D.C.: U.S. Department of Justice, Office of Policy Development.

Baumer, Terry L., M. G. Maxfield, and R. I. Mendelsohn. 1993. "A Comparative Analysis of Three Electronically Monitored Home Detention Programs." *Justice Quarterly* 10:121–42.

Baumer, Terry L., and Robert I. Mendelsohn. 1992. "Electronically Monitored Home Confinement: Does It Work?" In *Smart Sentencing: The Emergence of Intermediate Sanctions,* edited by James M. Byrne, Arthur J. Lurigio, and Joan Petersilia. Newbury Park, Calif.: Sage.

Beck, Allen, et al. 1993. *Survey of State Prison Inmates, 1991.* Washington, D.C.: Bureau of Justice Statistics.

Becker, Gary S. 1968. "Crime and Punishment: An Economic Analysis." *Journal of Political Economy* 76:169–217.

Beha, James A., II. 1977. "'And Nobody Can Get You Out': The Impact of a Mandatory Prison Sentence for the Illegal Carrying of a Firearm on the Use of Firearms and on the Administration of Criminal Justice in Boston." *Boston University Law Review* 57:96–146 (part 1), 289–333 (part 2).

Bentham, Jeremy. 1843. *The Works of Jeremy Bentham,* vol. 4, edited by John Bowring. London: Simpkin, Marshall.

———. 1948, 1789. *Introduction to the Principles of Morals and Legislation,* edited by Wilfrid Harrison. Oxford: Oxford University Press.

Biles, David. 1993. "Noncustodial Penalties in Australia." *Overcrowded Times* 4(1):7–9.

Block, Michael K. 1989. "Emerging Problems in the Sentencing Commission's Approach to Guidelines Amendments." *Federal Sentencing Reporter* 1:451–55.

Blomberg, Thomas G., William Bales, and Karen Reed. 1993. "Intermediate Punishment: Redistributing or Extending Social Control?" *Crime, Law, and Social Change* 19:187–201.

Blumstein, Alfred. 1994. "Prisons." In *Crime,* edited by James Q. Wilson and Joan Petersilia. San Francisco, Calif.: ICS.

Blumstein, Alfred, Jacqueline Cohen, Susan E. Martin, and Michael Tonry, eds. 1983. *Research on Sentencing: The Search for Reform,* 2 vols. Washington, D.C.: National Academy Press.

Blumstein, Alfred, Jacqueline Cohen, and Daniel Nagin. 1978. *Deterrence and Incapacitation: Estimating the Effects of Criminal Sanctions on Crime Rates.* Washington, D.C.: National Academy Press.

Blumstein, Alfred, Jacqueline Cohen, Jeffrey Roth, and Christy Visher. 1986. *Criminal Careers and "Career Criminals."* Washington, D.C.: National Academy Press.

Boerner, David. 1985. *Sentencing in Washington: A Legal Analysis of the Sentencing Reform Act of 1981.* Seattle: Butterworth.

———. 1993. "The Legislature's Role in Guidelines Sentencing in 'The Other Washington.'" *Wake Forest Law Review* 28:381–420.

———. 1995a. "Sentencing Policy in Washington." *Overcrowded Times.* 6(3):9–12.

———. 1995b. "Sentencing Guidelines and Prosecutorial Discretion." *Judicature* 78(4):196–200.

Bogan, Kathleen M. 1990. "Constructing Felony Sentencing Guidelines in an Already Crowded State: Oregon Breaks New Ground." *Crime and Delinquency* 36:467–87.

———. 1991. "Sentencing Reform in Oregon." *Overcrowded Times* 2(2):5, 14–15.

Bogan, Kathleen, and David Factor. 1995. "Oregon Guidelines, 1989–94." *Overcrowded Times* 6(2):1, 13–15.

Bottomley, A. Keith. 1990. "Parole in Transition: A Comparative Study of Origins, Developments, and Prospects for the 1990s." In *Crime and Justice: A Review of Research,* vol. 12, edited by Michael Tonry and Norval Morris. Chicago: University of Chicago Press.

Bottoms, Anthony. 1995. "The Philosophy and Politics of Punishment and Sentencing." In *The Politics of Sentencing Reform,* edited by Chris Clarkson and Rod Morgan. Oxford: Oxford University Press.

Breyer, Stephen. 1988. "The Federal Sentencing Guidelines and the Key Compromises upon Which They Rest." *Hofstra Law Review* 17:1–50.

———. 1992. "The Key Compromises of the Federal Sentencing Guidelines." In *Sentencing, Judicial Discretion, and Training,* edited by Colin Munro and Martin Wasik. London: Sweet & Maxwell.

Bright, Myron. 1993. "These Sentences Defy Reason, but as I Have Already Noted—Such Is Our System." *Overcrowded Times* 4(3):20.

Brody, S. R. 1976. *The Effectiveness of Sentencing: A Review of the Literature.* London: H.M. Stationery Office.

Bureau of Justice Statistics. 1992*a. Prisoners in 1991.* Washington, D.C.: Bureau of Justice Statistics, U.S. Department of Justice.

———. 1992*b.* "Four Percent More Prisoners in First Half of 1992." News release. Washington, D.C.: Bureau of Justice Statistics, U.S. Department of Justice.

———. 1994*a. Prisoners in 1993.* Washington, D.C.: Bureau of Justice Statistics, U.S. Department of Justice.

———. 1994*b.* "State and Federal Prison Population Tops One Million." Press release dated October 27, 1994. Washington, D.C.: U.S. Department of Justice.

Bynum, Timothy S. 1982. "Prosecutorial Discretion and the Implementation of a Legislative Mandate." In *Implementing Criminal Justice Policies,* edited by Merry Morash. Beverly Hills, Calif.: Sage.

Byrne, James M., and Linda M. Kelly. 1989. *Restructuring Probation as an Intermediate Sanction: An Evaluation of the Massachusetts Intensive Probation Supervision Program.* Final report to the National Institute of Justice. Lowell, Mass.: University of Lowell, Department of Criminal Justice.

Byrne, James M., Arthur J. Lurigio, and Joan Petersilia. 1992. *Smart Sentencing: The Emergence of Intermediate Sanctions.* Newbury Park, Calif.: Sage.

Byrne, James M., and April Pattavina. 1992. "The Effectiveness Issue: Assessing What Works in the Adult Community Corrections System." In *Smart Sentencing: The Emergence of Intermediate Sanctions,* edited by James M. Byrne, Arthur J. Lurigio, and Joan Petersilia. Newbury Park, Calif.: Sage.

Cabranes, José. 1992. "Sentencing Guidelines: A Dismal Failure." *New York Law Journal* (July 27), p. 27.

Canadian Sentencing Commission. 1987. *Sentencing Reform: A Canadian Approach.* Ottawa: Canadian Government Publishing Centre.

Carlson, Kenneth. 1982. *Mandatory Sentencing: The Experience of Two States.* National Institute of Justice, U.S. Department of Justice. Washington, D.C.: U.S. Government Printing Office.

Carrow, Deborah M. 1984. "Judicial Sentencing Guidelines: Hazards of the Middle Ground." *Judicature* 68:161–71.

Carrow, Deborah M., Judith Feins, Beverly N. W. Lee, and Lois Olinger. 1985. *Guidelines Without Force: An Evaluation of the Multi-Jurisdictional Sentencing Guidelines Field Test.* Report to the National Institute of Justice. Cambridge, Mass.: Abt Associates.

Carter, R. M., J. Robinson, and L. T. Wilkins. 1967. *The San Francisco Project: A Study of Federal Probation and Parole.* Berkeley: University of California Press.

Casale, Silvia G. 1981. *Fines in Europe.* Fines in Sentencing Working Paper no. 10. New York: Vera Institute of Justice.

Clarke, Stevens H. 1984. "North Carolina's Determinate Sentencing Legislation." *Judicature* 68:140–52.

_____. 1987. *Felony Sentencing in North Carolina 1976–1986: Effects of Presumptive Sentencing Legislation.* Chapel Hill: Institute of Government, University of North Carolina at Chapel Hill.

Clarke, Stevens H., Susan Turner Kurtz, Glenn F. Lang, Kenneth L. Parker, Elizabeth W. Rubinsky, and Donna J. Schleicher. 1983. *North Carolina's Determinate Sentencing Legislation: An Evaluation of the First Year's Experience.* Chapel Hill: Institute of Government, University of North Carolina at Chapel Hill.

Clarkson, Chris, and Rod Morgan. 1995. *The Politics of Sentencing Reform.* Oxford: Oxford University Press.

Clear, Todd. 1987. "The New Intensive Supervision Movement." Paper presented at the annual meeting of the American Society of Criminology, Montreal, November.

Clear, Todd R., and James M. Byrne. 1992. "The Future of Intermediate Sanctions: Questions to Consider." In *Smart Sentencing: The Emergence of Intermediate Sanctions,* edited by James M. Byrne, Arthur J. Lurigio, and Joan Petersilia. Newbury Park, Calif.: Sage.

Cohen, Jacqueline. 1983. "Incapacitation as a Strategy for Crime Control: Possibilities and Pitfalls." In *Crime and Justice: An Annual Review of Research,* vol. 5, edited by Michael Tonry and Norval Morris. Chicago: University of Chicago Press.

Cohen, Jacqueline, and Michael Tonry. 1983. "Sentencing Reforms and Their Impacts." In *Research on Sentencing: The Search for Reform,* vol. 2, edited by Alfred Blumstein, Jacqueline Cohen, Susan Martin, and Michael Tonry. Washington, D.C.: National Academy Press.

Cole, George F. 1992. "Monetary Sanctions: The Problem of Compliance." In *Smart Sentencing: The Emergence of Intermediate Sanctions,* edited by James M. Byrne, Arthur J. Lurigio, and Joan Petersilia. Newbury Park, Calif.: Sage.

Cole, George F., Barry Mahoney, Marlene Thornton, and Roger A. Hanson. 1987. *The Practices and Attitudes of Trial Court Judges Regarding Fines as a Criminal Sanction.* Washington, D.C.: National Institute of Justice.

Committee on Justice and the Solicitor General. 1993. *Crime Prevention in Canada: Toward a National Strategy.* Ottawa: Canada Communication Group.

D.C. Superior Court, Sentencing Guidelines Commission. 1987. *Initial Report of the Superior Court Sentencing Guidelines Commission: The Development of Felony Sentencing Guidelines.* Washington, D.C.: D.C. Superior Court, Sentencing Guidelines Commission.

Dailey, Debra L. 1992. "Minnesota's Sentencing Guidelines—Past and Future." *Overcrowded Times* 3(1):4, 12–13.

Davis, Kenneth Culp. 1969. *Discretionary Justice—A Preliminary Inquiry.* Baton Rouge: Louisiana State University Press.

Dawson, Robert O. 1969. *Sentencing.* Boston: Little, Brown.

Delaware Sentencing Accountability Commission. 1989. *The First Year.* Wilmington: Delaware Sentencing Accountability Commission.

DiIulio, John J. 1990. "Crime and Punishment in Wisconsin." *Wisconsin Policy Research Institute Report* 3(7):1–56.

_____. 1994. "Let 'Em Rot." *Wall Street Journal* (January 26), ed. page.

DiIulio, John J., and Anne M. Piehl. 1991. "Does Prison Pay?" Unpublished manuscript. Princeton, N.J.: Princeton University, Center of Domestic and Comparative Policy Studies.

Doble, John, Stephen Immerwahr, and Amy Robinson. 1991. *Punishing Criminals: The People of Delaware Consider the Options.* New York: Edna McConnell Clark Foundation.

Doble, John, and Josh Klein. 1989. *Punishing Criminals: The Public's View. An Alabama Survey.* New York: Edna McConnell Clark Foundation.

Doob, Anthony. 1994. "Sentencing Reform in Canada." *Overcrowded Times* 5(4):1, 11–13.

_____. 1995. "The United States Sentencing Commission's Guidelines: If You Don't Know Where You Are Going, You May Not Get There." In *The Politics of Sentencing Reform,* edited by Chris Clarkson and Rod Morgan. Oxford: Oxford University Press.

Duff, R. A. 1986. *Trials and Punishments.* Cambridge: Cambridge University Press.

Dunworth, Terence, and Charles D. Weisselberg. 1992. "Felony Cases and the Federal Courts: The Guidelines Experience." *Southern California Law Review* 66:99–153.

Erwin, Billie. 1987. *Evaluation of Intensive Probation Supervision in Georgia.* Atlanta: Georgia Department of Corrections.

Erwin, Billie, and Lawrence Bennett. 1987. *New Dimensions in Probation: Georgia's Experience with Intensive Probation Supervision.* Research in Brief. Washington, D.C.: National Institute of Justice.

Fagan, Jeffrey. 1993. "The Political Economy of Drug Dealing Among Urban Gangs." In *Drugs and the Community,* edited by Robert C. Davis, Arthur J. Lurigio, and Dennis P. Rosenbaum. Springfield, Ill.: Thomas.

Federal Courts Study Committee. 1990. *Report.* Washington, D.C.: Administrative Office of the U.S. Courts.

Federal Judicial Center. 1994. *Planning for the Future: Results of a Federal Judicial Center Survey of United States Judges.* Washington, D.C.: Federal Judicial Center.

Federal Sentencing Reporter. 1990. May issue. New York: Vera Institute of Justice.

Flanagan, Timothy J., and Kathleen Maguire, eds. 1990. *Sourcebook of Criminal Justice Statistics—1989.* Washington, D.C.: U.S. Department of Justice, Bureau of Justice Statistics.

_____. 1992. *Sourcebook of Criminal Justice Statistics—1991.* Washington, D.C.: U.S. Department of Justice, Bureau of Justice Statistics.

Florida Legislature. 1991. *An Alternative to Florida's Current Sentencing Guidelines—A Report to the Legislature and the Sentencing Guidelines Commission.* Tallahassee: Florida Legislature, Economic and Demographic Research Division, Joint Legislative Management Committee.

Folkard, M. S., et al. 1974. *IMPACT Vol. 1: The Design of the Probation Experiment and an Interim Evaluation.* London: H.M. Stationery Office.

_____. 1976. *IMPACT Vol. 2: The Results of the Experiment.* London: H.M. Stationery Office.

Ford, Daniel, and Annesley K. Schmidt. 1985. *Electronically Monitored Home Confinement.* Research in Action. Washington, D.C.: National Institute of Justice.

Fox, Richard. 1991. "Order Out of Chaos: Victoria's New Maximum Penalty Structure." *Monash University Law Review* 17:106–31.

Frankel, Marvin. 1972. *Criminal Sentences: Law without Order.* New York: Hill & Wang.

Frankel, Marvin, and Leonard Orland. 1984. "Sentencing Commissions and Guidelines." *Georgetown Law Journal* 73:225–47.

Frase, Richard. 1991*a.* "Sentencing Reform in Minnesota: Ten Years After." *Minnesota Law Review* 75:727–54.

———. 1991*b.* "Defendant Amenability to Treatment or Probation as a Basis for Departure Under the Minnesota and Federal Guidelines." *Federal Sentencing Reporter* 3:328–33.

———. 1993*a.* "Implementing Commission-based Sentencing Guidelines: The Lessons of the First Ten Years in Minnesota." *Cornell Journal of Law and Public Policy* 2:279–337.

———. 1993*b.* "Prison Population Growing under Minnesota Guidelines." *Overcrowded Times* 4(1):1, 10–12.

———. 1994. "Purposes of Punishment under the Minnesota Sentencing Guidelines." *Criminal Justice Ethics* 13(1):11–20.

———. 1995. "State Sentencing Guidelines: Still Going Strong." *Judicature* 78(4):173–79.

Freed, Daniel J. 1992. "Federal Sentencing in the Wake of Guidelines: Unacceptable Limits on the Discretion of Sentencers." *Yale Law Journal* 101: 1681–1754.

Freed, Daniel J., and Marc Miller. 1989. "Intrigue at the U.S. Sentencing Commission: The Battle over Part-Time Commissioners." *Federal Sentencing Reporter* 2:156–58.

Freiberg, Arie. 1992. "Truth in Sentencing?: The Abolition of Remissions in Victoria." *Criminal Law Journal* 16:165.

———. 1993. "Sentencing Reform in Victoria." *Overcrowded Times* 4(4):7–9.

———. 1995. "Sentencing Reform in Victoria. A Case Study." In *The Politics of Sentencing Reform,* edited by Chris Clarkson and Rod Morgan. Oxford: Oxford University Press.

Gebelein, Richard S. 1991. "Sentencing Reform in Delaware." *Overcrowded Times* 2(2):5, 12–13.

Gendreau, Paul, Francis T. Cullen, and James Bonta. 1994. "Intensive Rehabilitation Supervision: The Next Generation in Community Corrections?" *Federal Probation* 58:72–78.

Gorta, Angela. 1992. "Impact of the Sentencing Act of 1989 on the NSW Prison Population." *Current Issues in Criminal Justice* 3(3):308–17.

———. 1993. "Truth-in-Sentencing in New South Wales." *Overcrowded Times* 4(2):4, 11–12.

Gottfredson, Don M., Leslie T. Wilkins, and Peter B. Hoffman. 1978. *Guidelines for Parole and Sentencing.* Lexington, Mass.: Lexington Books.

Gottlieb, David J. 1991. "A Review and Analysis of the Kansas Sentencing Guidelines." *Kansas Law Review* 39:65–89.

———. 1993. "Kansas Adopts Sentencing Guidelines." *Overcrowded Times* 4(3):1, 10–13.

Grebing, Gerhardt. 1982. *The Fine in Comparative Law: A Survey of 21 Coun-*

tries. Occasional Paper no. 9. Cambridge: University of Cambridge, Institute of Criminology.

Greene, Judy. 1995a. "Massachusetts, Missouri, and Oklahoma Establish Sentencing Commissions." *Overcrowded Times* 6(3):1, 18–22.

———. 1995b. "Phoenix FARE Program Implements Day-Fine System." *Overcrowded Times* 6(2): 6, 18–19.

Greenwood, Peter, with Allan Abrahamse. 1982. *Selective Incapacitation*. Santa Monica, Calif.: RAND.

Griset, Pamela L. 1991. *Determinate Sentencing: The Promise and the Reality of Retributive Justice*. Albany: State University of New York Press.

Harvey, L., and K. Pease. 1987. "The Lifetime Prevalence of Custodial Sentences." *British Journal of Criminology* 27:311–15.

Hart, H. L. A. 1968. *Punishment and Responsibility: Essays in the Philosophy of Law*. Oxford: Oxford University Press.

Hay, Douglas. 1975. "Property, Authority, and the Criminal Law." In *Albion's Fatal Tree: Crime and Society in Eighteenth Century England,* edited by Douglas Hay, Peter Linebaugh, and E. P. Thompson. New York: Pantheon.

———. 1980. "Crime and Justice in Eighteenth and Nineteenth Century England." In *Crime and Justice: An Annual Review of Research,* vol. 2, edited by Norval Morris and Michael Tonry. Chicago: University of Chicago Press.

Heaney, Gerald W. 1991. "The Reality of Guidelines Sentencing: No End to Disparity." *American Criminal Law Review* 28:161–233.

Heumann, Milton, and Colin Loftin. 1979. "Mandatory Sentencing and the Abolition of Plea Bargaining: The Michigan Felony Firearms Statute." *Law and Society Review* 13:393–430.

Hillsman, Sally. 1990. "Fines and Day Fines." In *Crime and Justice: A Review of Research,* vol. 12, edited by Michael Tonry and Norval Morris. Chicago: University of Chicago Press.

Hillsman, Sally, and Judith A. Greene. 1992. "The Use of Fines as an Intermediate Sanction." In *Smart Sentencing: The Emergence of Intermediate Sanctions,* edited by James M. Byrne, Arthur J. Lurigio, and Joan Petersilia. Newbury Park, Calif.: Sage.

Hillsman, Sally, Joyce Sichel, and Barry Mahoney. 1984. *Fines in Sentencing: A Study of the Use of the Fine as a Criminal Sanction*. Washington, D.C.: National Institute of Justice.

Holmes, Oliver Wendell. 1889. "Law in Science and Science in Law." *Harvard Law Review* 12:443–63.

Home Office. 1989. "Criminal and Custodial Careers." Statistical Bulletin No. 32. London: H. M. Stationery Office.

———. 1990. *Crime, Justice, and Protecting the Public*. London: Home Office.

———. 1994. *Criminal Statistics, England and Wales*. London: H.M. Stationery Office.

Honderich, Ted. 1989. *Punishment: The Supposed Justifications*. Cambridge: Polity.

Ifill, Gwen. 1991. "Senate's Rule for Its Anti-crime Bill: The Tougher the Provision, the Better." *New York Times* (July 8, national ed.), p. A6.

Jareborg, Nils. 1995. "The Swedish Sentencing Reform." In *The Politics of Sentencing Reform,* edited by Chris Clarkson and Rod Morgan. Oxford: Oxford University Press.

Johnson, Bruce D., Terry Williams, Kojo A. Dei, and Harry Sanabria. 1990. "Drug Abuse in the Inner City: Impact on Hard-Drug Users and the Community." In *Drugs and Crime,* edited by Michael Tonry and James Q. Wilson. Vol. 13 of *Crime and Justice: A Review of Research,* edited by Michael Tonry and Norval Morris. Chicago: University of Chicago Press.

Joint Committee on New York Drug Law Evaluation. 1978. *The Nation's Toughest Drug Law: Evaluating the New York Experience.* A project of the Association of the Bar of the City of New York and the Drug Abuse Council, Inc. Washington, D.C.: U.S. Government Printing Office.

Kansas Sentencing Commission. 1990. *Report to the Special Committee on the Judiciary* (July 26, 27, 1990). Topeka: Kansas Sentencing Commission.

_____. 1991. *Recommendations.* Topeka: Kansas Sentencing Commission.

Kant, Immanuel. 1887, 1797. *Rechtslehre,* Part Second, 49, translated by E. Hastie, Edinburgh.

Karle, Theresa Walker, and Thomas Sager. 1991. "Are the Federal Sentencing Guidelines Meeting Congressional Goals? An Empirical and Case Law Analysis." *Emory Law Review* 40:393–444.

Killias, Martin, André Kuhn, and Simone Rônez. 1995. "Sentencing in Switzerland." *Overcrowded Times* 6(3):1, 13–17.

Kleiman, Mark A. R., and David Cavanagh. 1990. "A Cost-Benefit Analysis of Prison Cell Construction and Alternative Sanctions." Unpublished manuscript. Cambridge, Mass.: Harvard University, Kennedy School of Government, Guggenheim Program in Criminal Justice Policy and Management.

Knapp, Kay A. 1984. *The Impact of the Minnesota Sentencing Guidelines: Three-Year Evaluation.* St. Paul, Minn.: Minnesota Sentencing Guidelines Commission.

_____. 1987. "Implementation of the Minnesota Guidelines: Can the Innovative Spirit Be Preserved?" In *The Sentencing Commission and Its Guidelines,* by Andrew von Hirsch, Kay A. Knapp, and Michael Tonry. Boston: Northeastern University Press.

_____. 1991. "Arizona: Unprincipled Sentencing, Mandatory Minimums, and Prison Crowding." *Overcrowded Times* 2(5):10–12.

_____. 1993. "Allocation of Discretion and Accountability within Sentencing Structures." *University of Colorado Law Review* 64:679–705.

Kramer, John. 1992. "The Evolution of Pennsylvania's Sentencing Guidelines." *Overcrowded Times* 3(4):6–9.

Kramer, John H., and Robin L. Lubitz. 1985. "Pennsylvania's Sentencing Reform: The Impact of Commission-Established Guidelines." *Crime and Delinquency* 31:481–500.

Kramer, John H., and Anthony J. Scirica. 1985. "Complex Policy Choices: The Pennsylvania Commission on Sentencing." Paper presented at the annual meeting of the Academy of Criminal Justice Sciences, Las Vegas, April.

Kress, Jack M. 1980. *Prescription for Justice: The Theory and Practice of Sentencing Guidelines.* Cambridge, Mass.: Ballinger.

Larivee, John J. 1991. "Day Reporting in Massachusetts: Supervision, Sanction, and Treatment." *Overcrowded Times* 2(1):7–8.

Lawrence, Pamela B., and Paul J. Hofer. 1992. "An Empirical Study of the Application of Relevant Conduct Guidelines. 1B1.3." Washington, D.C.: Federal Judicial Center.

Lear, Elizabeth T. 1993. "Is Conviction Relevant?" *UCLA Law Review* 40:1179–1239.

Lieb, Roxanne. 1991. "Washington State: A Decade of Sentencing Reform." *Overcrowded Times* 2(4):1, 5–8.

_____. 1993. "Washington Prison Population Growth Out of Control." *Overcrowded Times* 4(1):1, 13–14, 20.

Lilly, J. Robert. 1993. "Electronic Monitoring in the U.S.: An Update." *Overcrowded Times* 4(5): 4, 15.

Lipton, Douglas, Robert Martinson, and Judith Wilks. 1975. *The Effectiveness of Correctional Treatment: A Survey of Correctional Treatment Evaluations.* New York: Praeger.

Lloyd, C. 1991. *National Standards for Community Service Orders: The First Two Years of Operation.* London: Home Office Research and Planning Unit.

Loftin, Colin, Milton Heumann, and David McDowall. 1983. "Mandatory Sentencing and Firearms Violence: Evaluating an Alternative to Gun Control." *Law and Society Review* 17:287–318.

Loftin, Colin, and David McDowall. 1981. "'One with a Gun Gets You Two': Mandatory Sentencing and Firearms Violence in Detroit." *Annals of the American Academy of Political and Social Science* 455:150–67.

_____. 1984. "The Deterrent Effects of the Florida Felony Firearm Law." *Journal of Criminal Law and Criminology* 75:250–59.

Lubitz, Robin L. 1993. "North Carolina Legislature Considers Sentencing Change." *Overcrowded Times* 4(2):1, 9–10.

Lurigio, Arthur J., and Joan Petersilia. 1992. "The Emergence of Intensive Probation Supervision Programs in the United States." In *Smart Sentencing: The Emergence of Intermediate Sanctions,* edited by James M. Byrne, Arthur J. Lurigio, and Joan Petersilia. Newbury Park, Calif.: Sage.

McCarthy, Belinda, ed. 1987. *Intermediate Punishments: Intensive Supervision, Home Confinement, and Electronic Surveillance.* Monsey, N.Y.: Criminal Justice Press.

McDevitt, Jack, and Robyn Miliano. 1992. "Day Reporting Centers: An Innovative Concept in Intermediate Sanctions." In *Smart Sentencing: The Emergence of Intermediate Sanctions,* edited by James M. Byrne, Arthur J. Lurigio, and Joan Petersilia. Newbury Park, Calif.: Sage.

McDonald, Douglas. 1986. *Punishment without Walls: Community Service Sentences in New York City.* New Brunswick, N.J.: Rutgers University Press.

_____. 1992. "Punishing Labor: Unpaid Community Service as a Criminal Sentence." In *Smart Sentencing: The Emergence of Intermediate Sanctions,* edited by James M. Byrne, Arthur J. Lurigio, and Joan Petersilia. Newbury Park, Calif.: Sage.

McDonald, Douglas, Judith Greene, and Charles Worzella. 1992. *Day Fines in American Courts: The Staten Island and Milwaukee Experiments.* Issues and Practices. Washington, D.C.: National Institute of Justice.

McDowall, David, Colin Loftin, and Brian Wiersema. 1992. "A Comparative Study of the Preventive Effects of Mandatory Sentencing Laws for Gun Crimes." *Journal of Criminal Law and Criminology* 83:378–94.

McIvor, Gill. 1992. *Sentenced to Serve: The Operation and Impact of Community Service by Offenders.* Aldershot: Avebury.

_____. 1993. "CSOs Succeed in Scotland." *Overcrowded Times* 4(3):1, 6–8.

MacKenzie, Doris Layton. 1993. "Boot Camp Prisons 1993." *National Institute of Justice Journal* 227:21–28.

_____. 1994. "Boot Camps: A National Assessment." *Overcrowded Times* 5(4):1, 14–18.

MacKenzie, Doris Layton, and Dale Parent. 1992. "Boot Camp Prisons for Young Offenders." In *Smart Sentencing: The Emergence of Intermediate Sanctions,* edited by James M. Byrne, Arthur J. Lurigio, and Joan Petersilia. Newbury Park, Calif.: Sage.

MacKenzie, Doris Layton, and A. Piquero. 1994. "The Impact of Shock Incarceration Programs on Prison Crowding." *Crime and Delinquency* 40:222–49.

MacKenzie, Doris Layton, and J. W. Shaw. 1990. "Inmate Adjustment and Change during Shock Incarceration: The Impact of Correctional Boot Camp Programs." *Justice Quarterly* 7(1):125–50.

_____. 1993. "The Impact of Shock Incarceration on Technical Violations and New Criminal Activities." *Justice Quarterly* 10:463–87.

MacKenzie, Doris Layton, and C. Souryal. 1994. *Multi-Site Evaluation of Shock Incarceration.* Report to the National Institute of Justice. College Park: University of Maryland, Department of Criminology and Criminal Justice.

Maguire, Kathleen, and Ann L. Pastore, eds. 1993. *Sourcebook of Criminal Justice Statistics.* Washington, D.C.: U.S. Department of Justice, Bureau of Justice Statistics.

Mair, George. 1988. *Probation Day Centres.* London: H.M. Stationery Office.

_____. 1993a. "Day Centres in England and Wales." *Overcrowded Times* 4(2):5–7.

_____. 1993b. "Electronic Monitoring in England and Wales." *Overcrowded Times* 4(5):5, 12.

_____. 1994. "Intensive Probation in England and Wales." *Overcrowded Times* 5(4):4–6.

Mair, George, and Claire Nee. 1990. *Electronic Monitoring: The Trials and Their Results.* London: H.M. Stationery Office.

_____. 1992. "Day Centre Reconviction Rates." *British Journal of Criminology* 32:329–39.

Mair, George, et al. 1994. *Intensive Probation in England and Wales: An Evaluation.* London: H.M. Stationery Office.

Mann, Coramae Richey. 1993. *Unequal Justice—A Question of Color.* Bloomington: Indiana University Press.

Martin, Susan. 1984. "Interests and Politics in Sentencing Reform: The Development of Sentencing Guidelines in Pennsylvania and Minnesota." *Villanova Law Review* 29:21–113.

Maxfield, M., and T. Baumer. 1990. "Home Detention with Electronic Monitoring: Comparing Pretrial and Postconviction Programs." *Crime and Delinquency* 36:521–36.

Meachum, Larry R. 1986. "House Arrest: Oklahoma Experience." *Corrections Today* 48(4):102ff.

Meierhoefer, Barbara. 1992. "The Role of Offense and Offender Characteristics in Federal Sentencing." *Southern California Law Review* 66:367–99.

Michael, Jerome, and Herbert Wechsler. 1940. *Criminal Law and Its Administration*. Chicago: Foundation.

Miethe, Terance D., and Charles A. Moore. 1985. "Socioeconomic Disparities under Determinate Sentencing Systems: A Comparison of Preguideline and Postguideline Practices in Minnesota." *Criminology* 23:337–63.

Miller, Frank W. 1969. *Prosecution*. Boston: Little, Brown.

Miller, Marc. 1995. "Rehabilitating the Federal Sentencing Guidelines." *Judicature* 78(4):180–88.

Minnesota Citizen's Council on Crime and Justice. 1989. "The Cost of Corrections in the State of Alabama." A Report Prepared for the Alabama Department of Corrections, Montgomery. Minneapolis: Minnesota Citizen's Council on Crime and Justice.

Minnesota Sentencing Guidelines Commission. 1980. *Report to the Legislature— 1 January 1980*. St. Paul: Minnesota Sentencing Guidelines Commission.

_____. 1991a. *Summary of 1989 Sentencing Practices for Convicted Felons*. St. Paul: Minnesota Sentencing Guidelines Commission.

_____. 1991b. *Report to the Legislature on Intermediate Sanctions*. St. Paul: Minnesota Sentencing Guidelines Commission.

_____. 1992. *Report to the Legislature on Controlled Substance Offenders*. St. Paul: Minnesota Sentencing Guidelines Commission.

_____. 1994. *Sentencing Practices: Felony Offenders Sentenced in 1992*. St. Paul: Minnesota Sentencing Guidelines Commission.

Moore, Charles A., and Terance D. Miethe. 1986. "Regulated and Unregulated Sentencing Decisions: An Analysis of First-Year Practices under Minnesota's Felony Sentencing Guidelines." *Law and Society Review* 20:253–77.

Moore, Mark H. 1990. "Supply Reduction and Drug Law Enforcement." In *Drugs and Crime,* edited by Michael Tonry and James Q. Wilson. Vol. 13 of *Crime and Justice: A Review of Research,* edited by Michael Tonry and Norval Morris. Chicago: University of Chicago Press.

Morris, Norval. 1974. *The Future of Imprisonment*. Chicago: University of Chicago Press.

Morris, Norval, and Michael Tonry. 1990. *Between Prison and Probation: Intermediate Punishments in a Rational Sentencing System*. New York: Oxford University Press.

Moxon, David. 1992. "England Adopts Day Fines." *Overcrowded Times* 3(3):5, 12.

_____. 1993. "England Abandons Day Fines." *Overcrowded Times* 4(4):5, 10–11.

Moxon, David, Mike Sutton, and Carol Hedderman. 1990. *Unit Fines: Experiments in Four Courts*. London: H.M. Stationery Office.

Moynihan, Daniel Patrick. 1993. "Iatrogenic Government—Social Policy and Drug Research." *American Scholar* 62(3):351–62.

Mullaney, Fahy G. 1988. *Economic Sanctions in Community Corrections*. Washington, D.C.: National Institute of Corrections.

Murphy, Jeffrey. 1973. "Marxism and Retribution." *Philosophy and Public Affairs* 2:217–43.

Nagel, Ilene H. 1990. "Structuring Sentencing Discretion: The New Federal Sentencing Guidelines." *Journal of Criminal Law and Criminology* 80:883–943.

Nagel, Ilene, and John Hagan. 1983. "Gender and Crime: Offense Patterns and Criminal Court Sanctions." In *Crime and Justice: An Annual Review of Research,* vol. 4, edited by Michael Tonry and Norval Morris. Chicago: University of Chicago Press.

Nagel, Ilene H., and Stephen J. Schulhofer. 1992. "A Tale of Three Cities: An Empirical Study of Charging and Bargaining Practices Under the Federal Sentencing Guidelines." *Southern California Law Review* 66:501–66.

Nagin, Daniel. 1978. "General Deterrence: A Review of the Empirical Evidence." In *Deterrence and Incapacitation,* edited by Alfred Blumstein, Jacqueline Cohen, and Daniel Nagin. Washington, D.C.: National Academy Press.

National Commission on Reform of Federal Criminal Laws. 1968. *Final Report.* Washington, D.C.: U.S. Government Printing Office.

National Conference of State Legislatures. 1993. *State Budget Actions—1993.* Denver: National Conference of State Legislatures.

————. 1994. *State Budget Actions—1994.* Denver: National Conference of State Legislatures.

National Institute of Justice. 1994. *Drug Use Forecasting (DUF)—1993 Annual Report.* Washington, D.C.: National Institute of Justice.

New York State Committee on Sentencing Guidelines. 1985. *Determinate Sentencing Report and Recommendations.* New York: New York State Committee on Sentencing Guidelines.

Newman, Donald. 1966. *Conviction.* Boston: Little, Brown.

North Carolina Sentencing and Policy Advisory Commission. 1993. *Report to the 1993 Session of the General Assembly of North Carolina.* Raleigh: North Carolina Sentencing and Policy Advisory Commission.

————. 1994. *Revised Summary of New Sentencing Laws and the State-County Criminal Justice Partnership Act.* Raleigh: North Carolina Sentencing and Policy Advisory Commission.

O'Connell, John P., and Beth Peyton. 1990. "Delaware Evaluated Sentencing Accountability Commission." *The CJSA Forum* 8:4.

O'Donnell, Pierce, Michael Churgin, and Dennis Curtis. 1977. *Toward a Just and Effective Sentencing System.* New York: Praeger.

Oregon Criminal Justice Council. 1991. *First-Year Report on Implementation of Sentencing Guidelines.* Portland: Oregon Criminal Justice Council.

————. 1994. *Structured Sentencing Process.* Portland: Oregon Criminal Justice Council.

Orland, Leonard, and Kevin R. Reitz. 1993. "Epilogue: A Gathering of State Sentencing Commissions." *Colorado Law Review* 64:837–47.

Padilla, Felix. 1992. *The Gang as an American Enterprise.* New Brunswick, N.J.: Rutgers University Press.

Palumbo, Dennis J., Mary Clifford, and Zoann K. Snyder-Joy. 1992. "From Net-Widening to Intermediate Sanctions: The Transformation of Alternatives to Incarceration from Benevolence to Malevolence." In *Smart Sentencing: The Emergence of Intermediate Sanctions,* edited by James M. Byrne, Arthur J. Lurigio, and Joan Petersilia. Newbury Park, Calif.: Sage.

Parent, Dale. 1988. *Structuring Sentencing Discretion: The Evolution of Minnesota's Sentencing Guidelines.* Stoneham, Mass.: Butterworth.

_____. 1989. *Shock Incarceration: An Overview of Existing Programs.* Washington, D.C.: National Institute of Justice.

_____. 1990. *Day Reporting Centers for Criminal Offenders: A Descriptive Analysis of Existing Programs.* Washington, D.C.: National Institute of Justice.

_____. 1991. "Day Reporting Centers: An Emerging Intermediate Sanction." *Overcrowded Times* 2(1):6, 8.

_____. 1994. "Boot Camps Failing to Achieve Goals." *Overcrowded Times* 5(4):8–11.

Pearson, Frank. 1987. *Final Report of Research on New Jersey's Intensive Supervision Program.* New Brunswick, N.J.: Rutgers University, Department of Sociology, Institute for Criminological Research.

_____. 1988. "Evaluation of New Jersey's Intensive Supervision Program." *Crime and Delinquency* 34:437–48.

Pease, Ken. 1985. "Community Service Orders." In *Crime and Justice: A Review of Research,* vol. 6, edited by Michael Tonry and Norval Morris. Chicago: University of Chicago Press.

Pennsylvania Commission on Sentencing. 1984. *1983 Report: Sentencing in Pennsylvania.* State College: Pennsylvania Commission on Sentencing.

_____. 1985. *1984 Report: Sentencing in Pennsylvania.* State College: Pennsylvania Commission on Sentencing.

_____. 1987. *1986–1987 Annual Report.* State College: Pennsylvania Commission on Sentencing.

_____. 1993a. *Sentencing in Pennsylvania—1991.* State College: Pennsylvania Commission on Sentencing.

_____. 1993b. *Sentencing in Pennsylvania—1992.* State College: Pennsylvania Commission on Sentencing.

_____. 1994. *Sentencing Guidelines Implementation Manual,* 4th ed. (August 12, 1994). Harrisburg: Pennsylvania Commission on Sentencing.

Petersilia, Joan, Arthur J. Lurigio, and James M. Byrne. 1992. "Introduction: The Emergence of Intermediate Sanctions." In *Smart Sentencing: The Emergence of Intermediate Sanctions,* edited by James M. Byrne, Arthur J. Lurigio, and Joan Petersilia. Newbury Park, Calif.: Sage.

Petersilia, Joan, and Susan Turner. 1993. "Intensive Probation and Parole." In *Crime and Justice: A Review of Research,* vol. 17, edited by Michael Tonry. Chicago: University of Chicago Press.

Pierce, Glen L., and William J. Bowers. 1981. "The Bartley-Fox Gun Law's Short-Term Impact on Crime in Boston." *Annals of the American Academy of Political and Social Science* 455:120–32.

Pound, Roscoe. 1910. "Law in Books and Law in Action." *American Law Review* 44:12–36.

President's Commission on Model State Drug Laws. 1993. *Final Report.* Washington, D.C.: U.S. Government Printing Office.

Proband, Stan C. 1993. "North Carolina Legislature Adopts Guidelines." *Overcrowded Times* 4(2):4, 11–12.

Public Agenda Foundation. 1993. *Punishing Criminals: The People of Pennsylvania Speak Out.* New York: Edna McConnell Clark Foundation.

Quinn, Thomas J. 1990. "Delaware Sentencing Guidelines Achieving Their Goals." *Overcrowded Times* 1(3):1–2.

———. 1992. "Voluntary Guidelines Effective in Delaware." *Overcrowded Times* 3(1):1, 9, 11.

Radzinowicz, Leon. 1948–68. *A History of English Criminal Law and Its Administration from 1750.* 4 vols. London: Stevens.

Reiss, Albert J., Jr., and Jeffrey Roth, eds. 1993. *Understanding and Controlling Violence.* Washington, D.C.: National Academy Press.

Reitz, Kevin. 1993. "Sentencing Facts: Travesties of Real-Offense Sentencing." *Stanford Law Review* 45:523–73.

Reitz, Kevin, and Curtis Reitz. 1995. "Building a Sentencing Reform Agenda— The ABA's New Sentencing Standards." *Judicature* 78(4):189–95.

Renzema, Marc. 1992. "Home Confinement Programs: Development, Implementation, and Impact." In *Smart Sentencing: The Emergence of Intermediate Sanctions,* edited by James M. Byrne, Arthur J. Lurigio, and Joan Petersilia. Newbury Park, Calif.: Sage.

Reuter, Peter, and Mark A. R. Kleiman. 1986. "Risks and Prices: An Economic Analysis of Drug Prices." In *Crime and Justice: A Review of Research,* vol. 7, edited by Michael Tonry and Norval Morris. Chicago: University of Chicago Press.

Reynolds, Carl. 1993. "Texas Commission Proposes Corrections Overhaul." *Overcrowded Times* 4(2):1, 16–17.

Rhodes, William. 1992. "Sentence Disparity, Use of Incarceration, and Plea Bargaining: The Post-Guideline View from the Commission." *Federal Sentencing Reporter* 5:153–55.

Rich, William D., L. Paul Sutton, Todd D. Clear, and Michael J. Saks. 1982. *Sentencing by Mathematics: An Evaluation of the Early Attempts to Develop Sentencing Guidelines.* Williamsburg, Va.: National Center for State Courts.

Roberts, Julian. 1994. "The Role of Criminal Record in the Federal Sentencing Guidelines." *Criminal Justice Ethics* 13(1):11–20.

Roberts, Julian, and Andrew von Hirsch. 1993. "Statutory Sentencing Reform: A Review of Bill C-90." Unpublished manuscript. Ottawa: University of Ottawa, Department of Criminology.

Robinson, Paul. 1987. *Dissenting View of Commissioner Paul H. Robinson on the Promulgation of Sentencing Guidelines by the United States Sentencing Commission.* Washington, D.C.: U.S. Government Printing Office.

Romilly, Samuel. 1820. *Speeches.* Excerpts reprinted in Jerome Michael and Herbert Wechsler, *Criminal Law and Its Administration.* 1940. Chicago: Foundation.

Rossman, David, Paul Froyd, Glen L. Pierce, John McDevitt, and William J. Bowers. 1979. *The Impact of the Mandatory Gun Law in Massachusetts.* National Institute of Law Enforcement and Criminal Justice, Law Enforcement Assistance Administration, U.S. Department of Justice. Washington, D.C.: U.S. Government Printing Office.

Rothman, David. 1980. *Conscience and Convenience.* Boston: Little, Brown.

Schulhofer, Stephen. 1980. "Sentencing Reform and Prosecutorial Power." *University of Pennsylvania Law Review* 126:550–77.

————. 1992. "Assessing the Federal Sentencing Process: The Problem Is Uniformity, Not Disparity." *American Criminal Law Review* 29:833–873.

Schulhofer, Stephen J., and Ilene Nagel. 1989. "Negotiated Pleas under the Federal Sentencing Guidelines: The First Fifteen Months." *American Criminal Law Review* 27:231–88.

Schwartzer, William W. 1991. "Judicial Discretion in Sentencing." *Federal Sentencing Reporter* 4:339–41.

Sechrest, Lee B., Susan O. White, and Elizabeth D. Brown, eds. 1979. *The Rehabilitation of Criminal Offenders: Problems and Prospects*. Washington, D.C.: National Academy Press.

Select Committee on Capital Punishment. 1930. *Report*. London: H.M. Stationery Office.

Shane-DuBow, Sandra, Alice P. Brown, and Erik Olsen. 1985. *Sentencing Reform in the United States: History, Content, and Effect*. Washington, D.C.: U.S. Government Printing Office.

Stephen, James Fitzjames. 1883. *A History of the Criminal Law of England*. Reprinted 1977. New York: B. Franklin.

Stith, Kate, and Steve Y. Koh. 1993. "The Politics of Sentencing Reform: The Legislative History of the Federal Sentencing Guidelines." *Wake Forest Law Review* 28:223–90.

Tak, Peter J. P. 1993. "Sentencing in the Netherlands." Paper prepared for the Colston International Sentencing Symposium, University of Bristol, Faculty of Law, May.

————. 1994a. "Sentencing and Punishment in the Netherlands." *Overcrowded Times* 5(5):5–8.

————. 1994b. "Sentencing in the Netherlands." *Acta Criminologica* 7:7–17.

————. 1995. "Netherlands Successfully Implements Community Service Orders." *Overcrowded Times* 6(2):4, 16–17.

Thomas, David A. 1995. "Sentencing Reform: England and Wales." In *The Politics of Sentencing Reform*, edited by Chris Clarkson and Rod Morgan. Oxford: Oxford University Press.

Tonry, Michael. 1979. "The Sentencing Commission in Sentencing Reform." *Hofstra Law Review* 7:315–53.

————. 1987. *Sentencing Reform Impacts*. Washington, D.C.: U.S. Government Printing Office.

————. 1988. "Structuring Sentencing." In *Crime and Justice: A Review of Research*, vol. 10, edited by Michael Tonry and Norval Morris. Chicago: University of Chicago Press.

————. 1991. "The Politics and Processes of Sentencing Commissions." *Crime and Delinquency* 37:307–29.

————. 1992a. "Salvaging the Sentencing Guidelines in Seven Easy Steps." *Federal Sentencing Reporter* 4:355–59.

————. 1992b. "Mandatory Penalties." In *Crime and Justice: A Review of Research*, vol. 16, edited by Michael Tonry. Chicago: University of Chicago Press.

————. 1993a. "The Failure of the U.S. Sentencing Commission's Guidelines." *Crime and Delinquency* 39:131–49.

————. 1993b. "The Success of Judge Frankel's Sentencing Commission." *Colorado Law Review* 64:713–22.

_____. 1993c. "Sentencing Commissions and Their Guidelines." In *Crime and Justice: A Review of Research,* vol. 17, edited by Michael Tonry. Chicago: University of Chicago Press.

_____. 1994. "Proportionality, Parsimony, and Interchangeability of Punishments." In *Penal Theory and Practice,* edited by R. A. Duff, S. Marshall, and R. and R. Dobash. Manchester: Manchester University Press.

_____. 1995a. *Malign Neglect: Race, Crime, and Punishment in America.* New York: Oxford University Press.

_____. 1995b. "Twenty Years of Sentencing Reform: Steps Forward, Steps Backward." *Judicature* 78(4):169–72.

Tonry, Michael, and John C. Coffee, Jr. 1987. "Enforcing Sentencing Guidelines: Plea Bargaining and Review Mechanisms." In *The Sentencing Commission and Its Guidelines,* by Andrew von Hirsch, Kay A. Knapp, and Michael Tonry. Boston: Northeastern University Press.

Tonry, Michael, and Kate Hamilton. 1995. *Intermediate Sanctions in Overcrowded Times.* Boston: Northeastern University Press.

Tonry, Michael, and Richard Will. 1988. *Intermediate Sanctions.* Final Report submitted to the National Institute of Justice. Castine, Maine: Castine Research Corporation.

Törnudd, Patrik. 1993. *Fifteen Years of Declining Prisoner Rates.* Helsinki: National Research Institute of Legal Policy.

_____. 1994. "Sentencing and Punishment in Finland." *Overcrowded Times* 5(6): 1, 11–13, 16.

Turner, Susan. 1992. "Day-Fine Projects Launched in Four Jurisdictions." *Overcrowded Times* 3(6):5–6.

U.S. Bureau of Justice Statistics. 1990a. *Prisoners in 1989.* Bureau of Justice Statistics Bulletin no. NCJ-122716. Washington, D.C.: U.S. Government Printing Office.

_____. 1990b. "Prison Population Grows 6 Percent During First Half of Year." Bureau of Justice Statistics press release, Washington, D.C., October 7.

U.S. Department of Justice. 1994. *An Analysis of Non-Violent Drug Offenders with Minimal Criminal Histories.* Washington, D.C.: U.S. Department of Justice, Office of the Deputy Attorney General. (Reprinted in *Criminal Law Reporter* 54:2101–55.)

U.S. General Accounting Office. 1990a. *U.S. Sentencing Commission: Changes Needed to Improve Effectiveness.* Testimony of Lowell Dodge before the Subcommittee on Criminal Justice of the Committee on the Judiciary, United States House of Representatives, March. Washington, D.C.: U.S. General Accounting Office.

_____. 1990b. *Intermediate Sanctions: Their Impacts on Prison Crowding, Costs, and Recidivism Are Still Unclear.* Gaithersburg, Md.: U.S. General Accounting Office.

_____. 1992. *Sentencing Guidelines: Central Questions Remain Unanswered.* Washington, D.C.: U.S. General Accounting Office.

_____. 1993. *Prison Boot Camps: Short-Term Prison Costs Reduced, But Long-Term Impact Uncertain.* Washington, D.C.: U.S. General Accounting Office.

U.S. Sentencing Commission. 1987a. *Supplementary Report on the Initial Sentencing Guidelines and Policy Statements.* Washington, D.C.: U.S. Sentencing Commission.

_____. 1987*b*. *Sentencing Guidelines and Policy Statements, April 13, 1987.* Washington, D.C.: U.S. Government Printing Office.

_____. 1990. *Annual Report—1989.* Washington, D.C.: U.S. Sentencing Commission.

_____. 1991*a*. *The Federal Sentencing Guidelines: A Report on the Operation of the Guidelines System and Short-term Impacts on Disparity in Sentencing, Use of Incarceration, and Prosecutorial Discretion and Plea Bargaining.* Washington, D.C.: U.S. Sentencing Commission.

_____. 1991*b*. *Special Report to the Congress: Mandatory Minimum Penalties in the Federal Criminal Justice System.* Washington, D.C.: U.S. Sentencing Commission.

_____. 1991*c*. *Annual Report—1990.* Washington, D.C.: U.S. Sentencing Commission.

_____. 1992*a*. *Sentencing Commission Guidelines Manual.* Washington, D.C.: U.S. Sentencing Commission.

_____. 1992*b*. *Annual Report—1991.* Washington, D.C.: U.S. Sentencing Commission.

_____. 1994. *Annual Report—1993.* Washington, D.C.: U.S. Sentencing Commission.

_____. 1995. *Annual Report—1994.* Washington, D.C.: U.S. Sentencing Commission.

U.S. Sentencing Commission Alternatives to Imprisonment Project. 1990. *The Federal Offender: A Program of Intermediate Punishments: Executive Summary.* Washington, D.C.: U.S. Sentencing Commission.

van Kalmthout, Anton M., and Peter J. P. Tak. 1992. *Sanctions-Systems in the Member-States of the Council of Europe: Deprivation of Liberty, Community Service, and Other Substitutes.* Boston: Kluwer.

von Hirsch, Andrew. 1976. *Doing Justice: The Choice of Punishments.* New York: Hill & Wang.

_____. 1985. *Past or Future Crimes—Deservedness and Dangerousness in the Sentencing of Criminals.* New Brunswick, N.J.: Rutgers University Press.

_____. 1986. *Doing Justice: The Choice of Punishments,* rev. ed. Boston: Northeastern University Press.

_____. 1988. "Federal Sentencing Guidelines: The United States and Canadian Schemes Compared." Occasional Papers from the Center for Research in Crime and Justice, no. 4. New York: New York University Law School.

_____. 1992. "Proportionality in the Philosophy of Punishment." In *Crime and Justice: A Review of Research,* vol. 16, edited by Michael Tonry. Chicago: University of Chicago Press.

_____. 1993. *Censure and Sanctions.* Oxford: Oxford University Press.

_____. 1994. "Sentencing Guidelines and Penal Aims in Minnesota." *Criminal Justice Ethics* 13(1):39–49.

von Hirsch, Andrew, Kay Knapp, and Michael Tonry. 1987. *The Sentencing Commission and Its Guidelines.* Boston: Northeastern University Press.

von Hirsch, Andrew, Martin Wasik, and Judith Greene. 1989. "Punishments in the Community and the Principles of Desert." *Rutgers Law Review* 20:595–618.

Walker, Nigel. 1991. *Why Punish?* Oxford: Oxford University Press.

Wallace, Scott. 1994. "Crime Bill Offers Funds to States for Prisons." *Overcrowded Times* 5(5):4, 12.

Washington State Sentencing Guidelines Commission. 1985. *Sentencing Practices under the Sentencing Reform Act.* Olympia: Washington State Sentencing Guidelines Commission.

_____. 1986. *Preliminary Evaluation of Washington State's Sentencing Reform Act.* Olympia: Washington State Sentencing Guidelines Commission.

_____. 1987. *Preliminary Statistical Summary of 1986 Sentencing Data.* Olympia: Washington State Sentencing Guidelines Commission.

_____. 1991. *A Statistical Summary of Adult Felony Sentencing, Fiscal Year 1990.* Olympia: Washington State Sentencing Guidelines Commission.

_____. 1992a. *A Statistical Summary of Adult Felony Sentencing.* Olympia: Washington State Sentencing Guidelines Commission.

_____. 1992b. *A Decade of Sentencing Reform: Washington and Its Guidelines, 1981–1991.* Olympia: Washington State Sentencing Guidelines Commission.

_____. 1993. *Implementation Manual—FY 1993.* Olympia: Washington State Sentencing Guidelines Commission.

_____. 1994a. *Implementation Manual—FY 1994.* Olympia: Washington State Sentencing Guidelines Commission.

_____. 1994b. *Statistical Summary of Adult Felony Sentencing—FY 1993.* Olympia: Washington State Sentencing Guidelines Commission.

Wasik, Martin. 1993. "England Repeals Key Provisions of '91 Sentencing Reform Legislation." *Overcrowded Times* 4(4):1, 16–17.

Wasik, Martin, and Richard D. Taylor. 1991. *Criminal Justice Act 1991.* London: Blackstone.

Wasik, Martin, and Andrew von Hirsch. 1988. "Non-Custodial Penalties and the Principles of Desert." *Criminal Law Review* 1988:555–72.

Watts, Ronald K., and Daniel Glaser. 1992. "Electronic Monitoring of Drug Offenders in California." In *Smart Sentencing: The Emergence of Intermediate Sanctions,* edited by James M. Byrne, Arthur J. Lurigio, and Joan Petersilia. Newbury Park, Calif.: Sage.

Weigend, Thomas. 1992. "Germany Reduces Use of Prison Sentences." *Overcrowded Times* 3(2):1, 11–13.

_____. 1993. "In Germany, Fines Often Imposed in Lieu of Prosecution," *Overcrowded Times* 4(1):1, 15–16.

Weisburd, David. 1992. "Sentencing Disparity and the Guidelines: Taking a Closer Look." *Federal Sentencing Reporter* 5:149–52.

Wesson, Marianne. 1993. "Sentencing Reform in Colorado—Many Changes, Little Progress." *Overcrowded Times* 4(6):1, 14–17, 20.

Wheeler, Stanton, Kenneth Mann, and Austin Sarat. 1991. *Sitting in Judgment: The Sentencing of White-Collar Criminals.* New Haven, Conn.: Yale University Press.

Wilkins, Leslie T., Jack M. Kress, Don M. Gottfredson, Joseph C. Calpin, and Arthur M. Gelman. 1978. *Sentencing Guidelines: Structuring Judicial Discretion—Report on the Feasibility Study.* Washington, D.C.: U.S. Department of Justice.

Wilkins, William W., Jr., and John R. Steer. 1990. "Relevant Conduct: The Corner-

Discretion—Report on the Feasibility Study. Washington, D.C.: U.S. Department of Justice.

Wilkins, William W., Jr., and John R. Steer. 1990. "Relevant Conduct: The Cornerstone of the Federal Sentencing Guidelines." *South Carolina Law Review* 41:495–531.

Wilson, James Q. 1975. *Thinking About Crime.* New York: Basic.

_____. 1983. *Thinking About Crime,* rev. ed. New York: Basic.

_____. 1990. "Drugs and Crime." In *Drugs and Crime,* edited by Michael Tonry and James Q. Wilson. Chicago: University of Chicago Press.

_____. 1994. "Crime and Public Policy." In *Crime,* edited by James Q. Wilson and Joan Petersilia. San Francisco, Calif.: ICS.

Wolfgang, Marvin, Robert Figlio, and Thorsten Sellin. 1972. *Delinquency in a Birth Cohort.* Chicago: University of Chicago Press.

Wright, Ronald F. 1991. "Sentencers, Bureaucrats, and the Administrative Law Perspective on the Federal Sentencing Commission." *California Law Review* 79:1–90.

_____. 1994. "Amendments in the Route to Sentencing Reform." *Criminal Justice Ethics* 11:58–66.

_____. 1995. "North Carolina Avoids Early Trouble with Guidelines." *Overcrowded Times* 6(1):1, 16–19.

Wright, Ronald F., and Susan P. Ellis. 1993. "Progress Report on the North Carolina Sentencing and Policy Advisory Commission." *Wake Forest Law Review* 28:421–61.

Yellen, David. 1993. "Illusion, Illogic, and Injustice: Real-Offense Sentencing and the Federal Sentencing Guidelines." *Minnesota Law Review* 78: 403–65.

Young, Warren, 1979. *Community Service Orders.* London: Heinemann.

Zedlewski, Edwin. 1987. *Making Confinement Decisions.* Research in Brief. Washington, D.C.: National Institute of Justice.

Zeisel, Hans, and Shari Diamond. 1977. "Search for Sentencing Equity: Sentence Review in Massachusetts and Connecticut." *American Bar Foundation Research Journal* 4:881–940.

Zimring, Franklin E. 1976. "Making the Punishment Fit the Crime: A Consumer's Guide to Sentencing Reform." *Hastings Center Report* 6:13–21.

Zimring, Franklin E., and Gordon Hawkins. 1991. *The Scale of Imprisonment.* Chicago: University of Chicago Press.

_____. 1995. *Incapacitation: Penal Confinement and the Restraint of Crime.* New York: Oxford University Press.

Index